AIRPORT URBANISM

Infrastructure and Mobility in Asia

Max Hirsh

UNIVERSITY OF MINNESOTA PRESS

MINNEAPOLIS • LONDON

The University of Minnesota Press gratefully acknowledges financial support for the publication of this book from the Future Cities Laboratory at SEC Singapore ETH Center.

A different version of chapter 2 was published as "Design Aesthetics of Transborder Infrastructure in the Pearl River Delta," *Journal of the Society of Architectural Historians* 73, no. 1 (March 2014): 137–52.

All photographs, maps, and illustrations are by the author, unless otherwise credited.

Published by the University of Minnesota Press
111 Third Avenue South, Suite 290
Minneapolis, MN 55401-2520
http://www.upress.umn.edu

Library of Congress Cataloging-in-Publication Data
Hirsh, Max, author.
Airport urbanism : infrastructure and mobility in Asia / Max Hirsh.
Includes bibliographical references and index.
ISBN 978-0-8166-9609-3 (hc)—ISBN 978-0-8166-9610-9 (pb)
1. City planning—Asia. 2. Airports—Asia.
3. Transportation—Planning—Asia. I. Title.
HT169.A78H57   2016
307.1´216095—dc23   2015036914

Printed in the United States of America on acid-free paper

The University of Minnesota is an equal-opportunity educator and employer.

22 21 20 19 18 17 16   10 9 8 7 6 5 4 3 2 1

Contents

Preface

Urban studies is going through a peculiar phase of both renaissance and crisis. On the one hand, the past decade has witnessed a resurgence in popular interest in urbanization. Dozens of universities and national governments—and, increasingly, many large foundations and corporations—have founded new institutes, or inaugurated think tanks and fellowship programs, devoted to advanced research on cities. Invariably, their mission statements lead off with the same dramatic set of pronouncements: "More than half of the world's population now lives in cities. By 2050, that figure will rise to 70 percent." "Cities accommodate more people today than at any point in history. One million new people join the world's cities every week." "Innovative research is needed to confront the challenges of rapid urbanization." That call to arms is repeated on a daily basis at conferences, symposia, and workshops; in newspapers, online publications, and exhibitions.

And yet, by and large the scholars and practitioners who have been trained to engage with the complexities of urbanization—architects and planners, urban historians, anthropologists and geographers—are not taking part in this wider conversation. Their absence is palpable in the technocratically inflected outputs of upstart urban research institutes: whose emphasis on data analysis and computer modeling produces technologically driven "solutions" to urban "challenges" that ignore social and spatial processes that cannot be captured by quantitative means. As previous periods of urban growth have shown—when the accumulation and quantification of data was posited as a way to comprehend and master all aspects of urbanization—a full-scale reliance on such methods overlooks critical issues related to popular opinion, aesthetic preferences, culturally specific mores, faith, informal social and economic arrangements, and many other phenomena that fly under the radar of statistical databases. Removed from the vast body of knowledge that scholars of the city have accumulated since the late nineteenth century, these institutions risk rehearsing failed development strategies from the past.

Why are urban scholars not participating in these discussions? In part, their absence can be attributed to a crisis of the discipline, or rather disciplines, that engage with questions of the urban. Historians of architecture and urban planning remain mired in a drawn-out elegy for modernism and the post–World War II Western welfare state, and for the stature that both accorded to the design professions. Architects, having refashioned themselves as taste-arbitrating "curators" in an attempt to recuperate that lost cultural capital, have struggled to formulate a coherent design agenda that engages with the socioeconomic intricacies of the contemporary city and their implications for urban form. In many disciplines in the arts and sciences, there is a widening gap between empirical research taking place in cities and rigorous attempts to theorize the processes of urbanization. Trapped in an ideological rut, these fields also display an unfortunate reductive tendency to subsume all dimensions of urban change under a critique of neoliberalism. Perhaps most problematically, urban research has become geographically decoupled from the principal loci of urbanization: with an army of scholars combing through archival minutiae in the metropoles of the late nineteenth and early twentieth centuries—New York, London, Paris—while a frighteningly scant number conduct research on the ground in the burgeoning twenty-first-century cities of Asia, Africa, and the Middle East. The transatlantic boundaries of their research place these scholars at a pedagogical disadvantage in the globalizing classrooms of undergraduate institutions and design schools, which are populated by a very large number of students whose careers will take them far beyond Europe and North America. Moreover, the same spatial mismatch between urban growth and urban studies can be observed in the professional sphere of applied research. With some notable exceptions, there are few contemporary equivalents to Louis Wirth or Otto Königsberger or the Metabolists working in places like Shenzhen and Singapore. In their stead, developers, technical service providers, and management consulting firms hailing from the financial sector—Aecom, KPMG, McKinsey—have reinvented themselves as urban experts, filling in a vacuum left by those who are trained to conduct urban research.

To a great degree, the crisis of urban inquiry is of a lexical nature. The art historian Mariët Westermann notes that urban scholars face "unfamiliar physical and social environments for which our conventional notions—and even our descriptive language of city and suburb, exurb, and so forth—are no longer relevant. The whole descriptive vocabulary of urbanism is in flux."[1] In a similar vein, the architectural historian Swati Chattopadhyay argues that "the central problem in theorizing cities today is a paucity of vocabulary. The structural changes that have occurred in cities around the world in the last two decades have strained the limits of our existing vocabulary. . . . The vocabulary has long been insufficient; the new urban formations merely have showed up its mythic claims."[2] There is, in other words, a common consensus that urban studies finds itself at a transitional moment, cognizant of the inadequacy of our inherited vocabulary and conceptual framework—but not yet able to formulate new ones that go beyond expressing wonderment at unfamiliar forms of urban development or chastising them for departing from historical norms. The old terminology, and with it the epistemology of urban inquiry, is no longer relevant; leading to a deeply problematic disconnect between the signifiers at our disposal and the urban processes that we, as scholars, seek to analyze. More recent attempts to engage with the urban implications of paradigmatic social and technological shifts—in particular as they relate to the accelerated cross-border movement of goods, people, capital, and ideas by both digital and physical means—resort to unhelpful binary taxonomies ("global" vs. "local") and fashionable ide-olects ("rescaling," "translocal") that accord too much agency to opaquely defined processes of "globalization" while ignoring cultural and historical relationships that have long bound cities to one another across great distances.

Above all, the terminology used in urban research simply isn't accessible to anyone besides a small disciplinary in-group. The oft averred commitment to inter-disciplinary research, methodologies, and pedagogies has not been accompanied by a counterpart attempt to develop inclusive forms of writing that can speak to a broader audience through language that is precise and incisive without being impenetrable to the uninitiated. While discipline-specific jargon is deployed to bolster claims of expert knowledge, its use ultimately alienates most readers and fails to communicate critical research findings. In the domain of urban studies, the unfortunate consequence is a continuous reinvention of the wheel, as related disciplines—here I am thinking of architecture and urban planning, and anthro-pology and geography—conduct research on and develop theories about closely related topics yet are incapable of making connections across disciplinary bound-aries due to a basic problem of mutual unintelligibility.

Airport Urbanism represents a modest attempt to address some of the chal-lenges outlined above. In the narrowest possible sense, it is a study of airport infra-structure in five East and Southeast Asian cities: one that analyzes the exponential leap in international air traffic since the 1970s and its implications for the planning and design of the contemporary Asian city. More broadly, the book has two ambi-tions. First, by investigating the transportation systems used by new members of the flying public, such as budget tourists, retirees, and migrant workers, it models a new understanding of cities that fundamentally reconceptualizes the relationship between global migration patterns, transport infrastructure, and urban form. Sec-ond, by productively recombining visual, archival, and ethnographic approaches from a variety of urban disciplines, it advances an alternative, humanities-based methodology that is suitable for conducting urban research in rapidly developing parts of the world such as China and Southeast Asia. In so doing, the book sets up a fruitful dialogue between those scholars who study the city's spatial and aesthetic dimensions and those who investigate its social, political, and economic contours.

Studying cross-border mobility and its myriad manifestations in the contemporary Asian city represents a particular challenge for the Western observer, who may not be accustomed to the varying levels of informality, frugality, and entrepreneurialism that penetrate everyday processes of transport and trade in such cities as Bangkok, Hong Kong, and Kuala Lumpur. But it is also a challenge for Asian scholars and urban policymakers, who have been reared in a context where modernization and cosmopolitanism have invariably been equated with the importation of, and adaptation to, Western models of urbanism. They have likewise been trained to think that informal, flexible, and temporary structural arrangements are embarrassing reminders of a penurious past—and should be replaced by formal, and ideally megastructural, systems as quickly as possible.

My own approach to these questions is strongly inflected by my experience growing up and working in five very different countries on three continents, a personal trajectory that provides a unique insight into the practicalities of international migration and into the mindset of those who are on the move. Through autobiographical vignettes that bookend the text, *Airport Urbanism* thus probes the topic from the perspective of both an urban scholar and an active participant. I begin with a short introduction that situates the book within an existing literature on mobility, migration, and urban infrastructure; and points to some of the problematic assumptions embedded in that literature that my book aims to remedy. Each of the chapters that follow studies a different dimension of aerial mobility, its physical manifestations in five Asian cities, and its ramifications for Asia's political and economic integration. The chapters zoom progressively outward in geographic scale: beginning with an analysis of physical changes in the urban fabric of Hong Kong, and then continuing with an investigation of transport systems that connect Hong Kong's airport to Mainland Chinese cities in the surrounding Pearl River Delta. The second part of the book focuses on Bangkok, Kuala Lumpur, and Singapore, studying the evolution of low-cost aviation networks in Southeast Asia, and concluding with a first-hand account of daily life as a migrant in Singapore.

What Is Airport Urbanism?

Traveling to West Berlin in the 1980s was never easy. Enclosed by a wall and surrounded by East Germany, the city relied on heavily guarded transit highways and air corridors to connect it to the outside world. I grew up in a lower-middle-class section of Berlin's Lichterfelde district, a few kilometers from the city's southern edge. Here the Wall appeared far less glamorous than it did downtown: no graffiti or frowning tourists, just a tidy affair of pale gray concrete running through the backyards of high-rise apartment blocks and garden allotments. We lived directly above a bar that was run by my best friend's grandmother. A Hungarian Jew who had come to Berlin as a Displaced Person in the 1950s, she offered to sign over her lease because she knew that my mother was looking for an apartment that was cheaper and closer to McNair Barracks, where my mom worked as a social worker for the U.S. Army.

After my parents separated, my father took a job at a small liberal arts college in the Swiss resort town of Lugano. Teaching introductory courses in Western civilization and Soviet history, he was not particularly well compensated. He lived on the ground floor of an apartment complex adjacent to the main railway line that connects Italy to northern Europe. The other side of the tracks was dotted with the five-star hotels and lakeside *lido* that had made his neighborhood—Paradiso—a famous summer holiday destination. My father led a slightly shabby life amid privileged surroundings: preparing TV dinners in a tiny kitchen, his view of the Lago di Lugano and the Alpine foothills disrupted by the silhouette of luxury condos and the endless rattling of freight trains.

For most of elementary school, I shuttled between West Berlin and Lugano with my sister, attending school in Berlin and visiting my father during vacations. The twenty-hour journey by train began around midnight at Bahnhof Zoo and was punctuated by a series of frosty border controls: olive uniforms, floodlit platforms, transit visas. Tired and achy from a night sprawled across three seats, we would wake up in the morning in Frankfurt and switch to a train to Basel; and then again to another train that, after snaking its way through the Alps, delivered us at Lugano's Stazione FFS in the early evening. We spent two days of each one-week vacation en route.

Flying to Lugano was out of the question. Due to West Berlin's special status, only three airlines—Air France, British Airways, and Pan Am—operated out of Tegel Airport, one for each occupying power. Fares were exorbitant and the schedules inconvenient: infinitely more expensive than the train, and involving just as many transfers. One day, however, my mother got a bit of advice from a friend: why not try Interflug, the East German airline? They offer cheap flights out of Schönefeld, East Berlin's airport on the other side of the Wall.

Desperate for hard currency, the East German airline offered cut-rate fares to destinations like Athens, Rome, Beirut, and Istanbul (Figure I.1). Using a fleet of transit buses, Interflug shuttled passengers from downtown West Berlin to the airport through a special border crossing in the Wall. Though heavily criticized by Cold War ideologues, the cross-border service proved immensely popular with low-income tourists and Turkish *Gastarbeiter,* or migrant "guest workers," who could not afford the airfares on flights leaving from Tegel. In effect, Interflug identified an

FIGURE I.1. An Interflug jet at Schönefeld International Airport, East Berlin, 1986. Photograph by Interflug.

incipient segment of the flying public: travelers who were willing to sacrifice their comfort and convenience if that was their only means of flying abroad—even if it meant supporting a Communist dictatorship that didn't allow its own citizens to leave the country. By the late 1980s, a quarter of all West Berliners flew through East Berlin every year.

And so on our next trip to see my father, we piled onto a transit bus that drove us, along with fifty other passengers, to Schönefeld. In the absence of passport checks—West Berlin did not recognize the Wall as a national boundary, and the East German guards were instructed to facilitate transfer traffic to Schönefeld—we proceeded swiftly to the airport and boarded an elderly Tupelov bound for Milan Malpensa, the closest major airport to Lugano. The flight was not especially pleasant—cranky stewardesses and aging Soviet technology not being a recipe for comfort—but less than two hours later we had landed in Italy. Two hours instead of twenty! I spotted my father in the arrivals hall, waiting to drive us across the border to Lugano, and fuming. Someone had stolen his hubcaps from the airport's parking lot.

While I was thrilled by the ability to fly, I struggled to understand the logic behind our trajectory, so much speedier but less intuitive than the journey by train. If we wanted to fly from West Berlin to Switzerland, why did we need to take a bus to East Germany, and then a plane to Italy, and then drive to the Swiss border checkpoint at Chiasso? These regular trips between West Berlin and Switzerland instilled me with an abiding interest in two larger questions. First, how does the proverbial "other half"—that is, those who are not members of the elite—fly? In college and later in graduate school, I discovered that there was a general assumption among scholars that only the wealthy could afford to fly across international borders or had the need to do so. Yet this supposition is not consonant with my own experience; nor does it reflect the experience of many friends and acquaintances who grew up between two very different places—New York and the Dominican Republic, Hong Kong and the Philippines, West Germany and Azerbaijan—yet were not born into wealth. Like me, they were neither particularly affluent nor dirt poor, but rather somewhere in between, muddling across borders via transport systems that had been designed for businessmen and civil servants but which, over the past thirty years, have become appropriated by an increasingly broad socio-economic spectrum of the population for an equally wide variety of reasons. These semiprivileged travelers fall into two distinct categories that don't square neatly with common conceptions of wealth and status: passengers who have enough money to travel abroad, but whose citizenship makes it difficult to do so, such as Indians and Mainland Chinese; and travelers who hold a privileged citizenship—e.g., U.S. or EU—but whose financial resources are limited. While most of them can't afford to take a plane every week, they all fly at least once a year. They're definitely not members of a global elite; but they know how to activate informal networks of friends and relatives, and how to navigate the baggage restrictions of low-cost carriers, in order to get where they need to go.

Flying between countries from an early age invested me with another enduring preoccupation. After the Wall fell and my mother moved back to the United States, I continued to travel to Europe to visit my father—less frequently and for longer stays, since we could only pay for one flight a year. Each time I flew, I noticed subtle changes: more security checks and fewer passport controls; the obsolescence of travel agents and proliferation of flatscreens; and construction, construction, construction at every airport through which I transited. These experiences led to me to a second set of questions. As the number of air travelers expanded exponentially, how have architects and planners redesigned airports—as well as entire cities—to accommodate much larger passenger flows? How have concomitant changes in migration regimes and border regulations informed urban design strategies? And what happens when the political framework governing those frontiers, as well as travel across them, abruptly changes?

When I began my research in Hong Kong, I did so because it seemed the perfect place to investigate these questions. Within three short decades, the city underwent a major transition in its political status, experienced a tenfold increase in passenger air traffic, and completely overhauled its airport infrastructure. Among transportation experts and design critics, the city was lauded for the overwhelming scale and precise execution of its ten-point Airport Core Program, which involved the construction of a brand-new airport; several suspension bridges; a thirty-four-kilometer road and rail corridor between the airport and downtown Hong Kong; and a series of land reclamation projects in the city's central business district.[1]

However, I quickly discovered a distinct discrepancy between what I had read in architectural journals and scholarly articles about Hong Kong's infrastructure and the perception of those who designed these spaces and used them on a regular basis. For instance, many of the people that I spoke to rarely rode Airport Express, the high-speed train, in spite of the fact that it is presented—by the airport, by urban scholars, and by architecture critics—as an integral and innovative component of the airport's infrastructure. When I mentioned this to the general manager of the airport authority, he laughed, noting that only a small proportion of travelers—perhaps 15 percent—actually used the train. "It's a lovely service, but it's not high volume. It's a great marketing strategy."[2] Instead, most passengers rely on a range of other legal and semilegal transport options—buses, minivans, ferries, "discount" taxis—that operate in parallel with Airport Express and that move passengers more cheaply between a much wider range of locations throughout the city.

Hong Kong and its twin city, Shenzhen, across the border in Mainland China, are likewise a fascinating laboratory for investigating how border regulations and migration restrictions influence the design and use of airport infrastructure. Due to significant differences in the way in which Hong Kong and the People's Republic of China regulate their airspace, Shenzhen's airport has effectively become a regional hub for cheap domestic flights on the Mainland, while Hong Kong's airport mainly services international routes. This gap has generated a brisk trade in cross-border traffic between the two cities and has led to a proliferation of transport networks designed for travelers whose movement across the Hong Kong–PRC frontier is limited by their citizenship or income. These incipient air passengers, and the so-called "transborder" systems that they use, have radically reordered the cross-border flow of goods and people in the Pearl River Delta.

Focusing on five cities in East and Southeast Asia—Bangkok, Hong Kong, Kuala Lumpur, Shenzhen, and Singapore—this book uses airport infrastructure as a lens for illuminating paradigmatic shifts in the design, use, and regulation of cross-border mobility, and it investigates how those changes have reshaped the spatial and typological order of Asian cities. In so doing, it uncovers an architecture of incipient global mobility that has been inconspicuously inserted into ordinary places and unspectacular structures that are not typically associated with the infrastructure of international aviation, such as shopping malls, suburban new towns, theme parks, and industrial seaports. These facilities cater to a growing population of what I call the *nouveaux globalisés*—new members of Asia's flying public, such as migrant workers, students, retirees, pilgrims, budget tourists, and traders from the Global South—who rely on a variety of low-cost and informal transportation networks in order to move cheaply and efficiently across national frontiers.

Low-Cost Globalization and the Rise of the Semiprivileged

The emergence of these *nouveaux globalisés* accounts for the double-digit year-on-year increases in air traffic that have become the norm across much of Asia. Their movement has been enabled by the simplification of passport controls, exit formalities, and visa requirements throughout the region; and by the concomitant rise of low-cost carriers, or LCCs, that have made international air travel significantly cheaper and more accessible to a vastly enlarged flying public. As a result, air travelers in Asia have become much more diverse in terms of their socioeconomic background, citizenship, trajectory, trip purpose, and age.[3]

These changes are borne out by a closer look at four passenger types—Mainland Chinese tourists, foreign students, expatriate retirees, and migrant workers—who, by dint of their citizenship, budget, or social status, are members of Asia's emerging class of semiprivileged travelers:

- Until the late 1990s, it was nearly impossible for most citizens of the People's Republic of China to travel abroad; as they lacked both the financial resources and the official permissions required to visit another country. The removal of legal restrictions placed on the movement of Mainland Chinese citizens abroad, coupled with the introduction of low-cost tourism, has enabled members of China's burgeoning middle class to take leisure trips to nearby countries in East and Southeast Asia.

• Globally, the number of young people studying abroad has quadrupled since 1980, as the traditional model of international higher education—whereby foreign elites came to study in the United States and Europe—has been augmented by more modest forms of academic mobility.[4] This is evident, for example, in the large population of talented but not necessarily wealthy and well-connected foreign students who have been attracted by lower financial and immigration barriers to universities in Australia, Hong Kong, Malaysia, and Singapore.[5]

• At the other end of the age spectrum, millions of retired and semiretired people spend several months a year outside their country of residence—typically in warmer, cheaper parts of Asia. Through targeted migration schemes, middle-income countries like Malaysia and Thailand actively promote the part-time residency of retirees from aging societies such as Korea, Japan, and Taiwan and from land-scarce city-states like Hong Kong and Singapore.[6] Rather than a marker of high social status in their home countries, this type of travel often appeals to the middle classes of advanced economies who can increase their standard of living—especially in terms of housing and medical care—at the cost of being far from friends and relatives.[7] In essence, these are less affluent people engaging in a type of petit bourgeois transnationalism: flying a great distance to get things that they can't afford closer to home.[8]

• Like students studying abroad, expatriate retirees constitute what geographers and anthropologists call "circular" migrants—that is, people who move at regular intervals between two or more places.[9] Circular migration differs significantly from traditional forms of immigration in that it involves a cyclical back-and-forth between countries rather than a permanent relocation from one to another. In that respect, their travel patterns resemble those of labor migrants such as maids, service-sector employees, and construction workers, who shuttle between their home countries—Bangladesh, China, the Philippines—to work under fixed-term contracts in wealthier places like the Gulf states and the "Four Asian Tigers."[10] That geographic shift frequently entails a counterpart socioeconomic dislocation, as many of those involved in cross-border migration have different class positions in the two countries between which they are commuting.[11] Thus, someone with a low social status in their place of work is often comparatively well off in their home town, using their income to support family members and engaging in strategic real estate investments in their place of origin.[12]

Visual Ethnographies of Aerial Mobility: An Urban Humanities Approach

The expanding spectrum of international travelers has profound implications for airport design: changes that are reflected in the development of transport systems and terminal programming aimed at specific clienteles such as children, the elderly, the religious, as well as those traveling on a tight budget or who have limited computer literacy (Figure I.2 and I.3). These design modifications significantly problematize the way in which scholars have analyzed the spatial manifestations of global mobility in the contemporary urban landscape. For while the shifting demographic contours of global migration have been well documented in an array of sociological and anthropological studies, scholars of the built environment have largely ignored concomitant changes in the urban infrastructure that a vastly enlarged flying public uses to travel from place to place.[13] In part, the absence of research on the transport systems used by incipient members of the flying public can be attributed to their relative invisibility: in aviation and migration statistics, which undercount the operations of budget airlines;[14] in visual representations of the airport; and at the limited number of global hubs, primarily in Europe, where scholars have conducted most of their research.[15] Students, retirees, migrant workers, and budget travelers are much more likely to use airlines, airports, and urban transportation systems that operate outside the mainstream infrastructure of international aviation. Low-cost carriers frequently bypass global airport hubs in favor of cheaper airfields: departing from Bangkok's older Don Mueang airport instead of the larger and newer terminal at Suvarnabhumi, for example; or flying out of secondary cities located in the hinterland of primate ones, such as Batam and Johor Bahru in the case of Singapore. And in places where budget airlines do operate out of major international airports—such as Kuala Lumpur—they often do so from low-cost terminals sited on remote parts of the airfield.

The absence of these passengers in scholarly accounts is likewise reinforced by their invisibility in public representations of the airport—and, by extension, from research on airports. Overwhelmingly, scholars of urban infrastructure have studied the expansion of global air traffic by analyzing its most obvious physical manifestations: transport megaprojects like "starchitect" passenger terminals, high-speed airport railways, and business-oriented "airport cities."[16] To a great extent, these studies rely on an interpretation of urban space that is mediated by visual images produced by architects, developers, and urban boosters. Two books—Manuel Castells's *The Rise of the Network Society* and Stephen Graham and Simon Marvin's *Splintering Urbanism*—epitomize this larger methodological approach. Castells, for example, used drawings made by Ricardo Bofill as visual evidence for locating the Barcelona airport within a "space of flows" designed for and inhabited by global managerial elites. In a similar vein, Graham and Marvin relied on ads

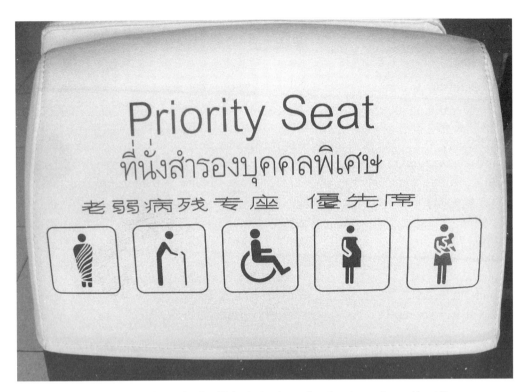

FIGURE I.2. Priority seating for monks, the elderly, the handicapped, and mothers at Suvarnabhumi Airport, Bangkok.

FIGURE I.3. Low-Cost Carrier Terminal at Kuala Lumpur International Airport.

clipped from in-flight magazines to highlight the "premium network spaces" of a "kinetic elite" impervious to the restrictions of national boundaries.[17] In effect, many scholars have availed themselves of only the most easily accessible visual materials: public representations of infrastructure systems such as maps, press kits, and architectural renderings (Figure I.4a and I.4b). To one degree or another, they all constitute some form of advertising. Investigations of the airport thus make use of a very narrow range of images, usually constructed by unreliable narrators who have a professional and/or financial stake in what is being depicted. Analyzing these images can tell us much about the stated intentions of their producers—public authorities, private developers, and the design firms that they engage. But public statements are rarely consonant with actual motivations. On the contrary, such PR materials aim to smooth over the cold calculations and irrational absurdities that drive the development of urban infrastructure systems—considerations that designers and developers freely acknowledge in private conversations, but take great pains to occlude in public presentations. To suggest that these images accurately represent how infrastructure systems operate in practice is a naïve assumption, yet one that remains widespread among urban scholars.[18]

These images depict airport infrastructure as clean, efficient, and exclusive; and mainly target wealthy business travelers. Accepting the ad copy contained in these visuals as the undisputed truth, scholars have identified airports—and their terrestrial support systems—as generic "non-places," designed to accelerate the "seamless" movement of an elite jet set through transport networks that are both socioeconomically and spatially segregated from the surrounding city.[19] In so doing, they have devised highly influential theories on the sociospatial dimensions of international mobility and its impact on urban form: arguing that the increase in cross-border air traffic has exacerbated the physical segregation between global and local, rich and poor, as well as mobile and immobilized constituents in the twenty-first-century city.[20] Their arguments have become unquestioned postulates in architecture culture and in the field of urban studies; and it has become de rigueur to cite them in any critical analysis of airports and air travel.[21]

Yet a close reading of airport infrastructure in Asia points to the existence of parallel transport networks, largely undetected by outside observers, that do not adhere to the master narrative outlined above (see Plate 1 and Figure I.5). While Asia's urban boosters are keen to broadcast their investments in transport facilities that cater to high-end consumers, the infrastructure systems used by the *nouveaux globalisés* are largely absent from official maps, ads, and brochures, and thus they remain unaccounted for in the urban scholarship on the physical dimensions of international mobility. But it is precisely these nontraditional travelers who have driven the exponential increase in global air traffic—and the expansion of airport infrastructure—over the past thirty years.

FIGURE I.4A AND I.4B. Advertising and renderings: the bread and butter of the aviation industry, and also of many infrastructure scholars. Drawing courtesy of Airport Authority Hong Kong.

Bearing these methodological shortcomings in mind, *Airport Urbanism* proposes to study the social and material conditions of global mobility through an expanded spatial and typological conception of the infrastructure of international aviation. Rather than focusing on iconic megaprojects and business-oriented transport nodes, the chapters that follow investigate the emergence of parallel transport systems that are designed to plug less-privileged people and places into the infrastructure of international aviation. Cheaper, rattier, and more geographically diffuse, these networks cater to passengers whose movement across international borders is limited by their income, citizenship, literacy, or place of birth. Studying their spatial and aesthetic composition in five Asian cities, the book deploys an experiential approach to the analysis of urban space in order to parse the broader impact of cross-border mobility on urban form. In so doing, it advances an explicitly inter-disciplinary research methodology: one that combines the illustrative tools of the design professions with humanities-based modes of historical and ethnographic inquiry. The book engages in an analysis of urban form, derived from the direct observation of passengers and planners, that brings the intentions of airport designers into dialogue with the spatial practices of its users. Much of the research was conducted while escorting travelers in transit and while accompanying architects and planners through the transport facilities that they designed. Illustrating those trajectories through maps and photographs, the book uses micro-level analyses of urban transport spaces in order to trace macro-level changes in the social, political, and aesthetic framework of cross-border mobility. At the same time, I juxtapose those images with descriptive accounts of the journeys that I took with a wide range of passengers—Filipino domestic helpers, Mainland Chinese tourists, businessmen and -women from Hong Kong and Malaysia, European retirees, African traders— from their point of departure in the city to their boarding gate at the airport. Drawing on archival documents, works of urban history, and long-form interviews with airport architects and planners, I then locate these image-driven mobile ethnographies within their broader cultural context through detailed historical accounts of the sites that they traverse.

The book does not pretend to be a full-scale ethnography based on systematic anthropological research; rather, it highlights the productive potential of deploying ethnographic methods in the study of urban form. In particular, I rely upon Johan Lindquist's notion of site-specific ethnographies as an open-ended form of knowledge production that "makes room for the unpredictable" research findings that inevitably arise from in-depth fieldwork; that "reduces the gap between description and theory" by concretizing abstract ideas about global mobility and its impact on the contemporary Asian city.[22] By combining visual and ethnographic modes of inquiry, *Airport Urbanism* builds on the methodological approaches of twentieth-century scholars and designers such as Paul-Henry Chombart de Lauwe, Donald Appleyard, Kevin Lynch, Yona Friedman, and William H. Whyte. These authors combined interviews and on-site observation with photographs, maps, and diagrams in order to generate new forms of evidence that drew attention to paradigmatic shifts in urban mobility patterns; and to the broader implications of those shifts for the design, use, and perception of the built environment.[23] Elaborating on their research methods and enriching them with the possibilities afforded by digital technologies, the book creates a visual and textual narrative of actual airport users in order to illustrate how small-scale urban infrastructure systems support complex socioeconomic interdependencies across international frontiers.

In both content and form, the book is thus conceived as an act of interdisciplinary translation: linking up related—yet thus far disconnected—scholarship on infrastructure and the user in the fields of architectural history and urban theory with research on mobility and migration taking place among historians, geographers, and anthropologists.[24] Designed to foster a productive conversation between the disciplines, it proposes a synthetic analysis of both the transport networks that enable the cross-border movement of people, and of the political and economic exigencies motivating their use. Throughout the book, those concerns coalesce around three key terms: *mobility, infrastructure,* and the *everyday.*

FIGURE 1.5. A road sign at the New South China Mall in Dongguan indicates the presence of an airport check-in terminal.

Mobility

On the most basic level, I use the term "cross-border mobility" to describe the movement of people across international frontiers for the purpose of work, study, leisure, and pilgrimage, and to visit friends and relatives.[25] Moreover, I draw on mobility as a useful umbrella term that encapsulates a range of interrelated forms of geographic displacement, such as migration and tourism. Thus defined, my conception of mobility is closely aligned with the term's use in the field of urban geography. In the founding issue of the journal *Mobilities*, Kevin Hannam describes the study of mobility as an investigation of "both the large-scale movement of people, objects, capital, and information across the world, as well as the more local processes of daily transportation, movement through public space, and the travel of material things within everyday life."[26] He calls upon scholars to study how "complex mobility systems . . . restructure both space and time" and more specifically how those systems effect changes in the physical and social organization of the contemporary city.[27]

That interest, prevalent today among both geographers and anthropologists, recalls the prominence accorded to mobility by modernist architects and urban planners: who framed some of their most prolific design strategies around the question of how to adapt the twentieth-century city to the mechanically enhanced modes of human mobility that were enabled by the automobile, the airplane, and the telephone. Mobility's primacy is evident in the influential designs of Le Corbusier, Richard Neutra, and Antonio Sant'Elia, who envisioned bombastic intermodal transport megastructures as the organizing nodes of the future city.[28] But it was also apparent in the more modest proposals of urban planners such as Colin Buchanan, Eugène Hénard, and Otto Wagner, whose studies of the relationship between transport systems and the inhabitants of cities led to fundamental modifications in urban design, such as the introduction of the traffic circle.[29] Throughout the post–World War II era, the question of mass mobility figured prominently in architectural discourse. Some critics, such as Reyner Banham and Melvin Webber, celebrated the liberating power of the automobile and the airplane and their potential to radically reshape both the physical landscape and dominant conceptions of urbanity.[30] Others, including Alison and Peter Smithson and Victor Gruen, as well as Kevin Lynch, Donald Appleyard, and John Myer, delivered a more measured evaluation, lauding the new design opportunities afforded by mass mobility, yet alerting their audiences to the significant adaptations needed to retrofit the prewar urban fabric to the age of the car and jet.[31]

All of these scholars and practitioners—and this brief overview by no means provides an exhaustive inventory—concerned themselves with the fundamental question of how changes in human mobility led to shifts in urban form. Many drew a direct connection between *geographic* mobility and *social* mobility, arguing that the former articulated the latter. Writing in 1958, Alison and Peter Smithson noted that "mobility has become the characteristic of our period. Social and physical mobility, the feeling of a certain sort of freedom, is one of the things that keeps our society together, and the symbol of this freedom is the individually owned motor car."[32] In other words, in the context of postwar plenty, the *geographic* mobility afforded by the popularization of the automobile served as a proxy for the *social* mobility of a rapidly expanding middle class. Echoes of that positivist sentiment, which remained largely unquestioned until the cultural upheavals of the 1960s, are audible in dominant attitudes toward mobility in the twenty-first-century Asian city. Much of that enthusiasm, however, has been directed not toward the automobile and the freeway, but rather toward the airplane and the airport. It is important to reflect on the fact that, until the very tail end of the twentieth century, the absolute majority of people living in Asia had never been on a plane and had never been outside their home country, either because airfares were unaffordable, or because foreign travel was forbidden by their government, or both. That that paradigm of immobility has shifted so rapidly continues to be both a source of wonder and a cause for celebration among residents of cities like Bangkok, Shenzhen, and Singapore.

The analogy drawn between literal *geographic* mobility and the more abstract notion of *social* mobility—defined as the "ability . . . of individuals . . . to move between different social levels or between different occupations"—did not arise until the second half of the nineteenth century, when the concomitant processes of industrialization and rural-to-urban migration led to a pronounced interest in the mechanisms underlying the movement of capital and labor. One of the earliest instances of that usage was in the *History of Agriculture and Prices,* published in 1866. In it, the economist Thorold Rogers speculated about the migratory potential of both capital *and* labor, presaging one of our current era's most enduring preoccupations: "If hereafter other regions of the world offer fairer prospects to capital, thither, in the increasing communion of nations, capital will inevitably flow. If hereafter the social dignity and material advantages of labour are vindicated in greater measure under other political and economic conditions than those which characterize our polity, thither labour, on which so many circumstances are now conferring mobility and expansion, will inevitably migrate."[33] Curiously, at the midpoint of the nineteenth century an older definition of mobility fell out of fashion. Up until then, "mobility" and its adjectival form "mobile" were widely understood to refer to the "common people," the "working classes," the "rabble."[34] (A remnant of that meaning can still be discerned in the abbreviated form *mob,* which retains the term's older signification.) Mobility was often invoked in contrast to "nobility": with the phonemic similarity of the two words underscoring their diametrically opposed social denotations. It was also used as a synonym for fickleness and instability, two negative attributes often ascribed to the erratic political allegiances of the masses. But from the 1840s onward, these several meanings gradually became lost, as workers' rights advocates adopted the term "mobility" as a badge of proletarian identification in an attempt to rid it of its pejorative connotations.[35]

It is significant that the meaning of mobility was inverted at the historical moment when England's cities were being reconfigured by the processes of industrial urbanization. As farmers left the countryside and poured into the factories and textile mills of Manchester, a contemptuous term for the "unwashed masses" was effectively reinvented as a conceptual signifier for both social advancement and the labor demands of industrial capitalism. In effect, the connotations surrounding the word "mobility" were upended when the flexible movement of the population came to be viewed not as an existential threat but rather as a crucial precondition for larger societal transformations.

A similar change in connotation can be observed today throughout East and Southeast Asia, where the geographic mobility of the masses—once eyed with great suspicion—has instead become an indisputable mantra of modernization. In the context of rapid urbanization, "mobility" appears to be recovering the archaic meaning outlined above: no longer a marker of distinction for a cosmopolitan elite, but rather a matter-of-fact necessity, and occasional indulgence, for a broad cross-section of the population. Undoubtedly, China offers the most vivid example of the paradigm shift in cultural attitudes toward mobility that has taken place in Asia since the end of the twentieth century. As the anthropologist Pál Nyíri notes in his book *Mobility and Cultural Authority in Contemporary China,* until the late 1970s China—like most socialist countries—strictly controlled the movement of its citizens through a bureaucratic system of household registration that severely limited the migration of rural peasants into urban areas. Tourism, too, was perceived as "an element of bourgeois lifestyle and was therefore taboo."[36] Uncontrolled geographic mobility, both within and across China's borders, was considered to be a socially and economically disruptive, and potentially incendiary, activity. However, the reformatory impulses initiated by Deng Xiaoping from the late 1970s onward brought with them a fundamental reconceptualization of individual mobility. No longer viewed with distrust, the movement of people came instead to be identified as a crucial "instrument of modernization and 'civilization.'"[37] Nyíri argues that that "public endorsement of mobility as an attribute of modernity [signaled] a major turnaround" from the PRC's historic attitudes toward the uncontrolled movement of its population: leading to a "valorization of . . . migration in China as an activity that turns . . . 'peasants into citizens,' making them more productive . . . and therefore more aligned with the expectations of the modernizing state."[38] As China's economy flourished, "a culture of leisure travel, once reviled but now promoted by the state, rapidly emerged as an attribute of modern urban lifestyle."[39] Chinese citizens, who had previously been forbidden from traveling abroad, were instead exhorted to do so for the purposes of work, study, and leisure. In the 1990s, state-run newspapers began publishing editorials that encouraged university students and manual laborers to go abroad, emphasizing their patriotic duty to subsequently return home with their accumulated capital and wisdom. Articles in *Worker's Daily* and *People's Daily* praised the "great army of Chinese labor . . . moving from here towards the world" and argued that "transnational work has not only brought in abundant revenue; it has also brought advanced thinking and management methods."[40] At the same time, the central government introduced three annual weeklong holidays, and designated dozens of countries as "approved" vacation destinations for its citizens, in an effort to stimulate foreign travel and "truly make tourism a part of the people's common consumer practices."[41]

The sociospatial implications of these policy shifts are central to the case studies in the first three chapters of this book, which examine the introduction, since 1980, of airport-related infrastructures that are designed to increase the global connectivity of three cities in China's Pearl River Delta. And while China provides the most striking instance of state-endorsed mobility, the fundamental shift in its policies toward cross-border travel is far from exceptional.[42] In Southeast Asia, the emergence of a middle class endowed with a modicum of disposable income, coupled with the attempt to create a common labor market within the ten member states of the Association of Southeast Asian Nations, or ASEAN, has likewise led to a radical reevaluation of mobility. The government of Singapore, for example, has embraced the influx of both skilled and unskilled foreign workers—who collectively constitute about 40 percent of the workforce—as a necessary precondition for the city-state's social and economic advancement. At the same time, poorer countries like Cambodia, the Philippines, and Indonesia encourage the back-and-forth migration of a wide range of laborers—maids, construction workers, nurses, IT professionals. Touting the economic significance of their remittances and the skills acquired abroad as critical components of nation-building, these governments declare overseas workers to be "foreign revenue heroes."[43] Meanwhile, Vietnamese authorities posit binational marriages as a win-win solution to the challenges of rural poverty in developing countries and rural depopulation in developed ones—leading to an exodus of women moving from Vietnamese villages to the countrysides of Taiwan and South Korea.[44] Throughout the region, tourism has become one of the defining emblems of modernization. Cities measure their importance by the volume of tourists flowing through the streets of their old quarters, which more often than not are ill equipped to handle the dramatic leap in visitors. Meanwhile, cheap T-shirts adorned with the names of big cities like Kuala Lumpur and Singapore have become a popular marker of cosmopolitan aspirations, suitable for everyday wear in the supermarket, shopping mall, and hawker center.

Infrastructure and the Everyday

Mass mobility, whether celebrated or excoriated, would not exist without a supporting network of roads, rails, and runways—in other words, without transport *infrastructure,* which forms the second key concern of the book. In so doing, I engage with an emerging interest in infrastructure in the fields of anthropology and urban geography: one that aims for a better understanding of the technical systems and material forms that enable the flow of goods and people across national frontiers. That concern is evident both in Brian Larkin's investigation of the political and aesthetic priorities that inform the planning and design of infrastructure networks; and in the discourse on "migration infrastructure," among such scholars as Lin Weiqiang, Johan Lindquist, Xiang Biao, and Brenda Yeoh, that studies the cross-border transport networks that crucially underpin intra-Asian migration flows.[45] These anthropological meditations are analyzed in greater detail in the two chapters on transborder ferry systems in the Pearl River Delta and low-cost aviation networks in Southeast Asia, where I bring them into dialogue with the firsthand perspectives of the architects and planners who design Asia's airports.

At the same time, I introduce recent attempts among architectural historians to reframe the study of infrastructure in the Asian context. From Shanghai to Istanbul, Dubai to Manila, infrastructure megaprojects—especially those that encourage the "smart" integration of physical and digital networks—are widely regarded as a motor of economic growth, a source of sociocultural transformation, and a one-stop solution for urban challenges of virtually any kind. Writing on India, Chattopadhyay notes:

> Infrastructure is the trope of modern urban thought; it is the basis for imagining, describing, and planning communities. It forms the very channels for the movement of commodities, power, and information that sustain cities. . . . The merit of a city's or region's or nation-state's infrastructure is seen to have a direct correlation to its economic and political robustness. In our daily lives it is everywhere and everything—the all-encompassing effects of capital, a litany of institutions, endless, proliferating circuits of technology.[46]

The primacy placed upon large-scale infrastructure projects by urban policymakers, and the melodramatic fatalism deployed to describe the economic woes that will beset a given city if a proposed project is *not* realized, help to explain why larger social and cultural preoccupations often crystallize around these plans.[47] Yet for all the understandable fascination with these megaprojects—they feed the self-aggrandizing impulses of both the architect and his municipal client, and they provide sustenance to the cultural pessimism of intellectuals—I am skeptical about whether they merit the level of attention that urban scholars have devoted to them. In shifting the focus away from these megaprojects, and from the motivations of urban elites that inform their development, I draw upon Chattopadhyay's call to "unlearn the idea of infrastructure" and to develop a "more expansive view" of infrastructure: one that sheds light on the widespread use of "invisible" systems of transport and communication, which operate outside the domain of formal transportation networks yet are crucial for day-to-day economic and social activities in the contemporary Asian city. Chattopadhyay delves into the unintentional, yet widely tolerated, appropriations of formal infrastructure systems, studying their "physical-material bases so as to grapple with the way [they are] used, manipulated, and undone by the majority in everyday practice." In so doing, she seeks to "not only make it possible to describe how modern infrastructures are appropriated and gnawed at to generate linkages and exchanges that were not intended, but also [to] pry open a window to a different conception of infrastructure" whose "deviance resides in its non-recognition in the eyes of the state. This is not just refusal but the inability of the state to comprehend these structures of exchange and linkages within its own logic."[48]

In effect, Chattopadhyay foregrounds user-driven appropriations of urban infrastructure that develop outside of, or in opposition to, formal processes of top-down master planning. In that sense, her study of Indian cities resonates with the notion of *everyday urbanism* articulated by the design theorists Margaret Crawford, John Chase, and John Kaliski.[49] My own study of infrastructure makes use of both halves of that term: deploying *urbanism* as a fruitful interdisciplinary approach to the city, capable of linking the "aesthetic, intellectual, physical, social, political, economic, and experiential" dimensions of urban life, and in so doing breaching disciplinary divides;[50] and relying on the concept of the *everyday* as an epistemological approach that assigns equal weight to both "lived experience" and "physical form" in its definition of the city.[51] As Crawford explains,

> Everyday space stands in contrast to the carefully planned, officially designated, and often underused public spaces that can be found in most . . . cities. These monumental spaces only punctuate the larger and more diffuse landscape of everyday life, which tends to be banal and repetitive, everywhere yet nowhere, obvious yet invisible. Ambiguous like all in-between spaces, the everyday represents a zone of social transition and possibility with the potential for new social arrangements and forms of imagination.[52]

The intellectual genealogy of everyday urbanism can be traced back to ethnographically informed theoretical concepts advanced by the French philosophers Henri Lefebvre and Michel de Certeau.[53] Rather than rejecting theoretical approaches to the city, Crawford insists instead that these theories are at their most incisive when they derive from observations of actual human beings moving through actual urban spaces. Lefebvre, for example, found in the banal and the trivial aspects of daily life a treasure trove of information for the urban scholar, as the spatial articulation of quotidian routines revealed much about their intersection with larger social, political, and economic processes.[54] De Certeau, meanwhile, emphasized the distinction between two very different modes of operation that characterize the use of urban space: *strategies,* based on place, and *tactics,* based on time. As Crawford notes, "strategies represent the practices of those in power.... They establish a 'proper' place, either spatial or institutional" where strictly defined activities can take place. By contrast,

> A tactic is a way of operating without a proper place, and so depends on time.... Tactics are the "art of the weak," incursions into the field of the powerful. Without a proper place, tactics rely on seized opportunities, on cleverly chosen moments, and on the rapidity of movements that can change the organization of a space.... By challenging the "proper" places of the city, this range of transitory, temporary, and ephemeral urban activities constitutes counterpractices to officially sanctioned urbanisms.[55]

In this book, I draw upon two foundational concepts of everyday urbanism that are particularly applicable to the contemporary Asian city: Crawford's interpretation of tactics, cited above, and her insistence on ethnography and experiential observations as the methodological basis for urban theory. As anyone who spends much time in East and Southeast Asia will observe, much of daily life in the city revolves around the deployment of temporally based tactics. Over the course of a day, a given patch of sidewalk may serve four or five different purposes: a breakfast spot at dawn; a vegetable stand in the late morning; a roadside café at lunchtime; a shady venue for a catnap during the afternoon heat; and a place to sell shoes, iPhone covers, and handbags at night. In effect, the extreme densities of cities like Bangkok and Hong Kong mandate an efficient use of public space that maximizes the quantity and variety of activities that can occur within a twenty-four-hour period. Moreover, spaces that are designed strategically for one specific purpose rarely remain loyal to that officially sanctioned function. In Hong Kong, one of the best examples of that phenomenon is on full display every weekend at the International Finance Centre, or IFC, a luxury shopping center and grade-A office tower complex built in the late 1990s to house the high-speed Airport Express station discussed in the next chapter. Every Sunday, its neatly manicured rooftop garden, outfitted with high-end bars frequented by the businessmen and -women who work in the IFC, transforms into one of dozens of semipublic spaces, located throughout Hong

Kong, where the city's 320,000 Filipino and Indonesian domestic helpers congregate on their weekly day off. Lounging on neatly arranged cardboard boxes that are assembled and disassembled within a span of eight to ten hours, they drastically expand these spaces' programmatic contours beyond their intended purposes, transforming relatively banal and monofunctional urban spaces into dynamic sites of "multiple social and economic transactions, where multiple experiences accumulate in a single location. These places where differences collide or interact," Crawford argues, "are the most potent sites for everyday urbanism."[56]

The conceptual framework of everyday urbanism has its limitations. While it is critical of "professional design discourse, which is based on abstract principles . . . and inevitably produces spaces that have little to do with real human impulses," it elides the fact that the intricately planned and centrally supervised infrastructure networks that are premised upon those abstract principles—roads and highways, for example—nevertheless provide the basic structuring elements upon which "everyday" activities rely.[57] In this book, I have tried to devote equal attention to both the infrastructure plans devised by design professionals and to their everyday appropriations by urban dwellers. In so doing, I argue that the movement of air passengers through Asian cities results from the complementary amalgamation of top-down infrastructure systems, designed by experts; and bottom-up mobility tactics, devised by new members of the flying public whose traveling needs are not always addressed by conventional modes of urban planning.

Tracing Global Mobility in the Asian City

The book's methodological insistence on site-based fieldwork addresses a more abiding problem embedded in studies of the infrastructure of global mobility. While the last decade has seen an outpouring of research on the hubs that dominated air travel in the postwar years—Amsterdam Schiphol, for example, or Chicago's O'Hare—very little scholarly work has been conducted in the world region where aerial mobility has expanded the most dramatically over the past thirty years: Asia.[58] For much of the twentieth century, American and European airports were at the forefront of developments in airport architecture and technology; and served as a model for developing countries around the world. By the early 1990s, however, they had ceded their vanguard role to a new generation of airports being built in Asia and the Middle East.

The shift toward Asia is reflected in an annual statistic compiled by the International Air Transport Association—the trade group of the aviation industry—which charts the "percentage of total scheduled revenue passenger-kilometers" (RPKs) by world region and between world regions. A common reference point of industry technocrats, RPKs represent the number of passengers that fly, multiplied by the distance that they fly. (Put another way, it is the total number of kilometers traveled by all passengers.) In the early 1990s, the majority of global air traffic was concentrated in North America and along the transatlantic corridor. Two decades later, however, the proportion of the world's air travel taking place within North America had declined by half, while Asia's share had nearly tripled.[59]

These statistics reflect the counterpart economic rise of Asia and relative stagnation of the West; the increase in trade between Asia, the Middle East, and Africa; and the growing population of transnational migrants living in Asian cities. They also testify to the reorientation of global aviation networks, and of investments in airport infrastructure, away from their historic bases in Europe and North America. While the geographic scope of airport design has moved on, scholarly research has—with some notable exceptions—clung narrowly to the transatlantic sphere.[60]

Based on five years of research in Asia, *Airport Urbanism* is the first book-length study on airport infrastructure whose primary focus lies outside the West. Much of the research was conducted in the Pearl River Delta. The urban region that includes Hong Kong, Shenzhen, and Guangzhou, the PRD represents an excellent case study for investigating the socioeconomic expansion of international air travel and its implications for architecture and urban design. Since 1980, the volume of air traffic in the PRD has increased by a factor of 50, a process enabled by the construction of five new airports across the region.[61] Endowed with autocratic modes of governance and a tradition of small-scale entrepreneurialism, the region evinces both top-down and bottom-up models of airport design and infrastructure planning. And divided into five distinct territorial entities that are politically separate yet economically interdependent, the PRD offers a unique lens for interrogating the design of airport infrastructure and the negotiation of cross-border mobility in complicated geopolitical contexts.[62] Finally, as one of the key centers of global production and trade, the Pearl River Delta is home to a socioeconomically diverse population of investors, merchants, tourists, and migrants, who rely on an equally heterogeneous mix of formal and informal transport systems in order to travel to, from, and around the region.

Chapter 1 focuses on several sites located along the thirty-kilometer road and rail corridor that connects Hong Kong International Airport (HKIA) to downtown Hong Kong: contrasting the normative projections that informed its planning and design in the 1980s and 1990s with the heterodox uses that characterized its day-to-day operations in the first two decades of the twenty-first century. Studying the development of a suburban new town and a subsidized network of airport shuttle buses, the chapter demonstrates how a housing estate and a transport system intended for employees of HKIA have been appropriated by budget air travelers—such as Mainland Chinese tourists, lower-middle-class Hongkongers, and Filipino domestic helpers—as an informal means of traveling cheaply to the airport. Using Melvin Webber's concept of "channel capacity," the chapter theorizes the insertion of these passengers into the everyday spaces of a suburban new town and critiques the failure of transport designers to adequately plan for their needs.

Chapter 2 investigates the development of an "upstream" check-in system that allows passengers in the Mainland Chinese province of Guangdong to fly through HKIA without going through Hong Kong's customs and immigration procedures. These facilities serve travelers whose movement across international frontiers is limited by their income or citizenship: such as Mainland tourists or traders from Africa and the Middle East. A sealed ferry then takes them across the border to Hong Kong where, isolated from other passengers, they proceed directly to their departure gate. Mapping the movement of passengers between the upstream ports and HKIA, the chapter uses the ferry terminals' spatial logic and aesthetic composition as a means of interpreting broader discrepancies in global migration regimes, and in the political and economic framework of the PRD.

The third chapter continues that theme through an investigation of cross-border buses that transport air travelers between Hong Kong and Shenzhen: Asia's largest special economic zone, and a prime example of a peculiar type of frontier urbanism that has emerged across the continent since the end of the twentieth century. I trace the history of the city's aviation infrastructure in order to investigate the tension between Shenzhen's aspirations to become a cosmopolitan global city and the constraints entailed by its subordination to regional economic interests and national security concerns. I argue that that tension has produced a variety of spatial and typological experiments that provide a unique insight into the distinctive social dynamics and spatial organization of Asia's special border zones.

Chapter 4 shifts the book's geographic focus toward Southeast Asia: a rapidly developing part of the world where low-cost aviation has effectively become the dominant mode of cross-border travel. Studying the emergence of budget airport facilities in Bangkok, Kuala Lumpur, and Singapore, the chapter models a regional geography of low-cost mobility and interrogates the influence of the budget airline industry on broader processes of urbanization and regional integration. Through an investigation of three distinct modes of engagement with low-cost mobility, the chapter identifies a tension between the populist narratives espoused by budget airlines and the airport designs produced by state planning agencies, who have only belatedly and begrudgingly responded to the pluralization of the flying public. In so doing, I posit the low-cost airport as a useful lens for interpreting broader contradictions in the planning, design, and use of Southeast Asian cities.

The book concludes with an account of my relocation to Singapore in 2012. Through observations of daily life in the city-state and interviews with its planning agencies, the final chapter examines the urban design challenges that Singapore has encountered as the number of short-term residents approaches parity with the permanent population. Reflecting on the preceding chapters, I identify three interconnected issues that are confronting the contemporary Asian city, and propose policy, design, and research strategies that address them. In so doing, I argue that the disciplines of architecture and urban planning, along with scholarly approaches to urban development in Asia, need to be fundamentally reconceptualized in order to engage with the changes that greater cross-border mobility has produced, and will undoubtedly continue to produce, in the domains of transport, housing, and recreation.

ONE

Parallel Lines

Over the past twenty years, Hong Kong has shed its roots as a colonial trading hub between China and the outside world and emerged as a global financial center: a place where everyone, from everywhere, comes to do business. That transition, spurred on by the former British colony's return to Chinese rule in 1997, has entailed a counterpart physical reprogramming of the urban landscape predicated on massive investments in infrastructure and land reclamation. The most dramatic (and costly) of those endeavors was the Airport Core Program: a ten-point urban redevelopment scheme that centered around the construction of a new airport—Hong Kong International Airport, or HKIA—built on the artificial island of Chek Lap Kok off the coast of Lantau, a sparsely populated region on the territory's southwestern fringe (Figure 1.1a and 1.1b). Built between 1992 and 1998, the Airport Core Program's ten projects also encompassed a thirty-four-kilometer high-speed rail and road corridor between HKIA and downtown Hong Kong; a suburban new town constructed on the periphery of the airport; and a land reclamation project in Victoria Harbour, studded with hotels, office towers, and shopping malls, that effectively increased the size of Hong Kong's central business district by more than 20 percent (see Plate 2). Throughout the 1990s, nearly all of the world's dredging equipment was stationed off the coast of Hong Kong, harvesting sand from the South China Sea upon which to build these various projects.[1]

Designed as a replacement for the minuscule colonial-era airport at Kai Tak, HKIA became, in little more than a decade, the world's busiest trans-shipment center for air cargo; and served more than 50 million passengers per year. Among the small but tightly knit community of airport designers, the Airport Core Program is well known for the infrastructural bravado underpinning its rapid construction and completion: a feat made possible by heaps of cash, top-down models of governance, and by Hong Kong's well deserved reputation for efficiency. By nearly any measure, Hong Kong's is one of the best airports in the world. Yet the Airport Core

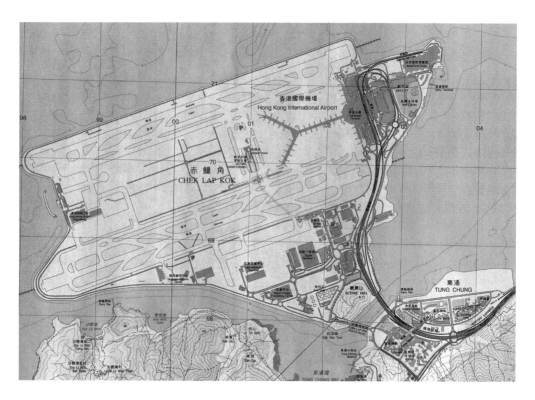

FIGURES 1.1A AND 1.1B. A map and aerial photograph of Chek Lap Kok, a man-made island built to house Hong Kong International Airport. Map courtesy of Survey and Mapping Office, Lands Department, Government of the Hong Kong Special Administrative Region. Photograph courtesy of Airport Authority Hong Kong.

Program's awe-inspiring panoply of bridges, tunnels, and intermodal transit hubs obscures an underlying tension between how these projects were planned and how they operate in practice: a persistent gap that can be attributed to the socioeconomic expansion of the flying public and the challenges that it presents for the design of urban infrastructure networks. Built primarily for foreign executives who are long on money and short on time, Hong Kong's airport infrastructure has struggled to keep pace with the growth in nontraditional passengers whose temporal and financial priorities, spatial practices, and aesthetic predilections differ significantly from those of the corporate business traveler.

This chapter focuses on three projects introduced under the auspices of the Airport Core Program: Airport Express, a high-speed rail line that links HKIA to two "in-town check-in terminals"; the Airbus network, a system of double-decker coaches that connects all of Hong Kong's eighteen districts to HKIA; and Tung Chung, a suburban new town built on the edge of the airport. Bringing the normative projections that informed the planning of these projects into dialogue with the heterodox uses that characterize their day-to-day operations, the chapter reveals how newer members of the flying public—such as budget tourists, students, and migrant workers—have appropriated transport networks and communal facilities intended for a local audience in order to move cheaply to and from the airport. I argue that the failure of Hong Kong's planners to anticipate the mobility demands of these less monied passengers led to an unintentional desegregation of the city's urban transport systems, which were designed according to a strict separation between local and long-distance traffic. In the conclusion, I draw upon Melvin Webber's concept of "channel capacity" in order to theorize the insertion of these passengers into the everyday spaces of a suburban new town; and to identify qualities of cosmopolitanism, centrality, and connectivity in buildings and neighborhoods that are usually considered to be parochial, peripheral, and disconnected. In so doing, I critique a common conception of urban form—prevalent among both scholars and practitioners—that imagines the contemporary Asian city as an amalgam of monofunctional urban spaces occupied by either hypermobile elites or subaltern, and intransient, local constituents.

Airport Express: "We have brought our new airport back to the city"

Most contemporaneous accounts of HKIA's construction identified it as a means of reassuring Hong Kong's inhabitants that their city would remain well connected to the world beyond China in spite of its absorption into the PRC.[2] According to this narrative, the new airport represented a massive infrastructural attempt to quell pre-millennial anxieties, and to stave off a widely feared economic collapse, in the run-up to the 1997 handover.[3] Less charitable observers perceived HKIA as the last-minute boondoggle of a departing colonial power, one that was intent upon draining Hong Kong's financial reserves before relinquishing the city to the Chinese.[4]

While both analyses circulated widely in the late 1990s, the decision to relocate Hong Kong's airport to Chek Lap Kok can be better understood as part of a broader movement among urban policymakers in Asia—who, confronted by exponential growth rates in air traffic, endeavored to replace existing inner-city airfields with much larger ones located far from the urban core, often on artificial islands in the sea. Executed throughout East and Southeast Asia, these relocation projects aimed to enable twenty-four-hour flight operations, to "reduce friction" with the airport's immediate neighbors, and to allow for greater flexibility in future expansion plans.[5] The first city to do so was Osaka, which opened the New Kansai Airport in Japan's Inland Sea in 1994. Similar airport island projects were realized concurrently in Hong Kong, which inaugurated HKIA in 1998; as well as at South Korea's Incheon Airport, which opened three years later.[6]

In fact, the site for Hong Kong's new airport—Chek Lap Kok, a distant island on Hong Kong's southwestern fringe—had been identified decades earlier, in a feasibility study conducted by the Los Angeles–based consultancy firm Ralph Parsons.[7] Written in 1975, the study speculated that the expansion in international trade and cross-border migration would give rise to a new generation of air terminals located far away from the cities that they served, and would demand significant innovations in the mobility systems used to convey passengers to and from the airport:

> In the area of ground transport, a major shift in emphasis to public transport could have a marked effect on terminal operations. . . . Processing of passengers and cargo in remote locations has not been very successful in the past, but increased dependence on public transport could make such solutions more palatable in future years, perhaps even essential. Airports located long distances from urban centers could possibly support ground vehicles operating on exclusive guideways to several distribution centers, conceivably operating directly from the aircraft parking stand.[8]

Until the early 1990s, Asian airports were planned along the lines of American precedents like Dallas–Fort Worth and Denver: enormous hubs surrounded by interstate highways and a low-density suburban landscape where most passengers drive to the airport.[9] However, that model proved difficult to replicate in the context of a hyperdense Asian city with extremely low rates of car ownership. Parsons's radical vision of a decentralized airport, predicated on multiple "distribution centers" located throughout the city and connected to the airport via dedicated "guideways," offered an attractive alternative and found its ultimate realization in downtown Hong Kong.

Indeed, the most innovative aspect of Hong Kong's new airport was not the terminal itself—which essentially elaborated on Norman Foster's earlier design for Stansted, London's low-cost hub—but rather its fundamental reconceptualization of the management of passenger flows between the airport and the city.[10] Whereas most travelers at Kai Tak had arrived by taxi or by bus, passengers at the new airport were invited to use Airport Express, a high-speed train that linked HKIA to two "in-town check-in terminals" in Kowloon and on Hong Kong Island (see Figure 1.2 and 1.3). Built between 1994 and 1998 by the city's Mass Transit Railway Corporation (MTRC), the train corridor spans 34km, much of which built on reclaimed land.[11] An article in *Architectural Record* noted,

> Although much media attention has been showered on the new . . . airport terminal, . . . the most profoundly felt modifications will reach deeply into the infrastructure of Hong Kong and Kowloon. . . . [A] departing traveler's airport "experience" will actually begin long before he or she ever reaches Chek Lap Kok. Arriving by subway, bus, ferry, taxi, or automobile, passengers will enter two new express-rail terminals—one in the Central district . . . and one in Kowloon. . . . At either station, the traveler checks luggage and receives a boarding pass at the In-Town-Check-In Hall before proceeding to a railway platform, from where trains will zip over to the airport.[12]

Airport Express thus outsourced basic aviation procedures from the airport itself and inserted them into the urban fabric of downtown Hong Kong. In so doing, the express train link promised to give travelers more control over where and how they spent the hours leading up to their flight. For example, people leaving late at night might drop their bags at the in-town check-in after work, meet friends for dinner,

FIGURE 1.2. An advertisement for Airport Express, the high-speed train that links Hong Kong International Airport to downtown Hong Kong. Image by MTRC.

FIGURE 1.3. Interior of an Airport Express train.

and then head back to Airport Express in time to fly out. As the designers of the Kowloon check-in terminal boasted: "For passengers, having checked in baggage and obtained boarding passes, the whole city becomes as much a part of the airport as the lounges, shops, and concourses of the airport terminal itself."[13] Both the airport's master plan as well as a more detailed railway feasibility study projected that the absolute majority of passengers would use Airport Express to get to HKIA.[14] The planning consultants who authored these studies argued that rising levels of GDP, and a corresponding increase in travelers' "value of time," would provide a reliable customers base for the rather pricey service which, for around 13 U.S. dollars each way, would shuttle business travelers and foreign tourists between the airport and "the principal air passenger destinations in the Territory," namely Hong Kong Island and southern Kowloon, the site of many international hotel chains. As the primary means of accessing the airport, the express line was accorded a "high profile" in the airport's layout—and in the extension of Hong Kong's central business district, which was designed around Airport Express's two downtown stations.[15]

These "in-town check-in terminals" presented a range of logistical quandaries.[16] Air passengers tend to travel with a large amount of personal belongings and are slower and less familiar with their surroundings than the average commuter.[17] Moreover, since few travelers would be able to access the check-in terminals by foot, the terminals needed to be designed as rapid redirection centers, allowing passengers to transfer quickly between the airport railway, taxis, and a dedicated system of hotel shuttle buses.[18] The stations were thus designed as a hybrid typology: combining the spaciousness and service standards of an international airport with the rapid transfer capabilities of an urban subway system (see Figure 1.4). Planners installed an armada of check-in desks where passengers could receive a boarding pass and surrender their bags. Their luggage, in turn, would be loaded onto a baggage car located at the end of each express train, transferred to the airport, and screened for security purposes upon arrival at Chek Lap Kok.[19] Maintaining HKIA's time-efficiency guidelines demanded voluminous departure and arrival halls; comparably sized spaces were likewise planned for baggage handling facilities behind the scenes. Bends and columns were to be avoided in order to accelerate passenger flow rates.[20] All of these facilities were to be given finishes of "a significantly higher standard, consistent with that of an international airport" (Figure 1.5).[21]

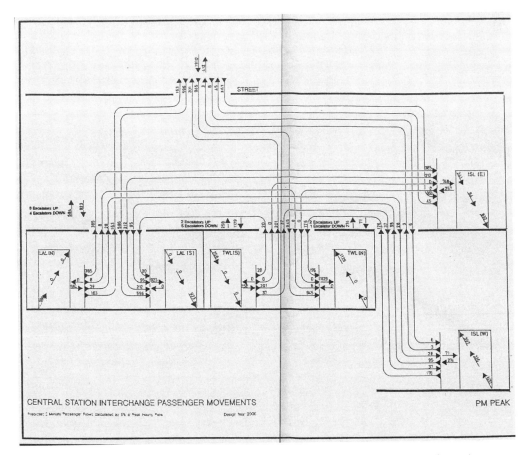

FIGURE 1.4. A map of peak-hour passenger flow projections at Hong Kong Station provides an insight into the material culture and technocratic mindset of airport planners. Map courtesy of Airport Authority Hong Kong.

FIGURE 1.5. Check-in hall at Hong Kong Station, the downtown terminus of the Airport Express line.

Combining the flexibility of a remote airfield with the convenience of a downtown air terminal, the Airport Express stations required a formal and programmatic extension of the airport terminal environment into the urban fabric of the inner city.[22] In 1992, the MTR selected the Hong Kong–based architect Rocco Yim and the global infrastructure firm Arup to design Hong Kong Station. The most visible icon of the Airport Core Program's ten projects, the station anchors the two skyscrapers of César Pelli's International Finance Centre (IFC), and was planned as the downtown terminus of the Airport Express line. Built on reclaimed land— the architects' initial site visits were made by boat—the eight-hectare plot increased the size of Hong Kong's Central district by more than 10 percent (see Plate 3 and Figure 1.6).[23] Following a logic of vertical zoning, the MTR located the site's transport infrastructure beneath a podium-level shopping mall that supports three office towers, two luxury hotels, and a serviced apartment complex.[24] The station's main hall houses check-in desks, flight departure displays, and luggage trolleys within a cantilevered terminal building whose pronounced horizontality stands in striking contrast to the extreme verticality of central Hong Kong's thickly settled forest of skyscrapers.[25]

The station was designed as the first impression of the city for the arriving air passenger: Hong Kong's "front door to the world" (Figure 1.7).[26] Yet despite the enormous amount of money and effort that went into building Airport Express, from the get-go Hong Kong Station suffered from disappointing passenger figures and poorly frequented commercial spaces. While planners had estimated that more than half of all travelers would use Airport Express to get to HKIA, by 2010 only about every fifth passenger did so.[27] The railway's underperformance was largely a function of the changing demographic profile of Hong Kong's flying public. Early plans for Chek Lap Kok noted that only a small fraction of Hongkongers could afford the cost of a plane ticket, and that its airport would be used, by and large, by businessmen and foreign tourists. Accordingly, planning consultants designed its airport infrastructure for a well-heeled, nonlocal audience that was not particularly familiar with Hong Kong's geography—hence Airport Express's oversimplified toponymy ("Hong Kong Station," "Kowloon Station"), its emphasis on shuttling passengers to hotels in the central business district, and planners' insistence that the railway be designed in the aesthetic vernacular of a business-class lounge. By the late 1990s, as air travel became cheaper and more accessible to the general population, planning consultants reluctantly began to identify the need for a more affordable means of accessing the airport that would serve a wider socioeconomic spectrum of passengers.

An influential transport study recommended the creation of a dedicated system of airport buses between HKIA and the main hotel zones and commercial districts in southern Kowloon and Hong Kong Island.[28] The consultants' assertions that

FIGURES 1.6. A photograph taken in 1996 shows the construction of Hong Kong Station and the extension of the central business district. Photograph courtesy of Information Services Department Photo Library, Hong Kong.

FIGURE 1.7. Night view of Hong Kong Station.

these buses were not needed in the New Territories—home to the majority of Hong Kong's population—were disproven at a series of public meetings, which revealed strong demand for direct airport links to and from peripheral new towns such as Sha Tin, Tsuen Wan, and Lam Tin.[29] Contradicting the wisdom of transport planners, these public consultations suggested that the airport's customer base had expanded into nearly every single one of Hong Kong's eighteen districts—reflecting a flying public that was much more geographically dispersed than previously assumed. In the wake of these findings, Hong Kong's government commissioned a fleet of double-decker "Airbuses" outfitted with luggage racks, comfortable seating, and television monitors that allow passengers to keep an eye on their belongings. Operated as a limited-stop express service, the Airbuses ferry passengers to the airport for about four U.S. dollars—one-third of the price of an Airport Express ticket (see Plate 4). Plying the traffic-clogged thoroughfares of Hong Kong Island and Kowloon, and weaving their way through the residential tower blocks of the New Territories, the Airbuses quickly became a common sight throughout the city (Figure 1.8).

One of the Airbuses' users is Anna, a thirty-nine-year-old Filipino cleaning woman I met through one of her clients.[30] When I first asked Anna if I could accompany her to the airport, she was understandably skeptical; she ultimately agreed, however, and asked me to phone her the night before her trip to make arrangements. When I call her on a Friday night, Anna is both exhausted from a long workweek as well as excited about her upcoming vacation: "My flight leaves at nine o'clock tomorrow morning. Do you know the Ramada Hotel in Sai Ying Pun? Good. Meet me in front of the Ramada at 6:30. Or maybe a little earlier. The bus will come at 6:35 and it only runs at thirty-minute interval."

At 6:20 the following morning, it's still dark outside as the first shift of workers shuffle to the tram stop, tired faces lit up by the sodium glow of street lamps. Anna is hurrying down Des Voeux Road toward a bus stop on the corner of Water Street. She is accompanied by her landlord, an affable Filipino in his late thirties, who is helping her with her luggage: a giant suitcase held shut with twine, a carry-on trolley, a blue IKEA tote bag stuffed with wooden shelves, a black Jimmy Choo purse, a courier bag, and a laptop.

"So many things!" her landlord exclaims.

Anna laughs. "All presents!"

She queues up behind a handful of other people waiting for the A12. When the bus arrives a few minutes later, it is completely packed with passengers, about half of whom are also Filipino. Every seat is taken, and the aisles are filled with cardboard boxes, much more than the appointed luggage racks can handle (Figure 1.9). There is just enough room for Anna and me to squeeze into the doorway. She frowns. "Normally the bus is not this full. But right now there are school holidays in the Philippines, and it's almost Easter."

Anna has been working in Hong Kong since 1999. Although she only travels back to the Philippines once a year, her life is evenly divided between the two places. Two of her siblings also work as domestic helpers in Hong Kong, while the rest of her family, including her two children, live in a small village in northern Luzon. Anna has timed her annual trip to coincide with the holidays and her daughter's high school graduation. "Once I went home for Christmas, but the ticket was so expensive. So I usually fly in April or May. I go back once a year, for three weeks. Two weeks is too short! But I am lucky—many people only go back every two years. My employer will pay for one ticket every two years, and I pay for the other. It's OK."

Like most Filipino women living in Hong Kong, Anna is a "foreign domestic helper" (FDH). For about 500 U.S. dollars per month—the "minimum allowable wage" set by the government—domestic helpers cook, clean, and care for children

FIGURE 1.8. Passengers wait for an Airbus at a bus stop in the Yau Ma Tei district of Kowloon.

FIGURE 1.9. The Airbus that Anna takes to get to the airport.

and the elderly six days a week.[31] There are more than three hundred thousand helpers living in Hong Kong, making up 8 percent of the workforce.[32] Most come from Indonesia and the Philippines. Their length of stay and freedom of movement are strictly regulated: FDHs live in Hong Kong on two-year fixed contracts and are guaranteed a return flight to their country of origin at the end of their term, paid for by the employer. This regulation has generated a brisk trade in "domestic helper fares" that can only be purchased by the helper's employer. Cathay Pacific, for example, offers round-trip flights to Manila for as little as 100 U.S. dollars, which includes an allowance for excess baggage.[33] These tickets cater to a very specific clientele: middle- and upper-class Hongkongers buying plane tickets for Southeast Asian servants who are loaded down with gifts for their relatives.

Officially, domestic helpers are required to live with their employers for two years before returning to their home country. Unofficially, many helpers spend decades in Hong Kong, work part-time for many customers, and sleep in illegal boarding houses in order to save more money for the remittances that they send home. Anna is a typical example, sharing a cramped four-room flat with five other helpers in a working-class section of Sai Ying Pun. During the fifteen years that she has spent in Hong Kong, Anna has become an expert in coordinating trips to the Philippines. "When I lived in Wanchai, I used to take the airport train. It is nice with the in-town check-in. But now that I live in Sai Ying Pun, the bus stops right in front of my door, so it is more convenient—and it's cheaper. The train and the bus both take the same amount of time. With the Airbus, there's no need to go to Central."

I ask Anna how her friends travel to the airport.

"Most of them go by airport bus. You can also take the E bus," Anna notes, referring to a network of heavily subsidized buses operated on behalf of the sixty thousand people working in and around HKIA. Intended for airport employees, E buses are much more spartan in their layout; and make frequent stops in the logistics centers, catering facilities, and office parks that cluster around the airfield. Fares are correspondingly cheap: for less than two U.S. dollars, passengers can travel between Chek Lap Kok and any of Hong Kong's major residential districts. "But the E bus takes fifteen minutes longer, makes lots of stops, and then when it gets to the airport . . ." Anna makes a weaving motion with her hand and grimaces. "So you must be patient. But it's very, very cheap!"

She pauses to think. "Oh, and another way you can go is by moving van. Because when your employer moves to a new flat, the helper organizes the move. You have to call up a moving company to come get the furniture. There are many companies to choose, so sometimes they offer you a deal: if you use my company, then the next time you need to go to the airport, we will drive you there for free." Gesturing to her luggage, Anna remarks, "This is very useful—people take a lot of things back to the Philippines!"

The bus accelerates as it enters the Lantau Link, an elevated highway that snakes its way through the port facilities of western Kowloon, along the same narrow strip of reclaimed land upon which the tracks of the Airport Express are built. Over the course of the half-hour ride to the airport, Anna outlines her upcoming trip. "I will fly to Manila, and then from Manila I take a flight to Tuguegarao. It's my first time taking a domestic flight in the Philippines. Normally I take the bus, which takes ten hours. But the flight is just one hour! And from Tuguegarao I take a bus to my home town—two more hours."

Her narrative is interrupted by the beeping of her cell phone. She extracts it from her handbag, frowns at the screen, and types a short reply. "It's from my sister in Manila. Philippine Airlines"—the operator of her flight to Tuguegarao—"only allow fifteen kilos free luggage, so I will leave the rest for her. She and her husband have a car in Manila. Her husband will meet me at the airport and I will give him my luggage, and then they will put it in the car and drive to my hometown tomorrow."

The bus marshals on, across two sets of suspension bridges, and zips down the highway that hugs the rugged coast of northern Lantau island, passing the skyscraper apartment blocks of Tung Chung before making a sharp turn onto Chek

Lap Kok island. Five minutes later, the A12 pulls up to the curb of the departures level at HKIA and Anna hauls her belongings onto a trolley. It is 7 a.m., and the terminal is swarming with passengers (Figure 1.10). Steering her overstuffed trolley toward Cathay Pacific's check-in desks, Anna recognizes two friends—also flying to Manila, but on a different flight—and wishes them a happy vacation.

Anna's trajectory on the Airbus points to the resourcefulness of nontraditional air travelers in devising alternate forms of transportation when existing systems cannot accommodate their needs: a disconnect between supply and demand that is best viewed through the lens of luggage. Baggage weighed heavily on the minds of the planners of Airport Express, and the accommodation of travelers' personal belongings figured prominently in the designs for the in-town check-in stations. But these facilities were not planned for someone like Anna, who transports the equivalent of her body weight in food, furniture, clothing, and electronics on each of her annual trips to the Philippines. The baggage habits of foreign domestic helpers like Anna suggest that there is an inverse relationship between how often people fly and how much they carry with them: evident when one compares the travel patterns of the frequent flyer—who tries to pare down his or her belongings to the

FIGURE 1.10. Foreign domestic helpers wait for a flight to Manila at Hong Kong International Airport.

bare necessities—to those of a migrant worker, who returns home once a year weighed down by dozens of presents for friends and relatives. In other words, those who have the fewest financial resources fly with the most amount of swag. Such practices have been codified in the added baggage allowances with which airlines like Cathay Pacific advertise their special domestic helper fares and are on full display in the baggage claim areas of Asian airports that are on the receiving end of transnational remittances: places like Ninoy Aquino International Airport in Manila, and Tân Sơn Nhất in Ho Chi Minh City, whose conveyor belts are perpetually clogged with the overstuffed boxes of the millions of workers returning home from abroad.

The lack of room for Anna on the Airbus indicates that conventional transport systems, while making provisions for the storage of luggage, fail to take into account the alternate temporal rhythms of Hong Kong's migrant workforce: as the Airbuses, along with the airport itself, become periodically overwhelmed by the Filipino holiday schedule and the gift-giving obligations that those celebrations entail. The recourse of domestic helpers to local moving vans thus presents an interesting alternative: as small-scale entrepreneurs, detecting an underserved clientele, cater to the nonstandard spatial demands of Filipino maids in order to secure the moving contracts of their employers. In effect, the moving van—an emblem of domestic relocation—becomes redeployed to serve the cross-border mobility practices of Hong Kong's low-wage transnational commuters.

Tung Chung: Mainland Tourists in the Airport Suburb

Shortly before arriving at the airport, Anna's bus passes through Tung Chung New Town: a dense cluster of high-rise apartment blocks that lines Chek Lap Kok's southern flank. Tung Chung was planned as an "airport support community," designed to house the sixty thousand pilots, flight attendants, and ground staff working at HKIA (Figure 1.11). The new town is also the terminus of the Tung Chung Line (TCL), a local subway line that shuttles commuters between Tung Chung and Hong Kong Station on a railway track that runs parallel to Airport Express. Both lines were planned with a distinct clientele in mind, distinguished by "the willingness to pay, the time of travel, and the need for luggage provision."[34] Whereas Airport Express provides a "business class style" environment aimed at air passengers, planners designed the Tung Chung Line to serve so-called "domestic" travelers: that is, the residents of Tung Chung as well as airport employees, who were expected to take the train to Tung Chung and then transfer to a fleet of shuttles to the various office parks and industrial facilities at Chek Lap Kok. Accordingly, Airport Express is faster and makes fewer stops, provides luggage carts on the platform and baggage racks inside the train, and is five times more expensive than the Tung Chung Line.

FIGURE 1.11. Built between 1992 and 1998, Tung Chung New Town was designed as a residential extension of Hong Kong's new airport at Chek Lap Kok. Photograph courtesy of Information Services Department Photo Library, Hong Kong.

The first new town to be built on one of Hong Kong's outlying islands, Tung Chung feels decidedly remote. Much like Airport Express, the housing development struggled to attract its intended users, as most airport employees preferred a longer commute to living on the city's extreme periphery. In fact, many continued to live in Kowloon City, the neighborhood surrounding the former site of Hong Kong's airport.[35] In their stead, Tung Chung became a magnet for what might uncharitably be described as B-grade expats: a new generation of middle-class foreigners who, displaced by the financial doldrums in the West, have found work in Hong Kong but do not enjoy the generous housing and travel allowances that were once de rigueur for expat workers (Figure 1.12). Particularly for singles and young families, the affordable rents and easy access to nature make Tung Chung an acceptable alternative to the astronomical cost of living on Hong Kong Island. The new town's unusual demographics are reflected in the district's census figures: while non-ethnic Chinese made up just 6 percent of Hong Kong's resident population in 2013, they composed one-quarter of those living in Tung Chung.[36] Hailing from Europe, North America, and Australia, these expats reside conspicuously within a new town that has a distinctly local, and distinctly suburban feel: a windswept landscape of middle-income shopping malls and wet markets, populated by young mothers with small children.

Coinciding with the construction of the new town, the Tung Chung Line was built to stimulate urban development on Lantau and to encourage HKIA's employees to relocate closer to the airport. Operating in parallel to the airport railway, the TCL connects Hong Kong Station to Tung Chung in about thirty minutes, making frequent stops in down-at-heel housing estates and industrial wharves along

FIGURE 1.12. Residents and air passengers in Tung Chung New Town.

Kowloon's western shore. Significantly, however, the line terminates at Tung Chung rather than continuing to the airport: a measure, implemented at the behest of planners, that aimed at preventing passengers from using the subway line as a cheaper substitute for Airport Express.[37]

In practice, however, that is precisely what happened. Opting for a compromise between price and speed, travelers of more modest means take the Tung Chung Line from Hong Kong Island or Kowloon to Tung Chung, cross the new town's central plaza, and head into a cavernous bus depot that houses a fleet of "E" buses (see Plates 5 and 6). This route is particularly popular among local students and lower-middle-class families—and among Mainland Chinese tourists who, chatting *sopra voce* in Mandarin, are a conspicuous presence on the Tung Chung Line. As discussed in greater detail in the next chapter, until the early 2000s it was all but impossible for most Mainlanders to visit Hong Kong. But with disposable incomes rising and immigration barriers falling, the city has been inundated with Chinese tourists. Whereas in the 1990s Hong Kong counted around 2 million annual visitors from China, by 2014 more than 40 million Mainland citizens traveled to Hong Kong each year, accounting for two-thirds of the city's overnight guests.[38] One of the main reasons why they come to Hong Kong is to shop: especially for global brands that—due to Hong Kong's status as a free port and the attendant absence of import and sales taxes—are both cheaper and more plentiful than on the Mainland.

One of the cheapest places to buy those goods is Citygate, a gigantic outlet mall that dominates Tung Chung's central plaza. Transferring between the subway and the bus on their way to the airport, many Mainland tourists make a quick detour to the mall. Designed by Anthony Ng Associates, a local architecture firm that also planned the ground transportation hub at HKIA, Citygate and the surrounding pedestrian plaza display a high degree of aesthetic continuity with the airport terminal down the road; as the shopping center's corridors, roof canopy, and structural supports recall an airport concourse rather than the dominant shopping mall typologies prevalent in Hong Kong's new towns (Figure 1.13). At Citygate, Mainland tourists arriving on the Tung Chung Line speed past expat moms and toddlers engaging in their daily kaffeeklatsch at the mall's various pastry shops. The Mainlanders, by contrast, are on a mission to buy as many discounted Western brands as possible before running to catch a flight at HKIA. On any day of the week, the outlet stores—Adidas, Tommy Hilfiger, Ralph Lauren—are mobbed, their narrow aisles blocked by suitcases and carry-on bags. On the plaza outside, Chinese tourists occupy every available seat at Starbucks, munching on homemade snacks packed tightly inside Tupperware containers. Others meander aimlessly around the enormous plaza, searching for onward transportation to the airport. (Since the buses that connect Tung Chung to HKIA are designed primarily for employees commuting to the airport, the signage system at Citygate's bus hub is a bit opaque, and certainly not consonant with those intended for nonlocal, first-time users.) After several stops in the freight, catering, and back office facilities that surround the airfield, the bus deposits travelers at the foot of the airport terminal at a nondescript bus stop, lined with gigantic exhaust fans and airport staff taking cigarette breaks, where a fresh batch of tourists and locals returning from abroad are waiting to make the reverse trip back to Tung Chung (Figure 1.14). Hauling their luggage behind them, the travelers cross the service road and walk beneath the elevated tracks of the Airport Express line to a bank of escalators that take them to the check-in desks on the departures level.

Conclusion

In his 1964 essay "The Urban Place and the Nonplace Urban Realm," the design theorist Melvin Webber investigated the leap in individual mobility, enabled by technological advances in transportation and telecommunication, and its impact on the spatial form and organizational logic of North American cities.[39] His essay attempts to analyze the changes in urban form entailed by the popularization of the automobile and the telephone—technologies that were by no means new but that had been a marker of social exclusivity for much of their existence and had only recently become affordable to the masses. Through their popularization, Webber

FIGURE 1.13. Interior of Citygate outlet mall, Tung Chung.

FIGURE 1.14. Passengers queue for the airport employee bus along Hong Kong International Airport's service road. The elevated tracks of the Airport Express line are visible in the background.

argued, the car and the telephone had radically expanded the territorial boundaries of the modern metropolis and had fundamentally altered the spatial logic of urban activities: replacing the densely populated "unifocal" city, predicated on a downtown area surrounded by concentric rings of settlement, with a multipolar metropolitan region whose inhabitants could quickly and easily interact with one another across great distances. In light of technological changes that were reformatting the scope and scale of urban activities, Webber suggested that what distinguished a given location as "urban" had become decoupled from its historical context—that is, the densely packed, inner-city streets that had facilitated social interaction—and could be more accurately measured through an activity-based conception of urbanity:

> The varieties of activity-related interactions occurring at a given urban space may be taken as an indication of the richness of the cultural and economic life of the people occupying that space. The quantity of information flowing within a given space may be taken as an indicator of probable levels of cultural productivity. Together, variety and quantity of information may yield an index to those elusive qualities of city life that have been intuitively attached to the term "urbanity."[40]

Disentangling urbanity from a particular physical form, Webber suggested that it was *accessibility* and *ease of interaction* that distinguished a given location as "urban": be it a skyscraper-lined downtown boulevard or a strip mall on the peripheral fringe. Significantly, he contended that these nascent urban nodes typically emerged when existing infrastructures could not accommodate an increase in the volume of activities, noting that "where channel capacities are inadequate to the communication or transportation loads and when relief is not in sight, locational adjustments inevitably follow."[41]

While Webber's comments referred to the challenges that mass car ownership posed to the postwar American city, they represent a useful conceptual tool for framing the changes to Hong Kong's urban landscape that have occurred as a result of the exponential leap in air traffic since 1980. In particular, his understanding of urbanity as a "set of spatially structured processes," whose "configurations of communication and transport channels" continuously evolve in response to broader social and technological changes, allows us to use shifts in transport flows in order to identify emerging centers of activity in unlikely places—such as Tung Chung, which has become an extension of the airport in a very different way from the one envisioned by the new town's master plan.[42] As planners' ambitions to turn Tung Chung into a bedroom community for airport employees failed to materialize, the infrastructure designed for them became filled with thrifty users who repurposed the new town into an inexpensive source of expat housing, and as an unofficial hub for cost-conscious tourists looking for a cheap way to get to the airport. Endowed with a modicum of disposable income and a bottomless well of status anxiety, these passengers are not the poorest of the poor. But their newfound stature on the cusp of the Chinese middle class is predicated on cutting corners and making compromises: taking a slow train to a distant mall in order to buy a pair of name-brand sneakers, and then hopping on a bus meant for airport employees (Figure 1.15). As a result, a steady flow of foreign visitors has been inserted into the pedestrian areas of one of Hong Kong's most remote new towns. In effect, these passengers have transformed Tung Chung into the suburban, petit bourgeois equivalent of the International Finance Center: that is, a locus of commerce and intermodal interchange that appeals to a lower-middle-class clientele of air travelers.

In thinking about how to plan a city that can accommodate residents, migrants, and visitors, it is perhaps more rational and straightforward to design separate spaces to cater to their often incongruent needs. But like the separation of functions entailed by modernist theories of urban planning, what might sound good on paper rarely works out in practice. In effect, a segregative approach to planning for locals, migrants, and visitors—intended to increase efficiency, as well as avoid potential frictions—rehearses both the dysfunctionally monofunctional aspects of modernist urban design as well as the segregation of native and nonnative urban

FIGURE 1.15. Mainland Chinese tourists at Tung Chung Station.

populations in nineteenth-century Asian port cities.[43] Here we have Hong Kong Station and the Airport Express, built to ensure the speedy movement of visiting air passengers; and there we have Tung Chung and the E buses, designed to satisfy the housing and transport needs of the local workforce that serves them. At the turn of the twenty-first century, these types of planning strategies led urban scholars to propose a disaggregated conceptual model of urban form: a city sharply divided by income, by levels of social and geographic mobility, and by local and global scales of interaction. That approach is evident, for example, in Stephen Graham and Simon Marvin's identification of "infrastructural bypass" as one of the archetypal facets of the emerging twenty-first-century city. Through the "development of a parallel infrastructure network that effectively connects valued users and places while simultaneously bypassing non-valued users and places," they argued, these infrastructural bypasses physicalize a broader program of urban restructuring: one aimed at integrating cities more efficiently into global networks of communication and exchange by accelerating the movement of high-income individuals between a limited number of economically strategic sites in the urban landscape while ignoring the transportation needs of less privileged segments of the population.[44]

These strategies of sociospatial and economic differentiation undoubtedly informed the planning of Hong Kong's Airport Express line, which was designed as a high-priced, high-speed shuttle between HKIA and the city's central business districts. But if we take a closer look at how that railway corridor operates in practice, it becomes clear that a monofunctional approach to urban development—one that sought to isolate the flow of air passengers from the everyday operations of the city—ultimately yielded underperforming and underutilized spaces, both in the transport facilities designed for travelers and in the residential complexes built for employees. These spaces did not, however, lie fallow, and were instead progressively activated and enlivened through an interpenetration of local and nonlocal functions that was neither intended by planners nor detected by scholars. Indeed, in the absence of systems that were planned for them, newer members of the flying public appropriated subsidized local transport infrastructures operated on behalf of airport employees, recombining them for rather creative and elaborate mobility strategies that make international travel more affordable. In so doing, they engendered an unintentional desegregation of an airport corridor whose planning rested on a strict division between transport systems designed for local residents and workers and those intended for air passengers. In effect, these passengers engage in an entirely different form of "infrastructural bypass" than the one imagined by Graham and Marvin, inasmuch as they deftly circumvent the more expensive top-down routing directives of airport authorities and transit regulators.[45] Mingling with the lower-middle-class expats who frequent Tung Chung's coffee shops, these passengers have injected a degree of what one might call *nonpedigreed cosmopolitanism* into a new town deep inside the New Territories: one that decouples the markers of jet-set privilege—air travel, name-brand shopping, expat housing—from its traditional socioeconomic basis. Located on the margins of Hong Kong, Tung Chung thus embodies a new type of urbanism that does not fit neatly into the established spatial and typological taxonomy of global cities: a cosmopolitan approach to urban space that eschews the extremes of both parochial protectionism and placeless homogenization.

TWO

Transborder Infrastructure

The history of international air travel is studded with big names and bold ambitions: a monograph-heavy hagiography of airport architects that celebrates the monumentality of their designs.[1] By and large, these studies have been dominated by meditations on the iconic nature of airport terminals and on what those icons are meant to convey: national pride and technophilic positivism in the modernist designs of Ernst Sagebiel, Eero Saarinen, and Paul Andreu; "global city" status and transnational connectivity in the starchitectural bravado of Norman Foster, Helmut Jahn, and Renzo Piano. Throughout the relatively short architectural history of air travel, scholars have thus focused primarily on its metonymic function as a vehicle for broadcasting broader technical, political, and economic ambitions. Those desires are readily on display at the dozens of airports being built across China, whose voracious appetite for large-scale infrastructure projects operates as a conspicuous shorthand for the country's expanding geopolitical intentions.

In recent decades, a wide range of architectural historians, urban theorists, and anthropologists have identified the iconic spaces of air travel as a prominent emblem of globalization and the attendant spatial and typological reprogramming of the urban landscape.[2] According to this approach, the architecture of aviation represents an integral component of what Manuel Castells has called the "space of flows": a global infrastructure of transport and communication, rendered in ferrovitreous bombast, that conveys transnational elites through an interconnected network of airport terminals, high-speed railways, and corporate financial centers.[3] Taking a similar approach, Graham and Marvin's influential volume *Splintering Urbanism* depicted airport infrastructure as a sequence of "secessionary network spaces" connected via "elite corridors" to "premium city cores." Designed for a "kinetic elite" impervious to the restrictions of national boundaries, these transport axes provided "seamless interchange for valued spaces and travellers between air and surface transport." In so doing, the architecture of air travel engendered conditions of "local bypass" whereby less privileged people and places became "delinked" and excluded from global networks of aerial mobility.[4]

Both Castells and Graham argued that these phenomena were most evident in the Pearl River Delta, which the former dubbed a "megacity in the making," emblematic of the lopsided social and spatial processes by which developing countries have been integrated into the global economy.[5] Examining urban growth in China, these authors fixed their gaze on the "showpiece infrastructure projects" commissioned by central governments and designed by European starchitects:

> On the eastern Chinese seaboard, arguably the most awesome process of urbanization ever seen on the planet is taking place. . . . [L]oose-knit sprawling spaces like the Pearl River Delta megalopolis . . . are growing at the astonishing rate of 20 percent per year. Widely scattered cities . . . are all laced together unevenly by gleaming new webs of infrastructure. . . . These infrastructures are being starkly configured to meet the needs and spaces of the powerful; lower-income and poorer spaces within the emerging cityscape remain very poorly served.[6]

For both authors, the Pearl River Delta and the architecture of air travel are, respectively, the defining geographic and typological apotheoses of top-down global economic integration in the developing world. Yet a close reading of the PRD's airport infrastructure, based on site visits and interviews with its designers and users, points to the existence of parallel air transport networks, largely undetected by outside observers, that do not cohere with the master narrative outlined above. In this chapter, I argue that the singular focus on iconic architecture has overshadowed the emergence of distinctly *uniconic* air transportation facilities that are designed to plug less privileged people and places into the infrastructure of global mobility. Cheaper, rattier, and more geographically diffuse, these transport networks cater to passengers whose movement across international frontiers is limited by their income, by their citizenship, or by both. These less privileged air travelers, and the so-called "transborder" systems that they use, have radically reordered cross-border flows of goods and people.

Transborder infrastructure is hardly the subject of international design competitions: operated by local entrepreneurs, it is typically found in marginal urban spaces and articulated in a definitively banal aesthetic register (see Plate 7). Yet its unremarkable setting and unexceptional design mask the extraordinary nature of the processes that it enables: namely, to abet the cross-border movement of people who have *just* enough money to travel abroad, but whose passports make it difficult to do so. A feature common to developing world regions where economic contours fail to coincide with political boundaries, transborder infrastructure represents a gray zone, both juridical and aesthetic, that permits discreet forms of exchange that are necessary for the operation of urban economies, yet are undesirable from the perspective of national security.[7] Investigating the development of transborder airport infrastructure in China's Pearl River Delta (PRD) over the past thirty years, the chapter interrogates its spatial logic and aesthetic composition in order to model a new understanding of urban space: one that illuminates an architecture of incipient global mobility that has been inconspicuously inserted into ordinary places and unspectacular structures throughout the PRD.

Specifically, it investigates the emergence of an "upstream" check-in system that allows travelers in Mainland China to fly through Hong Kong International Airport (HKIA) without going through Hong Kong's customs and immigration procedures (Figure 2.1). A joint venture between the airport and Mainland Chinese ferry operators, these "upstream" facilities have been inserted into neighborhoods that are not typically associated with the infrastructure of international air travel. At the upstream terminal in Guangdong province, travelers print their boarding pass, check their luggage, and proceed through Chinese emigration. A sealed ferry then transports them across the border to Hong Kong, where they are transferred to an underground train that takes them directly to their departure gate. Isolated from other passenger flows, these transborder travelers technically never enter Hong Kong.

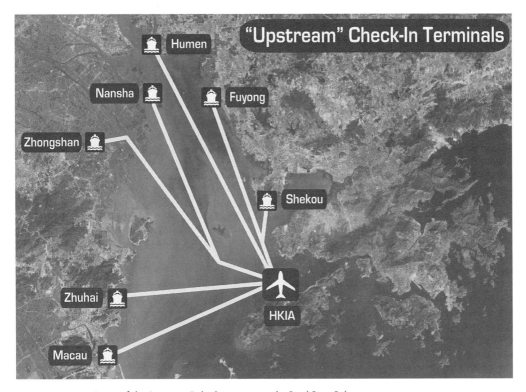

FIGURE 2.1. A map of the "upstream" check-in system in the Pearl River Delta.

FIGURE 2.2. Transborder air passengers who have just arrived from cities in Africa, Asia, and the Middle East travel aboard an automated people mover at Hong Kong International Airport.

Upstream check-in caters to relatively new members of the flying public: Mainland Chinese tourists, for example; as well as traders from Africa, South Asia, and the Middle East (Figure 2.2). Mapping the movement of these *nouveaux globalisés* between the industrial city of Dongguan and HKIA, this chapter traces the historical origins of the upstream check-in system, probes its spatial and aesthetic features, and locates it within a broader tradition of transborder infrastructural engagements with complex geopolitical conditions. By reconceptualizing the aesthetic and typological contours of international air travel, the chapter posits the upstream network as a useful tool for advancing an alternative theory of the impact of global mobility on urban form.

One Country, Two Airspaces

In 2003, Hong Kong International Airport opened an experimental "cross-boundary ferry terminal" called SkyPier. Housed in a provisional structure on HKIA's periphery, SkyPier sought to address the haphazard regulation of international air travel in the Pearl River Delta—regulations that are predicated on fundamental contra-dictions in the region's political and economic frameworks. Over the past thirty years, the PRD has become one of the primary loci of global production and trade.[8] The PRD's central role in the world economy has brought with it an exponential increase in the demand for international air travel to and from its industrial cen-ters. Moreover, the removal of legal restrictions placed on the movement of Main-land Chinese citizens abroad, coupled with the introduction of low-cost tourism in Asia, has enabled members of China's incipient middle class to take leisure trips to nearby countries like Thailand, Malaysia, and Vietnam. In recent decades, the number of Chinese tourists traveling abroad catapulted from 2 million in 1991 to nearly 120 million in 2014, with a disproportionately large share hailing from the prosperous industrial regions of Guangdong.[9] At the same time, the PRD has become a magnet for low-end traders from the Global South who come to its fac-tory towns in search of cheap textiles, plastic goods, and electronic components.

Taken together, the demand for air travel has grown at an exponential rate. Yet that demand conflicts directly with the security and migration concerns of local and national political entities—a disconnect reflected in the complex regulation of the PRD's aerial and terrestrial boundaries. On the ground, the PRD is divided into five distinct political entities,[10] each governed by its own migration and secu-rity regulations. For many travelers, this represents a logistical obstacle: nearly all foreigners require a visa to enter China, and all Mainland Chinese need an entry permit to visit Hong Kong. Many visitors from the developing world require both. Moreover, China's conservative approach to civil aviation severely limits the opera-tion of foreign airlines in Chinese airspace, such that relatively few international flights are available from cities like Guangzhou and Shenzhen; the taxes on these flights are also considerably higher than in Hong Kong.[11] Foreign airlines thus find it cheaper and easier to fly through HKIA.

Thus there exists a peculiar gap in supply and demand for international air travel in the Pearl River Delta. In an attempt to move goods and people across these varying jurisdictions, local transport authorities and entrepreneurs have turned to so-called "transborder" infrastructural strategies such as SkyPier as a means of mediating between the region's dissonant political and economic geographies. These transport facilities aim to smooth over the limitations placed on individual mobil-ity by extending the extraterritoriality of the airport to a network of "upstream" check-in facilities located throughout the PRD. In effect, this "upstream" check-in system circumvents both land and air restrictions by transporting passengers to the airport by sea.[12] An investigation of the Hong Kong–Macau Ferry Terminal in Dongguan interrogates the unlikely genesis of one of these ports, and illustrates how the upstream ferry system works in practice.

Dongguan Humen: "The Path to the World"

Outside of Southern China, very few people have heard of Dongguan—yet it is highly likely that anyone reading this book is wearing a piece of clothing, or using an electronic device, that was manufactured there.[13] A sprawling city of nearly 6 million residents, Dongguan consists of dozens of former villages and rural townships that occupy the hilly terrain on the Pearl River's eastern shores, sandwiched between the much larger cities of Guangzhou and Shenzhen. Seventy kilometers north of HKIA, Dongguan's upstream check-in terminal is located on a sleepy tributary of the Pearl River in the city's Humen district (Figure 2.3).

A short drive from the garment factories and fabric markets that have given Humen the dubious reputation as the "fashion capital" of the world, the terminal's surroundings are decidedly slow-paced and countrified. Flanked by aging tenements, a failed toy mall, and a wholesale seafood market, HKIA's check-in counters are housed in a repurposed ferry terminal that was never intended for international air traffic. The river floats by lazily, its surface covered in weeds and household trash. Across the street, squat apartment blocks sit cheek by jowl with a village wet market in a warren of narrow alleyways (Figure 2.4a and 2.4b). On one side of the

FIGURE 2.3. A map of the surroundings of the Hong Kong–Macau Ferry Terminal, Humen Town, Dongguan.

FIGURES 2.4A AND 2.4B. Tenement housing and a village wet market across the street from the upstream check-in terminal.

street, women sell live chickens and puppies in cages; on the other side, passengers check in for flights to Bangkok and Dubai (Figure 2.5).

To understand how an airport check-in terminal came to be built in such an unlikely context, it is important to consider the seminal role that international migration has played in the region's urban development. Blessed with an expansive seacoast, a long tradition of foreign trade, and proximity to British-controlled Hong Kong, Guangdong has historically been one of the main sources of Chinese emigration.[14] From San Francisco to Singapore to Sydney, millions of Overseas Chinese can trace their genealogy back to towns and villages in Guangdong, their common ancestral origins solidified by the enduring use of the Cantonese language in diaspora communities around the world. Emigration has been a defining facet of the region for centuries: deployed by local communities as both a tool for upward mobility and as a logical response to periodic bouts of political turmoil throughout the nineteenth and twentieth centuries. In the immediate post–World War II period, civil war and the establishment of Communist control provoked a massive wave of emigration that lasted throughout the 1950s, when thousands of Guangdong residents fled to Hong Kong and Taiwan. Encouraged

FIGURE 2.5. Chickens and puppies for sale in a village wet market, Humen Town, Dongguan.

by the contemporaneous repeal of racially discriminatory immigration policies in Australia, Canada, and the United States, many people subsequently settled beyond Asia, strengthening existing communities abroad and intensifying the Cantonese diaspora's global reach.

Dongguan's recent urban development is largely the product of these overseas communities' reengagement with Mainland China and in particular with the villages of their ancestors. The area occupied by present-day Dongguan represents the ancestral home of a vast number of overseas Chinese—by last count nearly 1 million strong.[15] In the 1980s, the region's strategic location at the heart of the PRD allowed Dongguan "to embark on a path of export-led industrialization by merging the capital and industrial facilities relocated from Hong Kong with the influx of interior cheap labor transferred primarily from the transportation hub in Guangzhou."[16] Encouraged by Deng Xiaoping's appeal for foreign direct investment, entrepreneurs from Hong Kong and Taiwan came to Dongguan in the 1980s to develop modern infrastructure systems, which were correctly perceived as the requisite precondition for the industrialization of the region. Based on village-based ancestral ties, these family connections formed the linchpin between local administrators and state-owned enterprises on the one hand and overseas investors on the other.[17] Dongguan thus became a laboratory of experimentation for new systems of transport and communication: in 1987, Dongguan became the first city in China to install a digital telephone system; ten years later, it designed and built its own municipal highway network, without intervention or subsidies from the central government.[18]

Crucially, these developments were based on interpersonal connections between local officials and overseas investors who could claim a common ancestral bond at the village level, which typically proved more expedient and reliable than operating through official channels at the national or provincial level.[19] The peripheral village locations where these infrastructure developments took place were well suited to investors' needs, as they provided both a source of cheap land and labor, and a less regulated environment in which to operate.[20] In subsequent decades, as Dongguan became a hub for the production of textiles, furniture, and electronic components, these villages developed into highly industrialized zones teeming with factories, wholesale trading markets, and densely packed migrant settlements. The boosterish narrative of Dongguan's rapid development masks the drab reality that permeates its distended landmass: a landscape of garish luxury hotels, KTV lounges, brothels, and down-at-heel tenements produced by a bottom-up, village-based "industrialization of the countryside."

It is within this context that the development of the ferry terminal in Humen needs to be understood. Opened in July 1984, the Hong Kong–Macau Ferry Terminal was part of a larger government-led investment program under which state-owned enterprises and local authorities used foreign loans from Hong Kong and Taiwan in order to upgrade Dongguan's substandard transport infrastructure.[21] The ferry service catered to overseas Chinese entrepreneurs shuttling between the inner city of Hong Kong and Dongguan. In the absence of direct flights between Mainland China and Taiwan, it was also used by Taiwanese businessmen, who flew to Hong Kong and then continued by boat to production sites in Dongguan.

Two decades later, the ferry terminal operator shifted its service approach: discontinuing service to downtown Hong Kong in 2003; and, in the same year, becoming the first Mainland port to experiment with HKIA's upstream check-in service. Rebranded as Shiziyang Sea Express, the ferries initially served the same clientele of Overseas Chinese entrepreneurs, who could now travel by boat directly from the airport.[22] Very quickly, however, they were joined by much larger legions of Mainland Chinese citizens, as well as by traders from Africa, the Middle East, and the Indian subcontinent. In effect, the terminal's refashioning reflected the leap in geographic scales that had taken place in industrial centers like Dongguan over the past twenty years: from regional kinship ties between Hong Kong, Guangdong, and Taiwan to global connections with far-flung destinations around the world.

Promoting itself as Dongguan's "path to the world," Shiziyang Sea Express transports more than 350,000 travelers per year from Humen to HKIA.[23] Most of the check-in terminal's customers are Middle Eastern garment traders heading to Dongguan's wholesale fabric markets, as well as Chinese tourists and salesmen traveling abroad.[24] Apart from articles of clothing that have achieved global consensus (jeans, sneakers, T-shirts), Humen specializes in the production of "Islamic fashion" (headscarves, abayas) as well as "ethnic apparel" for markets in the Middle East and South Asia (kaftans, kurtas).[25] These emerging economies represent some of the main export destinations for Chinese products. Traders from these countries flock to the PRD, and their primary port of entry is Hong Kong. Yet for many of them—Pakistanis, Syrians, Bangladeshis—traveling to Dongguan requires two separate visas: one for Hong Kong and one for China. Depending on their citizenship, the application process is either expensive and time-consuming, or virtually impossible.

The remaining travelers are Mainland tourists embarking upon or returning from holidays abroad. Weighed down by excess baggage, they are members of China's incipiently mobile middle class. They fly through Hong Kong because international flights there are cheaper than in Mainland China. Yet their access to the airport is complicated by Hong Kong's immigration policies, which require that all Mainland Chinese citizens apply for a visa in order to enter the city; and by the vestiges of China's *hukou*, or household registration, system, which defines how often Mainland citizens can travel to Hong Kong according to where they were born and what kind of company they work for.[26]

This is where upstream check-in comes in. Brochures distributed at Humen terminal invite passengers to "travel hassle-free like never before: For ferry transfer passengers, immigration and customs procedures are not required at HKIA" (Figure 2.6). All that travelers need is a "valid air ticket with confirmed seat for same-day departure" and a "valid passport for intended destinations/onward destinations." One caveat: the ferry is "only for transit, passengers who want to enter HK city are not accepted."[27] Ubiquitous signs, posted in broken English throughout the facility, warn potential passengers: "Airport Route just for transit, passenger can not enter Hong Kong City." Moreover, only passengers who can show evidence of a same-day plane ticket and a valid passport and visa for their final destination—New York, Tokyo, Dubai, anywhere besides Hong Kong—are allowed onto the ferry.

Caught on the one hand between a keen desire and newfound financial ability to see the world beyond China, and on the other hand by a legal status that complicates foreign travel, such passengers experience what the anthropologist Pál Nyiri has dubbed the "frustrated mobility" of the twenty-first-century Chinese tourist—a juxtaposition between "the image of the borderless "globally modern Chinese" and the often humiliating experiences in which the mobility of PRC passport holders is frustrated by an immobilizing global migration regime. . . . A People's Republic of

FIGURE 2.6. Advertisement at Hong Kong–Macau Ferry Terminal, Dongguan.

China passport is indeed among the worst to have when applying for a visa or arriving at a border."[28] Here again, upstream check-in promises to flatten, or circumvent, local and national restrictions placed on individual mobility. A prominently featured poster invites passengers to "indulge in an ultimate sea-air experience! Bringing the world to your doorstep. . . . Free yourself from further immigration checks in Hong Kong! A perfect beginning for a hassle-free sea-air journey!" That enthusiastic tenor is tempered by signs posted throughout the terminal reminding travelers that "Hong Kong airport route is only for passenger transit in Hong Kong airport, passengers can't get in Hong Kong by this route."

The contrast between Sea Express's PR materials—photographs of majestic ships and soaring planes—and the reality of the upstream terminal's design is jarring (see Plate 8). The interior of the check-in hall is unfinished, its walls covered haphazardly in cream tile redolent of a highway rest stop. The path from the check-in area to the departures hall leads through a serpentine sequence of narrow corridors, the route marked only by a series of potted poinsettias (Figure 2.7). These give out on a cramped departure, customs, and security hall decorated with neoclassical light fixtures. On one visit to the terminal, a security guard napped on a folding chair in the corner in between ferry departures.

SkyPier: Extraterritorial Kit of Parts

Once they have boarded the ferry, upstream travelers are considered "transborder" air passengers.[29] Shuttling across the mouth of the Pearl River Delta on the one-hour ride to the airport, they are neither in China nor in Hong Kong, but rather in an extraterritorial maritime corridor that functions as an extension of international airspace. As such, the upstream terminals represent the physical border between the People's Republic of China and the outside world. Deep inside Chinese territory, travelers are shunted through remarkably flimsy design elements never intended to denote an international frontier—a wire fence, a wooden pier, a PVC door.

Whether they depart from Dongguan or any of the other Mainland check-in terminals, the journey ultimately takes passengers to the SkyPier terminal at HKIA (Figure 2.8). Designed by a joint venture among Skidmore, Owings, and Merrill, the Hong Kong-based architectural firm Aedas, and local design consultant OTC, the terminal is promoted by the airport authority as "an important facility to strengthen Hong Kong's connection with the Pearl River Delta (PRD), making it easier and more convenient for people to travel between HKIA and the PRD. . . . Travellers using the SkyPier—including international passengers and PRD residents—are not required to go through immigration and customs formalities at HKIA, thus cutting travel time and making their air-to-sea or sea-to-air transfers even more hassle-free."[30] SkyPier processes 2.5 million people a year traveling to and from upstream ports in the PRD—about every twentieth passenger flying through HKIA.[31] Arriving

FIGURE 2.7. Corridor between the check-in and departure halls at Hong Kong–Macau Ferry Terminal, Dongguan.

FIGURE 2.8. A rendering of the SkyPier terminal at Hong Kong International Airport. Image courtesy of Airport Authority Hong Kong.

ferries dock at two pontoon bridges floating in the sea in front of SkyPier. The pontoon is designed as a mobile kit of parts, consisting of a deck, a ramp, and a crane. These are connected, via a moveable bridge and a series of hinges, to the curtain wall of the terminal.[32] Passengers proceed up the ramp and into a "Sea Module,"[33] and then on to a security screening room on the lower level (see Plate 9 and Figure 2.9).[34] While they must present a boarding pass, they do not go through immigration or customs checks. After they clear security, passengers walk to a tax refund counter, where they collect a cash reimbursement of 120 Hong Kong dollars (U.S.$15). As transfer passengers, they are exempt from Hong Kong's departure tax and are thus entitled to a refund. Significantly, the refund indirectly subsidizes the price of the ferry ticket, thus making it affordable for less affluent customers.[35]

Travelers then enter the atrium of the Automated People Mover station, or APM (Figure 2.10). Here they may gaze, briefly, onto HKIA—their only opportunity to see the airport's exterior during the entire journey. Next, passengers take an escalator down to the APM platform and board the train. The train shuttles them through a tunnel beneath the airport's check-in halls and ground transportation center (Figure 2.11 and 2.12). After 1.1 kilometers and four minutes, upstream

FIGURE 2.9. Security screening room at SkyPier, Hong Kong International Airport.

FIGURE 2.10. Automated People Mover station at SkyPier, Hong Kong International Airport.

FIGURE 2.11. An Automated People Mover travels between SkyPier and the passenger terminal building at Hong Kong International Airport.

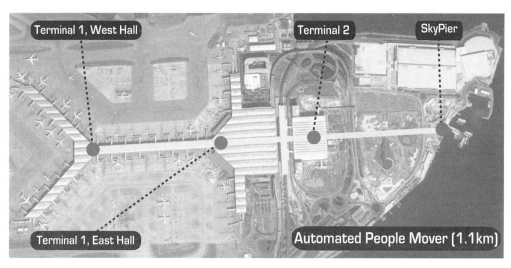

FIGURE 2.12. A map of the Automated People Mover that connects SkyPier to Terminal 1 at Hong Kong International Airport.

travelers emerge on the airside of Terminal 1. From here, passengers take escalators up to the departures level and to their respective gates. At no point can they enter the city of Hong Kong.

At the same time as passengers move through SkyPier, Mainland ferry staff bring their luggage, housed in pallets, up to the deck. Prohibited from interacting with their Hong Kong colleagues, the Mainland Chinese crew attach the pallets to a crane, which then hoists the luggage across to SkyPier (Plate 10).[36] Because the dimensions of the Mainland pallets do not conform to international aviation standards, the luggage is then "repalletized" before being transferred through an underground baggage tunnel that runs parallel to the APM to the airport terminal (Figure 2.13).[37] Separated by less than five meters from the ferries, airport employees are forbidden from communicating with the Mainland ferry crew; who, in turn, must remain aboard the ships and pontoons at all times, and are not permitted to enter SkyPier.

FIGURE 2.13. Mainland Chinese ferry staff transfer luggage to the ground floor of SkyPier, where it is subsequently "repalletized" by Hong Kong airport staff.

SkyPier's organizational logic reveals much about the design aesthetics of transborder infrastructure. As its designers note rather gingerly, "the opportunity for 'grand' architectural expression in SkyPier is minimal at best. There are no pretensions that this building is striving to make a great architectural statement."[38] Accessible only by ferry and underground train, it cannot be entered at the ground level, either by passengers or by employees. The building can only be seen at a distance—either on approach from the sea, or from the rear of Terminal 2. Moreover, the word "SkyPier" itself is not actually used in airport wayfinding systems, as its designers worried that the term might be confusing to the uninitiated.[39] From the user's perspective, then, SkyPier is a building without a name that can't be accessed from the city in which it is located, and which can only be viewed from afar.

In effect, the terminal supplants the notion of a border as something static and two-dimensional with one that conceives of it as flexible and divisible in sections. Both the pontoon and the APM neatly underline these spatial reconfigurations. Inherently temporary, the pontoon formalizes a pragmatic approach to international mobility that deploys flexible infrastructures and adjusts territorial boundaries to enable the cross-border movement of goods and people. Like the entire upstream system, it is a prosthetic extension of the airport, made up of modular and mobile components that extend and collapse according to user demand. Tolerant of a messy, ambiguous present, the pontoon allows travelers to rapidly traverse international boundaries while also marking the limitations placed on the movement of the Mainland ferry crew. You are no longer in China, it says; but you're also not in Hong Kong. The pontoon functions as an intermediary agent between the two, with the rational movement of the luggage crane obviating the need for direct interaction between Mainland and Hong Kong Chinese staff. It is a *Mechanisierung der Konfliktaustragung,* to paraphrase the German historian Jürgen Reulecke,[40] predicated on a floating element that can be detached and removed—or infinitely expanded.

The design of the Automated People Mover, or APM, further underscores that spatial fluidity. The APM transports passengers who do not have permission to enter Hong Kong: their right to remain is provisory, their presence tolerated as long as they remain in motion. The construction of a cross-boundary plane below the surface of the airport—a literal and figurative undermining of Hong Kong's spatial integrity—enables the conveyance of these passengers. In effect, SkyPier's designers devised a sectional approach to territory that both pays homage to and circumvents Hong Kong's border regulations. By divorcing the use of its infrastructure systems from a concomitant right to access the city, Hong Kong can operate as a transfer hub for passenger flows to China without compromising its security and migration policies.

The discourse of "upstream" travel naturalizes profoundly technical and technocratic processes. In so doing, it avoids uncomfortable questions—Why are some

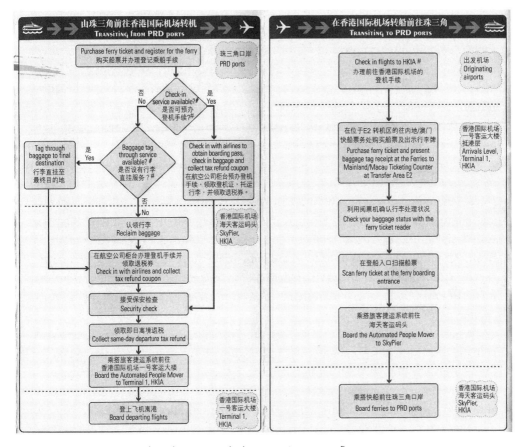

FIGURE 2.14. A poster explains the upstream check-in system's passenger flow sequence.

passengers allowed into Hong Kong while others are not? Why is access to foreign travel determined by one's place of birth? What is the nature of the boundary between Hong Kong and Mainland China?—and reduces them to a sequence of banalities: check-in, security screening, tax refund. That process is abetted by a simplified visual language that masks complex territorial reconfigurations beneath a Taylorized logic of flow charts, acronyms, and modular components (Figure 2.14). Passengers are not moving between the People's Republic of China and Hong Kong, but rather between PRD and HKIA.

Rethinking the Spatiality of Global Mobility

A visit to the Pearl River Delta's upstream check-in terminals demands a reevaluation of the dominant scholarly approaches to the infrastructure of global mobility. As noted in the introduction, scholars have primarily theorized it through a mediated analysis of its most obvious physical manifestations: that is, the iconic airport terminal and the attendant panoply of terrestrial transport links that connect it to the city's business districts. "Superseding the logic of any specific place" and "escaping the sociopolitical control of historically specific local/national societies," these spaces catered to the aesthetic sensibilities of a global elite "whose identity is not linked to any specific society but to membership of managerial circles of the information economy across a global spectrum."[41] The architecture of air travel is thus one of "placeless" social and aesthetic uniformity, engendered by deracinated elites and neoliberal regimes of urban governance.

In this chapter, I have argued that opportunistic retribalization—that is, a revival of transnational cultural and linguistic ties predicated on a shared village-based provenance—led to the formation of an ad-hoc transport system, designed cheaply and anonymously, to connect Hong Kong and Dongguan in the 1980s. While these installations initially aimed to abet the transfer of capital and industrial expertise from Hong Kong and Taiwan into Mainland China, these spaces were subsequently reprogrammed in order to serve the travel demands of those engaging in low-end forms of cross-border mobility, such as budget tourism or trading in Third World *shmatta.*

What we see at SkyPier and across the Pearl River Delta is a much messier articulation of international mobility, and of airport infrastructure, than the one in the established literature. In Dongguan, tourists and traders with less than desirable passports check in for international flights at a terminal that is indistinguishable from the factories, tenements, and village markets surrounding it. From here, passengers proceed to SkyPier, which essentially functions as an intermodal purgatory for the region's semiprivileged air travelers (see Plate 11). These are not upscale facilities designed for a kinetic elite, but rather infrastructural experiments that offer a limited form of mobility to people who have the "right" financial resources but the "wrong" travel documents. That conditional mobility is made possible by extending international airspace to a network of Mainland ferry piers; and, in the process, exploiting maritime space in order to evade the migration restrictions of terrestrial borders.

Extraterritorial, explicitly underdesigned, and ephemeral, the SkyPier terminal would, at first glance, seem to validate the "non-place" axioms that have become so popular in architectural discourse over the past twenty years. Yet to make such an assertion would be to ignore the contrast between SkyPier and its typological foil, the upstream check-in terminal in Mainland China. On paper, the upstream terminals are ostensibly built to the same design standard as the Hong Kong airport. In reality, they reflect the broader tendencies of contemporary Chinese urbanism: improvised, rough around the edges, and juxtaposed with an extreme diversity of urban practices. These findings suggest that a unifying, monolithic conception of how economic globalization affects urban form and architectural production is both inaccurate and unhelpful when applied outside the relatively exceptional context of the Western welfare state. McGee and Lin have argued that a formalist approach to globalization—that is, one that asserts a socioeconomic homogenization thesis based on the convergence of global architectural vernaculars, and which tends to privilege the study of flagship urban developments—masks the very different means by which those structures are built and used in a non-Western context:

> Despite the growing convergence in *urban forms* under the Chinese and American contexts, Chinese urbanization as locally constituted *processes* remains significantly distinct from what has been observed in the West. . . . A new and innovative approach with local sensitivity and historical contingency is in order for a better understanding of urbanization within the different regional contexts of the globalizing world. . . . If the processes of urbanism are no less significant than the urban forms, then it will not be possible to understand fully Chinese urbanism without careful studies of what has been taking place in many of the rapidly growing quasi-legal peri-urban regions where things can get done relatively easily, cheaply, and expeditiously.[42]

Observing contemporary Chinese attitudes to mobility and migration, Nyiri has written that "the conflicting imperatives of encouraging the cross-border movement of goods and of controlling the flows of individuals sometimes results in elaborate farces that are invisible to the uninitiated outsiders." Beguiled by the spectacle of China's airport megaprojects, scholars have thus far failed to identify the cleverly concealed spatial correlates of these "elaborate farces." In Dongguan, this has entailed the insertion of international aviation infrastructure into a decidedly nonpremium urban context—precisely because the flows that the upstream check-in system enables are both necessary for socioeconomic cohesion yet undesirable from the perspective of national security. The terminal's barebones layout tersely acknowledges the indispensability of the upstream check-in system, yet it discourages a broader reflection upon the strange set of political and economic contradictions that led to its genesis. The proliferation of these terminals is emblematic of the tolerance for pragmatic rule-bending that characterizes development on both sides of the Hong Kong–PRC divide—an unspoken willingness to ignore gray areas, both juridical and spatial, and a flexible attitude toward ideology aimed at harmonizing dissonant political and economic interests.[43]

Both in its rhetorical style and aesthetic vocabulary, Hong Kong's airport likes to present itself as a neutral mediator between China and the rest of the world. But just as Ludwig Feuerbach criticized Christianity for the distorting effects of its reliance on mediating institutions, so too is Hong Kong's *abgeleitete Mobilität* a simulacrum for unfettered freedom of movement.[44] It reflects the pragmatism—some might say moral relativism—endemic to a world region whose economic contours fail to coincide with its political boundaries. In this respect, contemporary developments in the PRD can be located within a tradition of creative infrastructural approaches to profoundly weird geopolitical contexts. Premised on territorial manipulations and typological flexibility, upstream travel rehearses a rather unlikely precedent from Cold War Berlin. In the 1970s and 1980s—as noted in the introductory chapter—the East German airline Interflug offered discounted airfares to residents of West Berlin. For about one-third less than the price of a normal ticket, West Berliners could fly in and out of East Berlin's Schönefeld airport to destinations like Athens, Rome, and Istanbul. Using transborder transit buses, Interflug shuttled passengers from West Berlin's central bus station to Schönefeld through a special border crossing in the Wall: a checkpoint located on the edge of a lower-middle-class suburb that was designated for the use of passengers transferring to the airport (Figure 2.15).[45]

Though heavily criticized by Cold War ideologues, the cross-border service proved immensely popular with Turkish "guest workers" and low-income tourists who could not afford the plane tickets on sale at the airport in West Berlin.[46] By the late 1980s, a quarter of all West Berliners flew through East Berlin every year.[47] Retrospectively identified as the first German *Billigflieger,* or budget airline,[48] the Interflug flights represented both a source of hard currency for the East German government and an opportunity for less privileged Berliners to become members of the flying public. The price was a degree of moral relativism on both sides: Should Interflug subsidize the Mediterranean vacations of West Berliners, while the East German government denied the right to travel abroad to its own citizens? And should West Berliners support a regime that had encircled them with a concrete barrier, only to subsequently offer them a cheap means of temporary escape? On both sides of the Wall, the answer was a resounding yes.

These types of infrastructural quasi-logics are endemic to situations where overarching political ideologies are not, or are no longer, consonant with socioeconomic realities on the ground. Under such conditions, transborder infrastructure is deployed in order to harmonize dissonant political and economic objectives. Hong Kong's upstream check-in system reduces extremely complex territorial manipulations to a discrete set of logistical procedures. In so doing, it smooths over the conflicting imperatives of free-market globalization and place-based protectionism— neither of which will disappear anytime soon. Such infrastructure strategies appeal to and are propelled by subaltern constituents caught in the interstices between competing ideologies. These interventions are more than just curious anomalies or footnotes to absurd historical situations: indeed, they entail a fundamental reordering of urban space. Transborder infrastructure removes passengers from the remote confines of the airport and inserts them into a variety of unusual locations— in Shenzhen, one of the terminals is surrounded by fish restaurants and banana

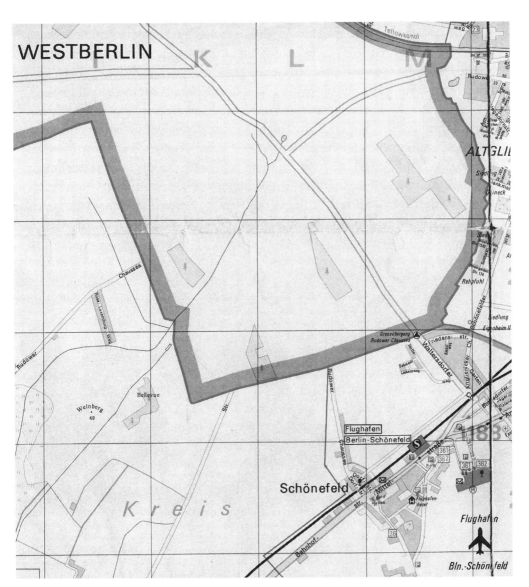

FIGURE 2.15. A map printed in East Germany in 1986 displays the transit corridor between West Berlin and Schönefeld airport. The black triangle in the lower right indicates the location of the border checkpoint for transit buses. Map by Tourist Verlag.

plantations—thus making the flow of international air traffic a facet of everyday urban life. In so doing, it invests these distinctly local venues with a global significance that explodes their spatial and typological definition.

Moreover, the development of transborder infrastructure typically portends both a rearticulation of existing mobility patterns, as well as a paradigm shift in political and economic structures.[49] By opening a small gap in the Berlin Wall, Interflug allowed low-paid "guest workers" to commute between Germany and Turkey, ushering in an aviation-based transnationalism long before it became commonplace. Similarly, Hong Kong's upstream check-in service exploits loopholes in the region's customs and security apparatus in order to expose incipient members of China's middle class to the outside world, and to abet the flow of low-end trade between developing countries on different continents. Scholars of the built environment would be well advised to study the vanguard role that such transborder infrastructure systems play in both anticipating and advancing systemic changes in the global flow of goods, people, and information.

THREE

Special Zones

Every morning before I start writing, I go for a short walk: past the temple to Tin Hau, the patron goddess of seafarers, after which my neighborhood is named, and down a short road toward Tai Hang. Tai Hang is a rapidly gentrifying micro-neighborhood, founded as a Hakka village in the nineteenth century, known for its many car repair shops and restaurants, and for a fire dragon dance performed each year during the Mid-Autumn Festival. At nights and on the weekends, Tai Hang is packed with mostly younger diners who queue up for the limited number of tables available at the neighborhood's ramen shops, *cha chaan teng*, and dessert cafés.

On weekday mornings, however, Tai Hang is fairly quiet, at least by the frenetic standards of Hong Kong Island. Old folks perch on stools and lawn chairs in front of their apartment buildings. Taxi drivers take a quick snack break and chat with mechanics working in the garages. Along Tung Lo Wan Road, the owner of a small workshop, which produces the distinctive red-and-blue striped canvas bags used to store and transport goods throughout China, washes the sidewalk in front of his store. He does so in the shadow of the thirty-three-story Metropark, a hotel owned by China Travel Service (CTS), the state-run tourism agency of the People's Republic of China. Those who are old enough to have visited the former East Bloc will undoubtedly recall the surly services and bureaucratic machinations of state travel bureaus—such as the Soviet agency Intourist—who held a monopoly on hotels and other tourism services geared toward foreign visitors. CTS is the Chinese equivalent: no longer the only game in town, but still a major provider of visas, transport, and accommodations. Its presence is particularly noticeable in Hong Kong, where CTS operates four hotels as well as an extensive network of cross-border buses that connect Hong Kong to the Mainland. At the Metropark in Tai Hang, a middle-aged woman dispenses bus schedules and tickets from a small booth next to the entrance of the hotel. A predominantly Mainland clientele congregates here throughout the day, towing toddlers, luggage, and shopping bags. Several times an hour, a sixty-five-seat CTS bus lumbers down Tung Lo Wan Road toward the Metropark, disrupting the steady flow of taxis and delivery trucks along Tai Hang's only access road. While there are frequent departures to nearby cities in Guangdong province, the most popular route takes passengers directly from my neighborhood to Bao'an International Airport, thirty kilometers north of the Hong Kong border on the western edge of Shenzhen.

CTS is one of four authorized operators of the cross-border buses that shuttle passengers between the Shenzhen airport and dozens of pick-up points located throughout Hong Kong Island, Kowloon, and the New Territories. The popularity of these cross-border buses testifies to the peculiar mobility regime that governs Shenzhen, China's largest special economic zone, or SEZ, and a prime example of a peculiar type of frontier urbanism that emerged throughout Asia at the end of the twentieth century. This chapter studies the emergence of Shenzhen's cross-boundary bus system in order to illuminate the crucial role that international mobility has played in the urban development of these special border cities. Tracing the history of Shenzhen's airport, its cross-boundary bus terminals, and its border control checkpoints, I use the evolution of the city's aviation infrastructure as a lens for investigating the tension between Shenzhen's aspirations to become a cosmopolitan global city and the constraints entailed by its subordination to regional economic interests and national security concerns. I argue that that tension has produced a variety of spatial and typological experiments that have fundamentally defined how Shenzhen is connected to the outside world, and that those experiments, in turn, provide a unique insight into the distinctive social dynamics and spatial organization of Asia's special border zones.

Founded in 1980, Shenzhen has enjoyed the most spectacular growth of any contemporary Asian city: transforming from a landscape of agri- and aquacultural villages to a sprawling metropolis of 15 million inhabitants in three short decades. Containing twice the population of Hong Kong in an urbanized area that measures more than a hundred kilometers from east to west, Shenzhen is exceptional both in terms of its proportions and in terms of the outsized role that the city played as a showcase of China's post-Mao economic reforms. But although it was an early pioneer of the special economic zone model in China, Shenzhen's status as a special border city is no longer exceptional. By the early twenty-first century, dozens of special border zones had been established throughout Asia. Many are located in previously underdeveloped regions, in the vicinity of seaports, border checkpoints, and major transportation hubs. Just as Shenzhen was chosen for its contiguity with Hong Kong, so too do other special border zones reference an existing city that is both proximate and prosperous. On the western banks of the Pearl River Delta, for example, the Zhuhai Special Economic Zone surrounds the former Portuguese colony of Macau on three sides. Twenty-five hundred kilometers to the south, Singapore is sandwiched between two zones: the Iskandar Malaysia growth corridor, which radiates outward from the gritty industrial city of Johor Bahru; and the Riau Islands, an Indonesian archipelago filled with factories, resorts, and myriad illicit activities. Smaller border cities, elevated to the status of special economic zones, can likewise be found all along China's external frontier. In the extreme north of Heilongjiang province, the special border development zone of Heihe faces the Russian city of Blagoveshchensk; while along the southern border of Yunnan, the special zone around Hekou serves as a beachhead for Chinese investments into Vietnam.[1] Similar zones dot Thailand's frontiers to Cambodia, Laos, and Myanmar.[2]

These special border zones vary in size and sophistication, and have served as one of the central loci of Asia's economic boom. They arise at the boundary between countries who share an interest in cross-border trade but who are at very different levels of economic development. Typically, the poorer partner provides access to cheap land and labor while the wealthier one supplies capital investments, managerial know-how, a robust consumer market, and technologically advanced production methods. These cities have evolved according to a widely imitated formula. As Jonathan Bach explains,

> Zones all offer variations on the same theme: a different regulatory regime than in the rest of the country, usually a confined geographic area that provides better infrastructure and good transport, and zone governance dedicated to business as the primary denizen of the zone. The zone thus becomes a privileged economic space for manufacturing, and later also services, because it became a kind of global space of exception to the tax, labor, and customs laws of countries worldwide, allowing a parallel system of global production to emerge that today employs 130 million people in direct and indirect jobs.[3]

The urban fabric of special border zones shares some common typological characteristics. Industrial estates and workers' dormitories intersect at odd angles with cheap restaurants and cavernous shopping malls filled with tailors, massage parlors, and pirated software. Drawing in migrants from distant provinces, these cities are famed for the variety of cuisines served in their restaurants. As sites of production within a larger global supply chain, special border zones depend on an integrated transport infrastructure in order to guarantee a continuous flow of goods, labor, and capital. Consequently, a disproportionate volume of urban activities concentrates around border checkpoints and transport hubs. Warehouses, shipping containers, and bus terminals figure prominently in a landscape populated primarily by migrant workers and itinerant businessmen. The border cities have, by the standards of their host country, a stratospheric level of per capita GDP. Over time, newer, consumption-oriented districts develop at some distance to sites of production, featuring luxury resorts, golf clubs, and gated condominiums. Theme parks, such as Shenzhen's "Window of the World," attract domestic tourists who are keen on experiencing a hint of "foreignness"—which is endemic to special border zones— without actually leaving the country.

Initial scholarly investigations of special border zones diagnosed them as ahistorical mutations, derived from and subservient to the neoliberal agenda of global capitalism. Aihwa Ong identified them as an example of "graduated sovereignty," wherein national governments accord special privileges to people and products within a restricted zone whose exemption from prevailing legal and financial norms undermines the contiguity of the nation-state while exacerbating socioeconomic inequalities between both people and places.[4] In a related line of thought, Keller Easterling conceptualized zones as a form of "extrastatecraft": a kind of neutral territory inserted at the margins of nation-states to accelerate cross-border flows of capital and production.[5] More recent reevaluations have pointed to a range of historical antecedents that fulfilled similar functions to today's special zones: the cities of the Hanseatic League, for example; or colonial settlements, leaseholds, and treaty ports such as Hong Kong, Dalian, and Jiaozhou.[6] Irrespective of their typological pedigree, in hub cities such as Hong Kong and Singapore—but also in smaller ones like Macau and Vientiane—the special border zone has become a defining facet of everyday life. Typically, the zone is everything, and has everything, that its inter-referenced twin does not. Macau is one of the densest cities in the world; Zhuhai is characterized by a superabundance of open space. Citizens of Hong Kong enjoy the rule of law; Shenzheners do not. Daily life in Singapore is clean, expensive, and boring; in Johor Bahru, it's dirty, affordable, and unpredictable. And yet, beyond their immediate region, special border cities are largely an unknown quantity. Most people will have heard of Hong Kong, Macau, and Singapore; far fewer will be familiar with Shenzhen, Zhuhai, and Johor Bahru. At once envied for their special status and derided for their frontier-town vulgarity, these cities occupy an ambiguous position within national hierarchies of wealth and status: prioritized, on the one hand, as focal points of macroeconomic development; yet deficient in the political clout, social capital, and cultural prestige enjoyed by national capitals and historic trading hubs. As a corollary, while these cities are extremely well connected within domestic transportation networks—the volume of labor migrants mandating reliable links to distant provinces—they are typically less accessible from abroad due to their subordination, within national infrastructure plans, to more established centers of political and economic power. A businessman from Frankfurt or Tokyo will thus need to fly first to Hong Kong or Singapore before transferring onward to Shenzhen or Batam.

PLATE 1. "Transborder" air passengers arrive by sea from Hong Kong International Airport at Fuyong Port, Shenzhen.

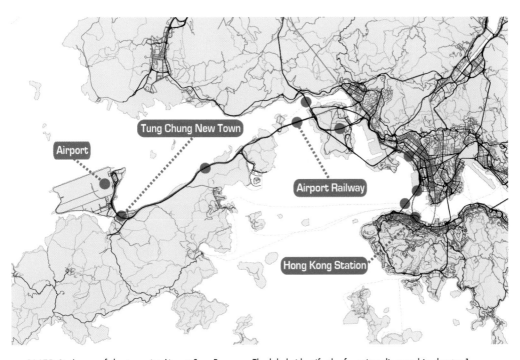

PLATE 2. A map of the ten-point Airport Core Program. The labels identify the four sites discussed in chapter 1.

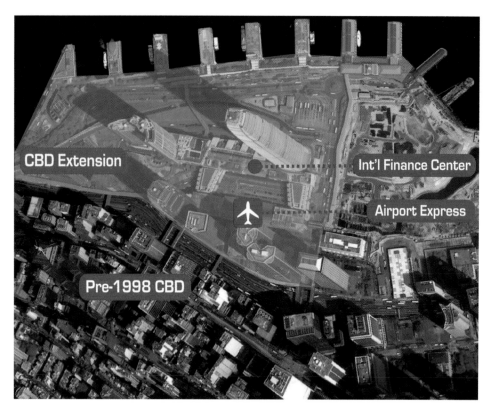

PLATE 3. Aerial view of the International Finance Centre and Hong Kong Station, the terminus of the Airport Express line.

PLATE 4. This map displays the cost of a one-way trip between Hong Kong International Airport and selected locations throughout Hong Kong. All prices are in Hong Kong dollars.

PLATES 5 AND 6. Tung Chung's Citygate Plaza is an unofficial transfer point for passengers traveling to Hong Kong International Airport.

PLATE 7. Hong Kong–Macau Passenger Ferry Terminal, Humen Town, Dongguan.

PLATE 8. Check-in hall at Hong Kong–Macau Passenger Ferry Terminal, Dongguan.

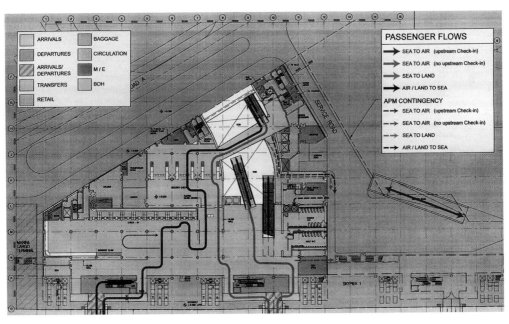

PLATE 9. Passenger flow model at SkyPier, Hong Kong International Airport. Image courtesy of Airport Authority Hong Kong.

PLATE 10. Luggage cranes at SkyPier, Hong Kong International Airport.

PLATE 11. Transborder passengers in transit at SkyPier, Hong Kong International Airport.

PLATE 12. A 2012 photograph of the construction site at Terminal 3, Shenzhen Bao'an International Airport, Shenzhen.

PLATE 13. A cross-border airport check-in terminal at Shenzhen Grand Theatre, Shenzhen.

Kingkey Banner Center, Shenzhen

Theme Park

Migrant Village

Airport Check-In

Shopping Mall

PLATE 14. Kingkey Banner Center in Shenzhen's Nanshan district hosts one of the city's four cross-border airport check-in terminals.

PLATE 15. A signboard at Kingkey Banner Center explains the sequence of steps necessary for passengers in Guangdong province to transfer to flights that depart from Hong Kong International Airport.

PLATE 16. Signs advertise low-cost flights to Chennai, Dhaka, and New Delhi in Little India, Singapore.

PLATE 17. A rendering of Singapore's future budget terminal envisions a fully automated check-in hall devoid of ticketing agents. Courtesy of Changi Airport Group.

PLATE 18. A rendering of the future forecourt of Changi International Airport, Singapore. Courtesy of Changi Airport Group.

PLATE 19. A stall in front of Singapore's Tekka Centre sells prepaid phone cards used by foreign workers from China, Southeast Asia, and the Indian subcontinent.

PLATE 20. Like many districts in Hong Kong, the urban fabric of Causeway Bay has been fundamentally altered by the influx of tourists and migrant workers from other parts of Asia. Here, a pharmacy hawks milk powder to Mainland Chinese tourists.

Indeed, most of the special border cities live in the shadow of their wealthier twins, dependent on the Other both economically and intellectually. What distinguishes Shenzhen from other special border zones—and the reason why it is the subject of this chapter—lies in the city's attempt to shed its reputation as Hong Kong's poorer, less developed foil; and to assert its autonomy on the international stage. Flush with cash and hubris, Shenzhen's urban ambitions had, by the early twenty-first century, gone global. With its status as a model for socioeconomic experimentation firmly entrenched within China, the city aimed to become, like Shanghai and Hong Kong, a "world-class" center for the international exchange of goods, services, and ideas. In the fields of architecture and urban design, Shenzhen's upwardly mobile aspirations were articulated in the city's active courtship of foreign architects, who were recruited to construct iconic public spaces and invest the city with sophisticated infrastructure systems. Articulating a deeply rooted sense of status anxiety, these show projects were a defining visual element of special border zones across Asia: a form of aesthetic globalization *avant la lettre*, designed into an environment where, until very recently, nonlocal faces were met with goofy grins and inquisitive stares. And in the specific context of the Pearl River Delta, these projects represented an attempt to transcend Shenzhen's regional reputation as the scrappy upstart. Having neither the administrative clout of Guangzhou—the capital city of Guangdong and the center of power in Southern China for several millennia—nor the cosmopolitan flair and global financial weight of Hong Kong, Shenzhen sought to deploy architectural bling in order to improve its regional stature and international visibility.

The competition for the expansion of Shenzhen's Bao'an International Airport, or SZIA, fit squarely within this paradigm. In 2007, the Shenzhen Airport Authority invited submissions from six foreign architects. The competition's brief called for the construction of a four-hundred-thousand-square-meter terminal that would double the capacity of the current airfield and would be capable of handling both domestic and international flights. Many of the competing architects, including Norman Foster, Kisho Kurokawa, and Meinhard von Gerkan, had previous experience with large-scale aviation projects.[7] Yet the winning entry came from the office of the Italian designers Massimiliano and Doriana Fuksas, making SZIA Fuksas's first airport project as well as their first foray into China.[8] For the members of the jury, composed of representatives from the airport authority and the planning bureau, technical expertise in airport planning was ultimately less important than architectural bravado: a spectacular design that would identify Shenzhen as a cutting-edge, cosmopolitan space of global connectivity.

Fuksas's striking terminal facade—a patterned glass and steel canopy, studded with hexagonal windows that deploy the parametric design technology en vogue in architecture culture—unquestioningly signaled Shenzhen's recently acquired wealth and its desire to increase its cultural capital (Plate 12).[9] Yet the functional goals underlying the airport's expansion—that is, to better connect Shenzhen with the rest of the world—have been hampered by the politics of national security and intercity rivalries within the Pearl River Delta. As noted in the previous chapter, China's military severely limits the operation of foreign airlines within Chinese airspace, and the nation's civil aviation authority channels most international flights through three designated airports in Beijing, Shanghai, and Guangzhou.[10] At the same time, an agreement between the airport authorities in Hong Kong and Shenzhen has led to a rough division of labor whereby Hong Kong International Airport (HKIA) serves as the twin cities' international gateway—with frequent departures to more than seventy countries—while SZIA functions as a hub for cheap domestic flights within China. Offering cut-rate fares and nonstop service to dozens of Chinese provincial capitals and secondary cities, SZIA attracts both Hongkongers flying to the Mainland and Mainlanders transiting to Hong Kong.[11] Despite the publicity surrounding the Fuksas terminal, inaugurated with much fanfare in 2013, the revamped airport thus offered surprisingly few international flights—an indication of the disconnect between the special border city's cosmopolitan ambitions and the requisite policy changes needed to turn Shenzhen into a global hub.

The recent influx of foreign visitors to Shenzhen, along with the much larger flows of passengers traveling between Hong Kong and the Mainland, has led to a rapid increase in the demand for international flights in Shenzhen and for China-bound ones in Hong Kong. Addressing the gap in supply and demand, the two airport authorities have sanctioned the development of "cross-boundary" airport bus terminals that allow passengers in Hong Kong to check in for flights departing from SZIA, and enable travelers in Shenzhen to do the same for flights leaving from HKIA. In both cities, passengers check in for their flights at cross-border terminals located inside shopping malls and transportation hubs, as well as at hotels such as the Metropark in my neighborhood. They then board a bus to the border and, after clearing customs and immigration, transfer to a second coach that takes them to the airport. The companies that operate these routes have developed a flexible and loosely organized network of city-to-airport bus and minivan services that piggyback on existing, non-airport infrastructures in order to shuttle thousands of air travelers across the Hong Kong–Shenzhen border every day. In the process, the infrastructure of aerial mobility has been extended far beyond the confines of the two airports and inserted into the everyday urban fabric of both cities.

Building Shenzhen, Building SZIA

Inaugurated in 1980, the Shenzhen Special Economic Zone was designed as both a laboratory and a model city: a laboratory for experimentation with market-driven modes of management and production; and a model city for displaying the benefits of Deng Xiaoping's policies of Reform and Opening, which aimed to transform the stagnant Chinese economy through an influx of foreign capital, expertise, and technical equipment. As noted in the previous chapter, much of that policy was predicated on engaging Overseas Chinese investors in Hong Kong, Singapore, and Taiwan. Guangdong, with its proximity to Hong Kong and with family links to Cantonese-speaking diaspora communities scattered throughout East and South-east Asia, played a substantial role in Deng's broader plans to jump-start the Chinese economy. As the historian Ezra Vogel notes,

> If there was a single magic potion for a Chinese economic takeoff, it was Hong Kong. Roughly two-thirds of the direct investment in China between 1979 and 1995 came through . . . Hong Kong. . . . Deng's experiment to open the 'great southern gate' between Guangdong and Hong Kong [became] China's most important channel through which flowed investment, technology, management skills, and ideas about the outside world.[12]

Planned as a linear city straddling the border to Hong Kong, Shenzhen was strategically sited at the foot of that "southern gate." Its intellectual genesis lay in the Chinese government's quiet study of special economic zones elsewhere in Asia, which provided a model through which Deng and Party officials in Guangdong sought to interact with foreign and Overseas Chinese investors.[13] Together, they

> proposed that the entire province be allowed to implement a special policy that would give Guangdong the flexibility to adopt measures to attract foreign capital, technology, and management practices necessary to produce goods for export. China would supply the land, transport facilities, electricity, and labor needed by the factories, as well as the hotels, restaurants, housing, and other facilities needed by foreigners. . . . The special policy for Guangdong and the unique leeway given to the special economic zones made these areas into incubators for developing people who would be able to function well in modern factories, stores, and offices in cosmopolitan settings.[14]

With its future inexorably tied to Hong Kong, Shenzhen's urban plan developed along a series of transport axes that ran perpendicular to the Hong Kong border (Figure 3.1). Huang Weiwen, formerly one of the city's chief planners, periodizes the history of Shenzhen's spatial layout according to the establishment of those so-called Shen-Kong transport corridors, outfitted with imposing border control checkpoints, that were designed to move goods and people efficiently between the two cities.[15] In the 1980s, Shenzhen's first cross-border transport axis developed in the city's Luohu district at the intersection of the border and the main north–south railway that connected Hong Kong to Guangzhou. The thrust of urban development moved progressively westward as new highways, commuter rail lines, and long-distance bus terminals opened in Futian district in the 1990s. That trajectory continued into the twenty-first century, as the focus of urban development coalesced around road and rail corridors in Nanshan district that connected the airport in Hong Kong to its counterpart in Shenzhen.

The development of Shenzhen's Bao'an International Airport, or SZIA, mirrored both the linear evolution of the city's urban fabric as well as the rollout of Deng's economic reform policies. Until 1978, all Chinese airports were directly controlled by the People's Liberation Army. As part of the Opening and Reform policy, China moved toward a market-driven approach to air travel, formalized by the separation of the civil aviation administration, or CAAC, from the military in 1980.[16] The CAAC subsequently transferred the responsibility for airport operation to local governments, broke up the national airline into several smaller entities, and encouraged the development of private regional carriers to compete with state-run ones.[17] Shenzhen was one of the most aggressive early adopters of the liberalized aviation regime. In the 1980s, the closest airport to Shenzhen was in Guangzhou, a four-hour drive away along bumpy country roads. Believing that aerial connectivity was a precondition for accelerating the city's economic growth, the municipality began

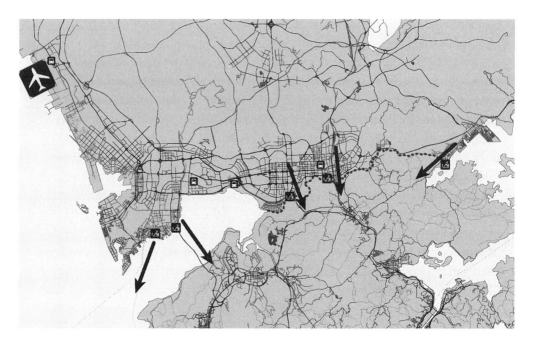

FIGURE 3.1. A map of Shenzhen displays the location of the city's airport, airport check-in terminals, and major border crossings. The dotted line demarcates the land boundary between Hong Kong and Shenzhen, while the arrows indicate the primary cross-border, or Shen-Kong, transport axes.

constructing its own airport in 1989, and it established its own carrier, Shenzhen Airlines, three years later.[18] At that time, responsibility for building major urban infrastructure projects in Shenzhen was delegated to the state-run architectural design institutes and urban planning bureaus of China's thirty-odd provinces and provincial-level municipalities, each of which was obligated by the central government to contribute to Shenzhen's urban development.[19] Boxy and functional, and designed by low-profile employees of the Northeast Institute of Architectural Design based in China's Manchurian rust belt, the original terminal served a very small number of civil servants and employees of state-owned enterprises commuting between Shenzhen and their home provinces.[20] When the airport opened in 1992, urban planners in neighboring Hong Kong expressed skepticism about the city's potential to support a major air hub, citing the underdeveloped state of Shenzhen's economy and the low income levels of its inhabitants.[21] Yet by the year 2000, Bao'an had become the fourth-largest airport in Mainland China, handling more than 6 million travelers a year. That figure quadrupled in the following decade: by 2013, more than 30 million passengers flew in and out of Shenzhen, placing it on a par with Barcelona, Newark, and Sao Paolo.[22]

In 1996, China's civil aviation authority reclassified SZIA as an international airport, a formal prerequisite for handling flights from abroad, which mandates the installation of customs and immigration facilities. Yet despite its upgraded status, national aviation policy has consistently omitted the city from the elite triumvirate—Beijing, Shanghai, Guangzhou—that constitute China's officially sanctioned gateways for international aviation.[23] The operation of international flights is further complicated by Bao'an's proximity to China's southern frontier, as the military does not allow commercial airplanes to fly across the border below five thousand meters.[24] As a consequence of these constraints, 96 percent of the flights that flew in and out of SZIA in 2014 were domestic. Of the eighty-two destinations served by SZIA, only eleven were located outside Mainland China, and the airport did not offer a single intercontinental flight.[25]

Prior to the opening of the Fuksas terminal in 2013, Shenzhen's inferior status within China's aviation hierarchy was rendered all too apparent by the airport's division into three separate buildings. The smallest was the "International, Hong Kong, Macau, and Taiwan Terminal," the politically correct, if somewhat convoluted, term used for nondomestic facilities at Mainland Chinese airports. The building felt like a mock-up or simulation of an actual airport. Prominent wall clocks displayed the current time in Paris, Berlin, Cairo, Moscow, New Delhi, Tokyo, Sydney, Los Angeles, and New York, yet the tiny terminal was more Potemkin than real, accommodating only a handful of flights to Southeast Asian cities, and at much higher prices than comparable routes from Hong Kong (Figure 3.2). Deafeningly silent, the "international" terminal never operated at full capacity.

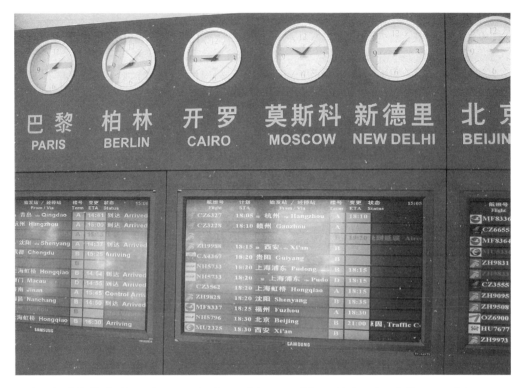

FIGURE 3.2. Clocks display the current time in capital cities around the world. Apart from Beijing, none of these destinations is linked to Shenzhen by air.

By contrast, a walk through the arrival halls of the two adjacent domestic terminals was tantamount to an aural and olfactory obstacle course. Security guards strutted around a mass of meeters and greeters, taxi touts, and thousands of passengers arriving from Chinese cities both large (Beijing, Shanghai, Chengdu) and small (Hailaer, Yibin, Zhangjiajie). On the departures level, booths staffed by highly motivated travel agents crowded around the main entrance to the departure hall. On one visit to the airport with a young woman named Yun Yun, a freelance musician from Hunan who had agreed to drive me around for the day, I was approached by a middle-aged salesman sporting a greasy comb-over.[26]

"Where do you want to go?" he bellowed.

We didn't actually want to fly anywhere—in fact, Yun Yun and I were late for an appointment on the other side of town—but I was curious what he might offer.

"Beijing," I replied.

"Beijing? Hold on." The man produced a printout from his shirt pocket. "Beijing . . . you can leave now, four o'clock, but you'll need to hurry. One thousand kwai." About 160 U.S. dollars.

"That's too expensive. Do you have something cheaper?"

He frowned and consulted his schedule.

"OK, if you leave at eight o'clock tonight the price is 800 kwai. Or 600 if you leave tomorrow morning."

We thanked him and said that we would need to think about it. As we turned toward the exit, a second man ran up to us and thrust a business card in Yun Yun's face.

"That salesman you were just talking to was quoting you the rack rate," he shouted excitedly. "My agency can get you a special price. Fifteen percent discount."

As we walked toward the parking lot, Yun Yun chuckled. "I've been living in Shenzhen for two years, and I've always booked my flights on Qunar"—the Chinese equivalent of Expedia. "I didn't know that you can just buy a ticket at the airport. It feels like I'm in a bus station!"

The actual bus station, however, is located downstairs, and serves an entirely different purpose. As passengers leave the baggage claim area and move toward the exit, they encounter a row of booths, similar to the ones occupied by the travel agents upstairs, that advertise cross-border bus and minivan services to HKIA and to Hong Kong's "urban area." Administered by no-nonsense saleswomen in form-unflattering orange and magenta uniforms, the booths are operated by four competitors: China Travel Service, mentioned in the introduction, and three local bus companies called Eternal East Cross-Border Coach Management, Trans-Island Chinalink, and Sino-way HK-China Express. Founded in the early 1990s by Hong Kong entrepreneurs to facilitate the growth in travel to and from Guangdong, these companies used their expertise in cross-boundary transport management as a springboard for developing transit connections to and from the region's airports.[27] These routes play a crucial role in the Pearl River Delta's aviation infrastructure. In 2013, 5 million people flying out of HKIA—about every tenth passenger—arrived at the airport on a cross-border bus originating in Guangdong province. A similar number of travelers made the reverse trip from Hong Kong to SZIA.[28] The staff working at these booths direct passengers bound for Hong Kong's "urban areas" toward a fleet of buses waiting outside the terminal. The coaches offer extraordinarily precise point-to-point connections to dozens of shopping malls, hotels, and new towns throughout Hong Kong Island, Kowloon, and the New Territories. Meanwhile, passengers who have just landed from elsewhere in China and are transferring to an international flight at HKIA shuffle toward the "Shenzhen–Hong Kong Airports Link Passenger Lounge." Adorned with the twin logos of the Hong Kong and Shenzhen airport authorities, the entrance to the waiting lounge is staffed by teenage greeters wearing identical neon orange polo shirts. Inside, two clerks sit at a desk advertising "FREE one stop check-in service" for travelers departing from Hong Kong's Chek Lap Kok airport. In an adjoining room, small groups of passengers loll about in oversized maroon armchairs, waiting to be transferred by bus to HKIA.

The Airport in the Urban Village

Shenzhen's airport is located on the city's northwestern haunch, a forty-five-minute drive from the skyscrapers of Luohu and Futian. Unless you happen to live near SZIA, or have just landed there from elsewhere in China, the airport's peripheral location makes it an inconvenient place to hop on a bus to HKIA. Recognizing this, in 2009 the cross-boundary bus companies began to develop a network of "in-town" check-in terminals that corresponded to the city's extensive, multipolar layout. Spread across the three central districts that border Hong Kong, these terminals were inserted into an unusual variety of urban spaces. In Futian district, the check-in terminal abuts the main entrance to the city's central bus station. Ten kilometers to the east, Shenzhen Grand Theatre, the city's largest performing arts center, houses an in-town check-in terminal between its box office and a shop selling watercolor prints and vases (Plate 13).[29] Finally, in Nanshan district, the "Hong Kong International Airport Check-In Service" is sandwiched between two of Shenzhen's quintessential typologies: a shopping mall and an urban village (Plate 14).[30]

Alternatively translated as "villages in the city," urban villages are the result of peculiar planning policies that guided Shenzhen's spatial development.[31] In 1980, more than three hundred villages existed on the territory that was designated as the future special economic zone. Huang notes that "these spaces existed outside the city's master plan in the cracks between designated [development areas]. Local villagers began to develop this space independently, outside of the plan, without municipal administration such as planning, design and building approval, quality control, property registration, and any other regulatory procedure."[32] Characterized by six- to eight-story buildings with extremely high plot ratios, warrens of narrow alleyways, and some of the cheapest rents in Shenzhen, urban villages attracted "low-income families, migrant workers, low-cost business, and entertainment service industries" (Figure 3.3).[33] In so doing, the villages "supplemented what the urban plans had clearly overlooked: sufficient housing for low-income workers and recent arrivals."[34] Although they account for less than 10 percent of Shenzhen's total land area, in 2007 more than half of Shenzhen's inhabitants lived in urban villages, producing population densities exceeding seventy thousand people per square kilometer.[35] Many of these villages have become the object of land speculation due to their prime location within Shenzhen's inner districts. Some have been razed and entirely replaced by office towers and high-end gated communities, while others have been "progressively enclaved" by a ring of shopping malls and condominiums built on their periphery (Figure 3.4).[36]

The latter condition accurately describes the immediate surroundings of the cross-border airport check-in terminal in Nanshan. Housed along a service road inside a multistory parking garage, the terminal is flanked on one side by an upscale

FIGURE 3.3. The edges of Baishizhou are lined with tenements, pool halls, restaurants, and car repair shops.

FIGURE 3.4. Kingkey Banner New Lifestyle Center, Shenzhen.

shopping mall and condominium complex called the Kingkey Banner New Lifestyle Center, and on the other side by Baishizhou, a sprawling urban village that provides an affordable home to thousands of migrant workers and young college graduates who power the city's services and manufacturing industries.[37] Like other urban villages, Baishizhou totters precariously on the edge of Shenzhen's relentless social and spatial cleavages, its densely packed tenements encircled by office towers and condo developments that cater to the special border zone's affluent middle and upper classes. Messy, lively, and overcrowded, Baishizhou's streets are lined with small shops devoted to plastic kitchenwares, cleaning supplies, and plumbing fixtures. Street vendors sell *jiaozi* and fish balls on wooden skewers in front of busy sheet metal workshops. At night, the road facing Kingkey Banner Plaza transforms into an outdoor eating and entertainment area, filled with seafood restaurants, pool halls, and noodle stalls.

Baishizhou's southern frontier is demarcated by a manicured plaza and promenade dotted with palm trees and skyscraper apartment buildings. At its center, the Kingkey Banner New Lifestyle Center was part of a crop of upscale shopping centers that were built by real estate developers all over Shenzhen in the late 2000s, often on former village land. The Kingkey Banner Center offers the typical accoutrements of the Chinese middle class: cleaned-up versions of dim sum parlors, exhibitions of luxury cars, and domestic clothing chains posing as foreign brands. Situated in between the mall and the tenements, the airport terminal consists of two small rooms: a reception area with a row of check-in counters where passengers can print out a boarding pass and buy a ticket for the bus and minivan transfers to the airport; and a small waiting lounge where they can verify their flight status on giant flatscreens that display upcoming departures at HKIA (Figure 3.5). Every fifteen minutes, a small group of female employees armed with clipboards, megaphones, and walkie-talkies shepherds passengers down a flight of stairs to the parking garage, where idling buses and minivans wait to take them across the border (see Plate 15 and Figure 3.6).

I met Jason on one of these buses.[38] He struck up a conversation with me, curious as to what the only non-Chinese person on the bus was doing in Shenzhen. Jason is in his early forties and from Hong Kong, where he works as a middle manager in the local office of a Mainland Chinese travel website. He spends four nights a week in a studio apartment in Kowloon and the rest of his time with his wife and two sons, who live in a condo in the Nanshan district of Shenzhen. "After we had our second child, my wife became very unhappy about how small our apartment was. We couldn't afford a larger place in Hong Kong, so she convinced me to start looking in Shenzhen. A few years ago, I would have never considered it. But nowadays there are actually a lot of nice flats going up, so we made the move and have not regretted it."

FIGURE 3.5. The access road to Kingkey's airport check-in terminal separates the shopping mall from the adjacent village.

FIGURE 3.6. Staff members of Eternal East communicate via walkie-talkie to track the imminent arrival of a cross-border airport bus.

Like me, Jason was on his way to HKIA. And like me, he had checked in for his flight at the Kingkey Banner Center in Baishizhou. "I work in the Hong Kong office of my company because I have good English skills. But most of my business travel takes me to China and Taiwan. Normally I will prefer to fly out of Hong Kong, but quite often I have to fly from Shenzhen instead. There are many more flights to China from here, and also it's easier to find a ticket on short notice. Especially if I'm going to a smaller city: a lot of them don't have direct flights to Hong Kong." He paused. "But this week I'm going to Taipei, so I'm flying out of Hong Kong. Flying direct from Shenzhen to Taiwan is expensive—it costs about three or four thousand [Hong Kong] dollars. If I go through Hong Kong, I can get a ticket for less than two thousand."

Fifteen minutes after our departure from Kingkey, the bus pulls into the eight-lane forecourt of the Shenzhen Bay border control checkpoint. Jason produces a credit card-sized Hong Kong ID from his wallet and glances anxiously at his watch. "I'm going to go to the front of the bus," he says apologetically. "Sometimes there's a wait at the border—especially on weekends, when a lot of people go back and forth between Hong Kong and China." As the bus decelerates into Shenzhen Bay's sprawling bus depot, Jason waves a hasty goodbye and sprints toward the entrance of the checkpoint.

The Airport at the Border

The border between Hong Kong and what later became Shenzhen was formally established in 1898, when Qing officials and their British counterparts established the Shenzhen River as the boundary between colonial Hong Kong and the Chinese Mainland. For much of its history, the border was porous and provided plenty of opportunities for the smuggling of both people and contraband. It continued to be permeable even after the establishment of the People's Republic of China in 1949, when hundreds of thousands of Chinese fled to Hong Kong. Stricter enforcement was not implemented until a mass exodus of Guangdong residents, escaping the famines induced by the Great Leap Forward in the early 1960s, obligated British officials to stem the flow of refugees.[39]

In 1997, the United Kingdom formally ceded its control over Hong Kong to the People's Republic of China, in what is commonly referred to as "the handover."[40] In the decades following the handover, the urban economies of Hong Kong and Shenzhen grew increasingly interdependent, as the governments of both cities initiated a series of regulatory changes and infrastructure projects designed to accelerate and simplify the movement of goods and people across the border. In an idealized future, the two cities will fuse together into one gigantic megalopolis: their physical integration emblematizing the harmonious rapprochement between Hong Kong and the Mainland.

Nevertheless, first-time visitors to the region are often surprised to find that the border between Hong Kong and Shenzhen is demarcated by a heavily patrolled no-man's-land lined with two parallel sets of fences and a string of guard towers (Figure 3.7). On the Hong Kong side, a rural "Frontier Closed Area" that can only be accessed by special permission serves as an additional buffer zone between the two cities.[41] Hugging the southern edge of downtown Shenzhen, the border is undoubtedly the most vivid spatial manifestation of the "One Country, Two Systems" policy that structures Hong Kong's relationship with China. Under that policy, Hong Kong's status as a Special Administrative Region guarantees it a high degree of autonomy in key areas of governance, including the ability to implement immigration and trade policies that are distinct from those on the Mainland. In the first five years after the handover, the fear of being overwhelmed by an influx of poor Mainlanders led Hong Kong to severely restrict access to the city for PRC passport holders, who could only enter the SAR as part of a registered tour group, or if they could demonstrate that they were coming to conduct legitimate business transactions. Moreover, until 2002 Hong Kong enforced a quota system that limited the total number of Mainland visitors to two thousand per day. That changed in 2003 when—reacting to a sharp decline in tourism following the outbreak of the SARS epidemic—Hong Kong introduced an experimental Individual Visit Scheme, or IVS, that allowed Mainlanders who held an urban *hukou* from four mid-sized cities in Guangdong to enter Hong Kong for up to seven days.[42] After a successful trial period, IVS was granted to *hukou* holders from all of Guangdong's cities, including Shenzhen; and

FIGURE 3.7. The border between Shenzhen and Hong Kong. In the background, a two-level pedestrian bridge connects the Futian border control point, located in Shenzhen, to its Hong Kong counterpart, Lok Ma Chau, located on the southern banks of the Shenzhen River.

beginning with Beijing and Shanghai in 2004, IVS was progressively extended to dozens of cities throughout China.[43]

The overarching motivation behind these policy changes was the growing purchasing power of PRC citizens: in effect, once a city or province achieved a respectable level of per capita GDP, Hong Kong's immigration authorities allowed its *hukou* holders to participate in IVS.[44] And in 2008, Hong Kong began issuing one-year, multiple-entry visas to Shenzhen *hukou* holders; as well as seven-day transit visas to any PRC citizen who could produce evidence of a plane ticket for a flight departing from HKIA. In essence, these measures represented vague proxies for wealth and status on the Mainland, with regulators seeking to profit from the growing affluence and free-wheeling spending habits of Chinese consumers, while at the same time excluding poorer Mainlanders who were likely to place a strain on Hong Kong's welfare systems. These shifts in Hong Kong's migration regime radically increased the number of Mainland visitors, whose shopping and leisure predilections represented both a crucial source of tourism dollars and a daily reminder of the inexorable social and cultural divide that separates Hong Kong from the Mainland. However, they did not much help the majority of Shenzhen's inhabitants, many of whom, as migrants, held a rural *hukou* and were thus effectively barred from entering Hong Kong. Rather, they exacerbated the inequalities embedded in Shenzhen's demographic composition, with the less than one-third of the population who have a Shenzhen *hukou* enjoying not only better access to municipal services, but also freer movement abroad. In response to complaints about the restrictiveness of its policies toward Shenzhen residents, in 2010 Hong Kong's immigration authority expanded the Individual Visit Scheme to employees of state-owned enterprises working in Shenzhen and, two years later, extended the scheme even more dramatically by granting entry permits to anyone who had been legally registered as a Shenzhen resident for at least one year.[45]

The relaxation of entry requirements for Mainlanders over the past decade required a substantial physical overhaul of Hong Kong's border infrastructure, as existing boundary control facilities became overwhelmed by the increase in cross-border flows that these policy changes entailed. Whereas at the turn of the twenty-first century only two thousand Mainlanders per day were permitted to enter Hong Kong via its land border with Shenzhen, a decade later more than half a million people were crossing between the two cities every day.[46] Hong Kong's transport and immigration authorities tried to reduce the pressure on Shenzhen's oldest checkpoints—Luohu and Huanggang—by constructing two new border crossings with streamlined immigration processes: Lok Ma Chau station, a terminal connected to Hong Kong's suburban KCR rail line, which opened in 2003; and Shenzhen Bay Border Control Point, a facility that anchors the Shenzhen side of the Western Corridor Link, a cross-border suspension bridge that opened in 2007.

These changes in the border infrastructure had significant implications for the operation of the cross-boundary airport buses. While most traffic to HKIA and SZIA had been channeled through the decaying border crossing at Huanggang, from 2007 onward the airport bus companies gradually shifted their operations to Shenzhen Bay.[47] The new checkpoint had two distinct advantages. Located on the far western end of Shenzhen, on an oblong parcel of reclaimed land at the southeastern tip of Shekou peninsula, Shenzhen Bay is closer to both SZIA and HKIA than any of the inner-city checkpoints. It was also the first "co-located" immigration and customs control point: a new type of border crossing, commissioned by Hong Kong's government-owned Architectural Services Department and designed by local engineering consultants, whose purpose was to expedite movement across the border by improving on the basic design of the twin cities' boundary control facilities (Figure 3.8).[48] Most border crossings between Hong Kong and Shenzhen consist of two parallel checkpoints, located several hundred meters from one another, where Mainland Chinese and Hong Kong immigration officers carry out two separate sets of customs, immigration, and quarantine (CIQ) inspections. By contrast, Shenzhen Bay combines, or "co-locates" Hong Kong and PRC formalities under one roof, a bureaucratic feat made possible through an elaborate process of jurisdictional and infrastructural gerrymandering. Though geographically in Shenzhen, the "co-located" facility is legally a part of Hong Kong and is jointly administered by immigration officers from both sides of the border.[49] On the Hong Kong–Shenzhen Western Corridor, a five-kilometer suspension bridge that connects Shenzhen Bay to Hong Kong, PRC law applies to the structural elements that anchor it to the seabed; while the bridge's deck is a territorial extension of the Hong Kong SAR. Spurred by the growth in cross-border air passengers, Shenzhen Bay's daily traffic grew by 20 to 30 percent a year; in 2014, nearly a hundred thousand people passed through the "co-located" facility every day.[50]

Due to the special role that Shenzhen Bay assumed in facilitating the movement of passengers between HKIA and SZIA, the border crossing effectively became a functional extension of the two airports. Located roughly at the halfway point between them, the checkpoint is flanked on both sides by massive bus depots and smaller airport check-in lounges, built into the ground floor of the boundary control building, for those passengers who have not yet received a boarding pass (Figures 3.9 and 3.10). These companies maintain separate fleets on both sides of the frontier in order to avoid the logistical complexities involved in bringing a bus across the border. In Shenzhen, as everywhere on the Mainland, vehicles drive on the right; in Hong Kong, reflecting the city's colonial heritage, they do so on the left. Moreover, authorities in Hong Kong and Guangdong province maintain separate vehicle licensing systems. A car registered in Hong Kong can thus only cross the border if the owner applies for a special cross-border license, denoted by a special

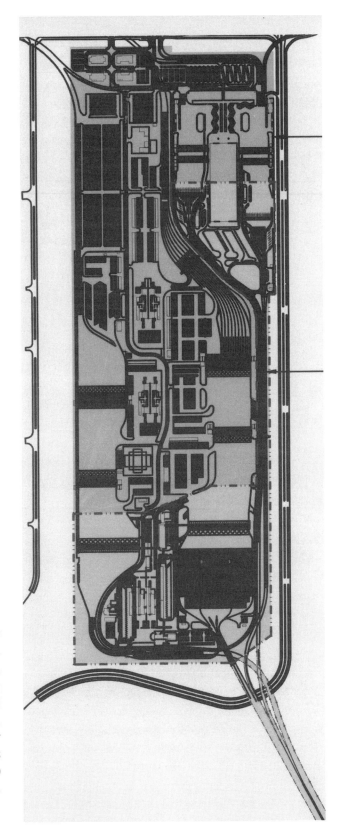

FIGURE 3.8. A diagram of Shenzhen Bay, the first "co-located" border checkpoint. The Immigration Department of Hong Kong administers the southern and eastern portions of the building, while the remaining area is under the jurisdiction of Mainland China's immigration authority. Map courtesy of Jonathan D. Solomon.

FIGURE 3.9. The Shenzhen Bay boundary control terminal is flanked by bus depots and airport check-in terminals on both sides of the checkpoint.

black plate that is affixed to the front and back of the vehicle. Buses arriving from the in-town check-in terminals deposit passengers at the entrance to the five-story checkpoint, where travelers then queue up at two sets of customs and immigration inspections. Depending on the time of day, the process takes between ten minutes and an hour. They then emerge on the other side of the checkpoint and board a second bus that takes Hong Kong–bound passengers to HKIA and China-bound ones to SZIA.

Disembarking at Shenzhen Bay, I follow in Jason's footsteps, joining a throng of passengers streaming out of half a dozen buses, and proceed through the sequence of immigration and customs inspections described above. I exit onto the Hong Kong side of the inspection terminal about twenty minutes later and speed walk along with hundreds of other travelers toward a second set of buses, idling in an identical bus depot, that are waiting to take passengers to HKIA. An employee of Eternal East intercepts me at the end of the concourse. Spotting the green sticker that a sales clerk at Kingkey Banner Center had applied to my jacket lapel, she steers me toward the appropriate departure bay. Jason waves to me from the back

FIGURE 3.10. An airport check-in terminal at the Shenzhen Bay border checkpoint.

of the bus as I board. "I was faster than you, but then I just ended up waiting here for ten minutes while the driver was on break." He points out the window toward a middle-aged man who is smoking and chatting with two of his colleagues. Eventually the driver throws his cigarette butt on the ground, climbs into his seat, reverses out of the departure slip, and makes a beeline for the checkpoint exit.

Jason and I sit in silence as we glide across the five-kilometer suspension bridge that spans the entrance to Shenzhen Bay. When we reach the other side, the bus enters Hong Kong's Frontier Closed Area, hurtling above villages and rice paddies on an elevated highway that snakes its way across the rural strip of land that separates Hong Kong from Shenzhen. As we speed through the enormous new towns that dot the rugged coastline of the New Territories, I ask Jason how often he travels outside of China. "I don't go abroad much on business—that's mainly for the more important people in the office!" He laughs. "But I do go on family vacations with my wife and kids. In the last few years we've been to Bangkok, to Malaysia, to Vietnam. For those trips, we always fly out of Hong Kong. There are some flights from Shenzhen, but they're much more expensive—double the price. Since there are four of us traveling, that makes a big difference."

"For family trips I usually take an airport minivan instead of the bus. It costs more, but it's also more comfortable, and easier to manage if you have a lot of luggage because you can stay inside the van when you go through the border. With the bus you have to get out with all of your suitcases, go through immigration, then get on a different bus. That can be a challenge with the kids."

In other words, for twice the price of a bus ticket, travelers can choose to ride in a seven-seat minivan, which has the distinct advantage of offering "on-vehicle CIQ clearance at Shenzhen Bay Port."[51] In effect, the differing price structure represents another proxy for passengers' wealth and status, as those who can pay for the more expensive van tickets are afforded both additional comfort and a less rigorous inspection. Rather than proceed to the border control building, the van drives through an imposing tollbooth-like structure, where the driver passes a thick wad of passports to a Mainland Chinese immigration officer sitting inside a small cubicle (Figure 3.11). Using a special set of mirrors, the officer checks the faces of each of the van's occupants against their passport photo, occasionally asking the driver to pull up or reverse in order to get a clearer view. The officer then returns the passports to the driver and waves him through to his counterpart from the Hong Kong Immigration Department, who repeats the procedure at an identical booth several meters away.

The final stop on the Hong Kong-bound airport buses is Terminal 2 at HKIA. "T2" was designed by the corporate architecture firm Skidmore, Owings, and

FIGURE 3.11. Air passengers traveling between Hong Kong and Shenzhen by minivan transit the border via tollbooths located next to the pedestrian checkpoint.

Merrill in partnership with the local design consultant OTC—the same team that collaborated on the SkyPier facility discussed in the previous chapter. The terminal is unusual insofar as it features most of the typical design elements of an airport terminal—check-in desks, shopping and entertainment facilities, lounges, immigration and security controls—yet it has no departure gates and is not connected to the airfield. Inaugurated in 2008, the terminal's primary purpose was to accommodate the needs of so-called "intermodal" air passengers: people transiting by bus, ferry, or minivan to and from Mainland China. In the early 2000s, these travelers constituted only a small fraction of all passengers flying in and out of Hong Kong and could be processed through a few service counters located in the arrivals hall of Terminal 1. A decade later, however, the proportion of Mainland passengers had grown to more than a quarter of all travelers at HKIA.[52] Unable to accommodate that growth within the existing terminal, Hong Kong's airport authority shifted them into a new building designed explicitly for their needs. Terminal 2 is anchored by the Mainland Coach Terminus: a spacious expanse of cross-border bus transfer desks, a "Hong Kong Shenzhen Airports Link Passenger Lounge," and a bus depot with thirty-four departure bays (Figure 3.12).[53] Illuminated signs advertise property developments in Shenzhen, while television screens indicate the departure times of buses bound for destinations across Guangdong province. Exiting the bus one final time, I accompany Jason through the passenger lounge and into a tunnel that leads to the main terminal at HKIA. Having already received his boarding pass in Shenzhen, he continues directly to security and immigration, and then on to his flight to Taipei.

Conclusion

Western observers of Chinese urbanism tend to focus on large-scale infrastructure projects like the Fuksas terminal at SZIA. Their attention is infused with an element of "megastructure porn": a visual attraction to the sheer scale of what is being built in China that readily ignores its structural flaws (such as the rapid senescence of shoddy building materials) and programmatic deficiencies (e.g., an international airport with few international flights). That fascination is likewise tinged with a deep nostalgia for a bygone era when Western governments, and the voting publics who elected them, demonstrated the political will to invest in major public works projects of their own.

From the perspective of the Chinese client, usually a municipality or a state-owned institution like an airport authority, megaprojects like the Fuksas terminal at SZIA are crucial not only for upgrading a city's basic infrastructure, but also for increasing their city's name recognition and cultural capital. Moreover, the timely completion of these "face" projects within the cycle of the five-year plan—which remains the basic temporal frame for China's economy—are essential for securing future promotions for the urban leaders involved. As central as these infrastructure projects may be to the design ambitions of the urban planner, or to the career aspirations of the politician, it is questionable whether they are really at the forefront of urban innovation—or whether, like many things in Shenzhen, they merely represent a shortcut to achieving global recognition through visually striking yet functionally inadequate architectural simulacra. In effect, the expansion of SZIA represented a highly formal approach to globalization devoid of the requisite content: an imitation of an international airport terminal that aestheticized rather than actualized Shenzhen's ambitions for cross-border connectivity. The parametric design of the Fuksas terminal, with its unabashed privileging of form over function, lent itself well to this pursuit, as it captured both the *arriviste*'s desire to show off newly acquired wealth, as well as Chinese leaders' obsession with bombastic displays of technological novelty.

Meanwhile, the bulk of Shenzhen's international air traffic is channeled through a network of exceptionally banal check-in terminals and bus depots whose ultimate

FIGURE 3.12. Cross-border buses terminate at the Mainland coach station inside Hong Kong International Airport's Terminal 2.

goal is nevertheless quite remarkable: namely, to compensate for the global connectivity that Shenzhen's megaprojects cannot provide. Like the "upstream" ferry terminals discussed in the previous chapter, these facilities are not the subject of international design competitions; rather, they are engineered by local technical service providers and are articulated in an explicitly understated aesthetic register that aims to deflect attention from the larger, transnational objectives informing their development. Tucked away into the corners and interstitial spaces of much larger structures, the check-in terminals are characterized by very little signage and almost no advertising. While they host hundreds of passengers per day, they are built to process travelers as quickly as possible, checking them in and loading them onto Hong Kong–bound buses in less than fifteen minutes.

In this chapter, I have opened up a dialogue between the Fuksas terminal and the cross-boundary bus terminals in order to shed light on the underlying processes that have guided Shenzhen's urban development at the beginning of the twenty-first century. In effect, the cross-border check-in system spatializes the inherent conflicts between the structures of a planned national economy, predicated on rigid geographic hierarchies, and the exigencies of a multipolar global capitalism that fetishizes unfettered point-to-point mobility across national frontiers. For the time being, Shenzhen's contact with the outside world is being channeled via HKIA. This mediated form of global connectivity is designed in equal measure to assuage Hong Kong's existential anxiety about its declining role as a broker between China and the West, as well as to placate the PRC's military and security apparatus, which is deeply reluctant to countenance any increase in cross-border activity over Guangdong's airspace. Thus, as Shenzhen seeks to extend its influence beyond the Mainland, it finds its aspirations circumscribed by the dictates of the military and by its subordinate role to established centers of international trade like Hong Kong and Guangzhou, who are loath to be bypassed by the upstart metropolis in their midst. Shenzhen exercises an extraordinary amount of autonomy within the confines of the special zone—but where its ambitions intersect with more powerful regional interests and national security concerns, it quickly becomes apparent that Shenzhen lacks the regulatory framework, and the political clout, to become a global city.

Economic elites in the Pearl River Delta have promoted investments in cross-boundary infrastructure as a means of achieving "win-win situations"—a diplomatic shorthand for the pragmatic compromises that are needed in order to circumvent the region's sociopolitical cleavages and intercity rivalries. Quite unintentionally, this strategy has become a source of inspiration for urban design, as the attempt to interpolate between Shenzhen's worldly ambitions and subaltern constraints has yielded a profusion of spatial and typological innovations. As the cross-boundary coaches channel passengers between the check-in terminals and the border, the flow of international air traffic along Shenzhen's streets and alleyways thus becomes a facet of everyday life in the city. In effect, the in-town check-in terminal represents the foil of the Fuksas project at Bao'an: aesthetically understated and deeply entrenched in the city's urban fabric, but also remarkably effective at providing Shenzhen with an infrastructure of international air travel.

As efficient as the cross-boundary coach system may be, it is undeniably time-consuming. Travelers are advised to arrive at the check-in terminal in Shenzhen three to four hours before their flight is scheduled to depart from Hong Kong. They then board a bus to the border, haul themselves and their luggage through two sets of customs and immigration controls, board another bus to HKIA, and proceed yet again through security and immigration. If the lines at the border are short and the buses leave promptly, the seventy-five-kilometer trip takes a little more than an hour; if there are hiccups along the way, the trip can be much longer. For a metropolis of 15 million inhabitants, with rising levels of income and an attendant eagerness to travel abroad, this is clearly not an ideal solution. Borne of the three traits that pervade urban development in the Pearl River Delta—pragmatism, improvisation, and entrepreneurialism—the cross-border check-in system points to the unavoidable conflict between those who would like to increase Shenzhen's global connectivity, and those who would like to arrest it.

In *The Anxieties of Mobility: Migration and Tourism in the Indonesian Borderlands,* the anthropologist Johan Lindquist studies the movement of migrant workers and working-class tourists on Batam, a special economic zone located off the coast of Singapore in Indonesia's Riau Archipelago. Focused on an island "located at the periphery of a global city," Lindquist's book seeks to "consider the social organization of human mobility from the vantage point of the spatial and temporal border between the 'developing' and the 'developed' worlds."[54] In so doing, he creates "an alternative topography of Southeast Asia . . . that allows us to understand Batam not strictly as a place that is 'offshore' in relation to Singapore, . . . but rather as a node in a system of human mobility that is territorially and culturally unbounded."[55] Lindquist's book serves as a useful model for probing the distinctive agency embedded in special border cities such as Batam and Shenzhen. While they originate as an economic appendage to established centers of wealth and power, over time these special zones take on a dynamic of their own and seek to assert autonomy from their more dominant twin city by engendering multidirectional mobility flows across the border. This phenomenon can be observed not just in Shenzhen, but also in other special border cities. In Malaysia, Johor Bahru has labored to shed its image as a supplier of cheap groceries and illicit activities for day-tripping Singaporeans—investing instead in middle-class housing developments and institutions of higher education in an attempt to attract a more cosmopolitan population of foreign students, young families, and retirees. Zhuhai, the special border city adjacent to Macau, has repositioned itself as a bucolic retirement destination, touting itself as the "Chinese Florida." And similar to the case of Shenzhen, which Mainland Chinese tourists fly through in order to get to Hong Kong, Batam is developing a new identity as a point of transit for Indonesia's emerging middle class, who fly to the island's Hang Nadim International Airport and then continue by ferry to spend their holidays in Singapore.[56]

Yet Shenzhen is unique among Asia's special zones insofar as it has already surpassed its conjoined twin in many respects. By the first decade of the twenty-first century, its population was more than twice that of Hong Kong; and with a median age of just thirty-three years, its residents were, on average, a decade younger than those across the border and more likely to be gainfully employed.[57] From an architect's perspective, the continued availability of both open space and open-minded clients made the prospect of building and designing in Shenzhen an appealing one. And while Hong Kong's residents were, on the whole, much wealthier, more educated, and cosmopolitan, it remained a city whose education system and stratified social hierarchies offered relatively few opportunities for upward mobility. For even the most grossly underpaid migrant worker, moving to Shenzhen afforded a dramatic step up in terms of economic status and prestige. And for a growing number of middle-class Hongkongers such as Jason, relocating to Shenzhen presented itself as a viable and even attractive alternative to Hong Kong's extremely confined living conditions.

Thus Shenzhen finds itself at an odd moment of urban adolescence: still subordinated to wealthier regional centers of power like Hong Kong and Guangzhou, yet faced with the prospect of greater autonomy in the not-too-distant future. How Shenzhen renegotiates its relationship with Hong Kong is instructive not only in terms of its role at the forefront of Mainland China's reconciliation with Hong Kong, but also insofar as it charts an evolutionary path for less developed special border cities elsewhere to follow. Until now, these zones' self-definition, as well as their perception from outside, was largely determined by practical exigencies: this city exists as a cheap place to produce T-shirts or assemble computer chips. Residents, too, saw their sojourn in the zone as a means to an end, connected to aspirations for social and material improvements in hometowns located far from their place of employment. Over time, however, these zones evolve, and the predominantly migrant population acquires a modicum of civic pride, along with more bourgeois expectations about life quality, that demand a certain normalization of the "special" border city. In so doing, however, they discover a peculiar contradiction in the mobility regimes that govern special zones. On the one hand, these cities owe their very existence to the privileging of movement—of goods, of people, of foreign capital; and their spatial layout revolves invariably around infrastructures of mobility—train stations, highways, air- and seaports—that connect them to the wider world. At the same time, residents of special zones find their cross-border mobility circumscribed by the vested interests of their interreferenced twin: established entrepôts such as Hong Kong and Singapore, who expend much energy in order to ensure that they will not be bypassed by their scrappy frontier-town double across the border. Unfettered mobility in border cities is likewise viewed negatively by the very national governments who created them, as they are unwilling to grant further autonomy to these special zones for fear that they will challenge the highly centralized power hierarchies, concentrated in capital cities like Beijing and Jakarta, that are endemic to the Asian nation-state.

The conflict between mobility and immobility can be seen most palpably in Shenzhen's continuous and simultaneous upgrading of its border control facilities and its cross-border transportation systems. That conflict is likewise echoed in the spatial tactics of Shenzhen's inhabitants: producing, among middle-class residents like Jason, a nonchalant attitude toward the region's complex and at times opaque regimes of cross-border movement. That blasé approach reflects what the historian Willem van Schendel has called the "everyday transnationality," common to people living in border cities, who "continually explore and challenge the territorial pretensions" of neighboring states.[58] In the case of Hong Kong and Shenzhen, the pragmatic attitude regarding where and when one flies out of which airport—if you're heading to Taipei or Bangkok, choose HKIA; for Kunming or Zhengzhou, better to pick Shenzhen—reflects a broader attitude of comparison and contrast between systems, cities, and currencies that is interwoven into quotidian routines in special border zones across Asia.

The writer Katha Pollitt has remarked upon the "strange internal logic" of a dream: the irrational chains of cause and effect that seem wholly plausible until the moment of awakening, when you realize the spurious nature of the causalities that your brain concocted while you were asleep.[59] Special border cities, too, have their own peculiar internal logic, as their organizing principles depend on creative rationalizations in order to make dissonant social, economic, and judicial regimes cohere with one another. In the overarching absence of historical precedents, those who dwell in special zones such as Shenzhen—cities that cannot be accurately described as either cosmopolitan metropoles or provincial hinterlands, existing instead in taxonomic limbo—do not perceive anything unusual about a 1.4 billion-U.S.-dollar international airport terminal that has almost no international flights, or about checking in for a trip to New York in a bus terminal located inside an urban village.[60] Rather, the contrast between highly representative yet ineffectual spaces of global connectivity, and hastily erected transport nodes that ingeniously evade regulatory restrictions on cross-border mobility, testifies to the compensatory design strategies devised by a municipality that is trying to transcend its hinterland role and interact directly with the outside world, but cannot do so just yet.

FOUR

Cheap Tickets

Every major Asian city features at least one mall dedicated to electronics, usually housed inside a slightly older but centrally located shopping center. In Bangkok, it's Pantip Plaza; in Singapore, it's the Sim Lim Tower; and in Kuala Lumpur, the capital of Malaysia, it's Plaza Low Yat. Located off of Jalan Bukit Bintang, a honky-tonk tourist strip lined with massage parlors, cheap hotels, and off-brand minimarts, Low Yat bills itself as "Malaysia's Largest IT Lifestyle Mall": six floors of mobile phones, digital cameras, laptops, computers, and flatscreen TVs, and an endless array of cables, chargers, and converters. Giant speakers on the ground floor blast auto-tuned top-40 hits while sales clerks stand around waiting for customers.

Off to one side of an atrium filled with camera shops and an anchor store called 3G Utopia, the AirAsia ticketing counter is tucked away near the back of the mall, inside a "concept store" run by a discount mobile phone provider.[1] Two clerks chat amiably in Malay on the AirAsia "side" of the shop, backlit by giant posters advertising new flight connections to Lombok, Indonesia, and Nanning, China. I approach one of them, a young woman wearing a white T-shirt and a black hijjab, and ask if I can buy a plane ticket in cash.

"Pay cash no problem," she answers.

"Also for a flight leaving today?" I ask.

"Flight leaving today can," she replies, lifting up four fingers. "But must be at least four hours before departure time."

"Do you have a schedule?"

"Schedule no have. You can check the flight timings over there."

She gestures toward an "AirAsia sales kiosk," a squat red machine that looks a bit like a computer terminal crossed with an ATM. The interface is a simplified version of AirAsia's online search engine. Prompts on the computer screen direct customers to use a rickety keyboard and mouse to enter the departure and arrival cities of the flight they are looking for. Once I've selected my flight, the computer instructs me to insert cash into a slot installed below the keyboard, reminding me to "pay the exact amount shown on the screen," as the terminal does not give change. Out pops my ticket, and I'm on my way.

It is difficult to overstate the impact that budget air travel is having on the social, spatial, and cultural dynamics of Southeast Asian cities. On routes between Singapore and Dhaka, Manila and Hong Kong, Kuala Lumpur and Jakarta, low-cost carriers (or LCCs) are the mode of choice for the migrant maids, nurses, and manual laborers who build Southeast Asia's metropoles, harvest the crops on its outskirts, and care for its inhabitants. In Singapore, their imprint is never far from the surface. At a busy intersection in Little India, Tamil- and Bangla-speaking construction workers peruse hastily printed A4-sized signs, affixed to a building façade with masking tape, that advertise cheap fares to Delhi, Dhaka, and Chennai (Plate 16). Across town on Orchard Road, the city's main shopping boulevard, the Filipino budget airline Cebu Pacific stages a flash mob–style "street dance."[2] Featuring a man dressed as an airplane and a phalanx of dancers writhing to Jennifer Lopez and Lady Gaga, the event quickly turns into an impromptu party for the thousands of Filipina maids who congregate on Orchard during their weekly day off.

Theorizing budget airlines as an integral component of what they term "migration infrastructure," the anthropologists Johan Lindquist and Xiang Biao have argued that low-cost carriers have effectively supplanted the complex bus and ferry itineraries that used to function as the dominant supply routes for migrant labor between Southeast Asia's boomtowns and impoverished hinterlands.[3] But what is perhaps more interesting is that the laboring underclass by no means predominates aboard these flights: mingling instead with an astonishing variety of other passengers. LCCs cater to college students and artists traveling on a tight budget. They tap into global routes of pilgrimage and piety, hosting Buddhist monks and *hajjis* en route to Mecca. They are popular among retirees, who visit children and grandchildren working abroad, and augment the purchasing power of their pensions by spending parts of the year in cheaper, hotter, and slower-paced locales.[4] Low-cost airlines also function as a social safety valve for the so-called "sandwich class" of wealthy cities like Singapore: enabling the shopping trips abroad for lower-middle-class residents who cannot afford many leisure activities and consumer products in their hometowns.

In this chapter, I argue that the advent of low-cost aviation has fundamentally reshaped the social and spatial dynamics of contemporary Southeast Asian cities— and that it has significantly reordered the functional interdependency of those cities by accelerating and expanding cross-border flows of labor, consumption, capital, and knowledge. I begin by investigating changes in Southeast Asia's mobility and migration regimes that have made it possible for budget airlines to thrive. The second part of the chapter focuses on architectural typologies and low-cost transportation systems that cater to an emerging clientele of what I call the *nouveaux globalisés:* people who have *just* enough money to travel abroad, but who lack the basic knowledge and technical equipment that is needed to fly, such as a credit card, Internet access, familiarity with check-in procedures, and a way to get to the airport. Studying the emergence of budget airport facilities in Kuala Lumpur, Bangkok, and Singapore, I distinguish between three distinct modes of engagement with low-cost mobility, which I term entrepreneurial populism, trickle-down infrastructure, and future city science fiction. In the conclusion, I identify a palpable tension between the populist narratives espoused by budget airlines and the airport designs produced by state planning agencies, who have only belatedly and begrudgingly responded to the pluralization of the flying public. In so doing, I posit the low-cost airport as a useful lens for interpreting broader contradictions in the planning and design of Southeast Asian cities. Specifically, I contend that infrastructure planners' reluctance to produce inclusive designs for a socioeconomically diverse audience provides a crucial insight into larger problems embedded in the planning of Southeast Asian cities. I argue that there is a perilous disconnect between the valorization of cross-border mobility and regional economic integration—advocated by the Association of Southeast Asian Nations (ASEAN) and its constituent member states—and the aesthetic goals of urban planners, who are keen to mobilize the symbolic value of airports as evidence of their cities' global connectivity and cosmopolitan stature, yet are loath to acknowledge the increasingly plebeian nature of the airport's clientele that has resulted from the liberalization of cross-border transportation and migration regimes.

The Origins of Southeast Asia's Low-Cost Airlines

Although Southeast Asia's budget airlines only emerged in the last two decades, their antecedents can be traced back to two historical precedents: the deregulation of the American airline industry that took place in the late 1970s; and the establishment of an integrated European airspace in the 1980s. For much of its history, civil aviation was heavily regulated by the dictates of the nation-state. Flights that crossed international borders were mainly operated by subsidized national airlines flying between capital cities.[5] National prestige and security trumped both convenience and profitability.[6] With the notable exception of chartered airplanes that flew during peak holiday seasons, international air routes were primarily maintained for state elites—diplomats, civil servants, military generals—and a small coterie of businessmen.

Transport historians identify the ratification of the U.S. Airline Deregulation Act (ADA) as a pivotal moment in the redefinition of global aviation networks. Signed into law by President Carter in 1978, ADA addressed a peculiar contradiction embedded in the regulation of domestic air traffic. Until the late 1970s, all interstate air travel was governed by a federal Civil Aeronautics Board (CAB), which set prices and authorized specific airlines to operate particular routes. Meanwhile, intrastate aviation—that is, air traffic that did not cross state lines—was largely unregulated. Taking advantage of that loophole, in the early 1970s several airlines began operating discounted flights within the borders of larger states like California, Texas, and Wisconsin.[7] This led to significant differences in ticket prices, as a one-hour *inter*state flight—between, say, Boston and Philadelphia—often cost twice as much as a one-hour *intra*state flight, for example, between San Francisco and Los Angeles.[8] The resulting discrepancy between intra- and interstate airfares, ushered in by locally operated low-cost airlines, created political pressure to reduce the cost of interstate air travel and ultimately led to the wholesale deregulation of domestic aviation.[9] Drawing on the American example, many countries with large domestic aviation networks—Canada, New Zealand, Australia, the UK, Japan—followed suit.[10]

In effect, the deregulation of domestic air travel in the United States originated in an effort to extend liberal models of intrastate air travel to flights that crossed state boundaries. The liberalization of air travel *within* one country subsequently led to efforts to deregulate flights *between* countries: as sympathetic governments applied the logic of airspace deregulation to the international scale. If domestic air travel was no longer subject to the oversight and control of the state, they argued, then why should international aviation remain heavily regulated? From the 1980s onward, the United States established so-called air service agreements and "open skies" treaties that gradually deregulated air travel between the United States and its allies in Europe and Asia.[11] Concurrent to these American-led efforts, European countries pursued parallel attempts to simplify cross-border air travel on the Continent: an ambition that reflected the political, financial, and cultural aims of the European Economic Community, the predecessor of the EU. Within that broader context, the creation of a Single Aviation Market—or SAM—was viewed as a crucial precondition for European integration.[12]

The Single Aviation Market was progressively implemented in a series of "packages" between 1988 and 1997.[13] Its significance lay in its pan-European commitment to what aviation technocrats refer to as the "freedoms of the air": nine core principles of deregulation that removed the limitations imposed by individual countries.[14] Upstart low-cost airlines were the first to experiment with this changing regulatory environment. In 1985, the Irish carrier Ryanair introduced flights between London's Gatwick Airport and Waterford, a small city in southeastern Ireland.[15] Cheaper and faster than cross-border ferries, the flights appealed to the large population of Irish guest workers living in the United Kingdom. Capitalizing on the effects of the Schengen Agreement, which created a pan-European zone of passport-free travel in 1995,[16] Ryanair and the budget airlines that followed opened up new international gateways in the provinces on former military bases that had been rendered obsolete by the end of the Cold War (see Figure 4.1). In so doing, they created parallel geographies of international aviation that catered to a new clientele of migrants, students, retirees, and budget tourists.[17] As the geographer Kathy Burrell notes, these flights "opened up travel, and most significantly migration opportunities" to a wide range of provincial locations across Europe, "transforming previously regionally focused towns and cities, by virtue of their airports, into international departure and arrival points."[18]

This brief digression into the annals of American and European aviation history is crucial in order to understand the changes in Southeast Asia's airspace and cross-border migration policies that took place at the turn of the twenty-first century. These shifts are part of a broader ambition to create a common market that encompasses the ten members of ASEAN. The motivations for doing so are similar to those that informed the formation of the European Union: economic development and regional integration through the free movement of goods and labor; and the suturing of historical wounds in a part of the world that remains starkly divided by ethnic, religious, national, and ideological cleavages. Since 2006, citizens of ASEAN countries no longer need a visa to visit any other member state.[19] Two years later, the ten countries agreed to remove restrictions on flights between capital cities. Further accords in 2010 and 2012 deregulated traffic between secondary cities and also made it easier for airlines to operate flights between ASEAN and Mainland China.[20] Taken together, these policies foreshadow the intent to create a Schengen-style regional visa zone, complemented by an ASEAN-wide Single Aviation Market based on the European model (Figure 4.2).[21]

FIGURE 4.1. Low-cost air travelers deplaning at Eindhoven Airport, the Netherlands.

FIGURE 4.2. A 2014 exhibition at Bangkok's Suvarnabhumi airport celebrated the loosening of restrictions on cross-border air travel between member states of ASEAN.

Against the backdrop of these changes, and drawing their inspiration from European and American antecedents, budget airlines began to emerge in Southeast Asia in the late 1990s. Counterintuitively, their development was abetted by the Asian Financial Crisis of 1997, which brought Southeast Asia's roaring fin-de-siècle economies to a standstill. In the ensuing economic downturn, the skyline of cities like Bangkok and Jakarta became dotted with the jagged hulks of unfinished skyscrapers and elevated railway lines, physical reminders of the wave of bankruptcies that swept across the region. The traumatic events that followed—thousands of people lost their jobs, property, and life savings—galvanized Asia's infant budget airline industry in two unexpected ways. First, as businesses were faced with much smaller travel budgets, they started to look for a cheaper alternative to Southeast Asia's state-run airlines. Second, national governments that had previously rejected the notion of a low-cost airline industry began issuing licenses to LCCs in order to counteract a sharp drop in air traffic.[22] Thus what was very bad from a macroeconomic perspective proved to be beneficial for Southeast Asia's budget airlines, which convinced both government regulators and passengers to experiment with a novel form of long-distance travel. In a macabre twist, these LCCs also profited from the financial crisis that followed the September 11 attacks on the World Trade Center. When American and European airlines declared bankruptcy and tried to recover their losses by reducing the size of their fleets, Southeast Asian budget carriers bought up second-hand planes and hired away staff who had been made redundant.[23]

The influx of technical equipment and expertise from the United States and Europe, coupled with the introduction of liberal regimes of cross-border mobility, effectively produced a favorable environment for these budget airlines. Their impact can be gauged by the so-called "LCC penetration rate," which measures the proportion of air traffic flown by low-cost carriers. Globally, they operate a quarter of all scheduled flights; in Southeast Asia, they account for 60 percent.[24]

These airlines emerged at the hands of a wide variety of actors who were already active in cross-border trade, running the gamut from Cebu Pacific, founded by the patriarch of an influential Filipino Chinese merchant family, to Vietjet, Vietnam's largest budget airline, owned by a corporation that previously functioned as an import–export agent for rice, textile, and electronics shipments to the Soviet Union (Figure 4.3). Undoubtedly the most visible actor is Tony Fernandes, a Malaysian entrepreneur descended from Goan and Malaccan Portuguese trading families. He studied and worked in the UK and then returned to Malaysia, where he tried to replicate the business model of European airlines like Virgin Atlantic and Ryanair. In 2001, Fernandes launched AirAsia as a cheaper and hipper alternative to Malaysia's old-fashioned national carrier, designed for the needs of a new set of lower- and middle-class consumers (Figure 4.4 and 4.5).[25] The airline's success lay in its application of the pop aesthetics and marketing techniques of mass culture to an industry and to an architectural typology—the airport—that had previously been conceived of as state-controlled infrastructures reserved for ruling elites. AirAsia became the most prominent budget airline in the region: easily recognized by the populist slogan emblazoned on its airplanes—*Now Everyone Can Fly*—and well known for its aggressive attempts to create an ASEAN-wide network of low-cost aviation.

FIGURE 4.3. A poster for the Vietnamese airline Vietjet advertises promotional fares for less than five U.S. dollars.

FIGURE 4.4. The Malaysian budget carrier AirAsia campaigned aggressively to reduce restrictions on cross-border flights that operate within ASEAN.

FIGURE 4.5. An AirAsia jet at Kuala Lumpur International Airport.

The In-Town Travel Center: Low-Tech Mobility and "Offline Distribution" at KL Sentral

LCCs like AirAsia owe much of their success to their emphasis on low-tech sales networks—known within the industry as offline distribution channels—that are designed for passengers who either don't know how to use a computer or lack the basic prerequisites—such as a credit card—for purchasing a ticket online. This is an important consideration in Southeast Asia, where a large proportion of transactions continues to be executed offline and in cash. As the introduction of affordable air travel outpaced the development of online banking systems, low-cost carriers developed creative strategies for extracting payments from their customers. In Thailand, for example, passengers on Nok Air can book a ticket by telephone. The airline replies by SMS with a six-digit reservation code and a request to make a payment in cash at any 7–Eleven within two hours' time. A similar system exists in Malaysia, where customers can pay for their plane tickets at petrol stations run by Petronas, the state-owned oil and gas company.[26]

The gap between the demand for budget travel and the inability of customers to purchase tickets online also gave rise to a new transport typology—the low-cost travel center—operated by individual airlines in downtown shopping districts, suburban malls, bus terminals, and railway stations. At these travel centers, staff advise passengers on how to book a flight, accept cash payments for existing reservations, and organize affordable bus transfers to the airport. AirAsia maintains more than forty of these travel centers across the region. In Bangkok, they are located inside six big-box stores owned by Tesco Lotus, the Thai equivalent of Target or Walmart. As a one-stop shop for groceries, clothing, and electronics catering to consumers on the lower end of the middle class, the warehouses are a logical point of sale for AirAsia's discount plane tickets, sold out of small shop fronts near the checkout lanes (Figure 4.6).[27]

AirAsia also manages eight travel centers in Kuala Lumpur—including the one at the Plaza Low Yet mentioned in the introduction. The largest outlet is at KL Sentral, an integrated transportation hub, shopping mall, condominium, and office tower complex that covers ten blocks on the southwestern edge of downtown Kuala Lumpur. Opened in 2001, KL Sentral is one of dozens of master-planned urban redevelopment projects tailored to the operational needs of multinational corporations that were built across Asia at the turn of the twenty-first century. Designed as "an exclusive urban centre built around Malaysia's largest transit hub, offering global connectivity, excellent investment opportunities, business convenience and an international lifestyle," KL Sentral's programmatic regime and organizational principles are clearly influenced by precedents like Hong Kong's International Finance Centre, discussed in chapter 1. Nominally planned by Kisho Kurokawa to coincide with his designs for the capital's new airport, the district centers around Stesen Sentral, the largest railway hub in Southeast Asia. Stesen Sentral is also the terminus of KLIA Ekspres, an in-town airport check-in facility and high-speed rail link that resembles a scaled-down version of Hong Kong's Airport Express.

FIGURE 4.6. The entryway and interior of a big-box store in central Bangkok that houses one of AirAsia's travel centers.

Near the main entrance of the station, in a nondescript corridor adjacent to the ticketing gates for commuter trains, the AirAsia travel center has the look and feel of a busy mobile phone shop (Figure 4.7). Sales clerks distribute waiting numbers, which are called up on a flatscreen behind the service counter. Customers are then assigned to a kiosk where they select a flight, enter their personal information, and pay for their tickets. Staff members stroll around the store, assisting customers who are less adept at using touch screens. On one visit to the travel center, the customers were a mixed bunch: single women, young couples, an elderly man, a student, mothers pushing strollers.[28] Most were making advance reservations, but some had arrived at the service center packed and ready to go to the airport.

After securing a ticket, the passengers follow a serpentine path through the railway station's arrivals hall, past the ticketing booth for the express train to KLIA, and descend a winding stairwell into a poorly lit and unventilated basement-level bus terminal (Figure 4.8). Here they join throngs of passengers who are boarding coaches bound for the airport, sixty kilometers to the south. Weaving their way through the mass of travelers, employees of two rival companies named AeroBus and SkyBus hawk tickets for the one-hour journey, at a cost of 3 U.S. dollars.

The Budget Airport Hub: Kuala Lumpur LCCT

In 2004, Fernandes convinced Malaysia's state-run airport authority to convert an empty cargo warehouse into a no-frills base of operations for AirAsia. The warehouse

FIGURE 4.7. An AirAsia travel center at KL Sentral, Southeast Asia's largest railway hub.

FIGURE 4.8. The basement level of KL Sentral. Twice an hour, buses shuttle between here and the Low-Cost Carrier Terminal (LCCT) at Kuala Lumpur International Airport.

was located on the outskirts of KLIA, a massive airport designed by the Japanese architect Kisho Kurokawa during the late 1990s. During its ten years of operation—it closed in 2014—Kuala Lumpur's Low-Cost Carrier Terminal was the undisputed mother ship of Southeast Asia's low-cost airline industry: processing more than 20 million passengers a year flying to every imaginable destination in the region, as well as to Australia, China, India, Japan, and Saudi Arabia.[29] The terminal's digital departure screens juxtaposed the names of Asia's capital cities and high-tech metropoles with those of vacation hotspots and obscure provincial towns, delivering a poetic roster of shoutouts that juxtaposed historic trade hubs with incipient ones, growth poles with sources of migrant labor:

YOGYAKARTA	TAWAU	KUALA NAMU	BINTULU
PEKANBARU	SURABAYA	PHUKET	KOTA KINABALU
BANGALORE	PENANG	KOTA BHARU	SINGAPORE
KUCHING	DENPASAR	JAKARTA	MACAU
KUNMING	CHENNAI	HONG KONG	TAIPEI
DON MUANG	GUANGZHOU	SIBU	
KOLKATA	SHENZHEN	MIRI	

The slow approach to the LCCT suggested the magnitude of traffic that flowed through it every day. At peak hours, cars, taxis, buses, and minivans were backed up several blocks before the main entrance came into view. Passengers waited stoically as the traffic inched forward, staring out onto the low-rise logistics parks that surround the LCCT. Unlike the main passenger terminal at KLIA, whose triumphal arches were designed by Kurokawa, the LCCT was entirely planned and built by a local construction company. The terminal building was an exercise in cheap and practical simplicity, and its original intent as a cargo hangar was still very much in evidence (Figure 4.9). Although the LCCT processed the same number of passengers each year as KLIA, it did so in a space that was less than one-fifth of the size of the full-fare terminal.[30] A colossal roof canopy enveloped the domestic and international check-in halls and extended across the five lanes of traffic that clogged the terminal's forecourt. Gigantic ceiling fans ventilated its unairconditioned interior, which was patchily illuminated by natural light pouring in through slits in the façade. Outfitted with the cheapest possible finishes, the terminal was deafeningly loud.

FIGURE 4.9. Passengers wait inside the main entrance of Kuala Lumpur International Airport's Low-Cost Carrier Terminal.

Thousands of shoes squeaked against linoleum floors, persistent alarms alerted disinterested staff members to the repeated unauthorized opening of emergency exits, and unintelligible announcements punctuated the din of passengers lackadaisically pushing their luggage carts from one queue to the next: queues at the fast-food outlets, queues at the ATM machines, queues at the check-in desks, queues to buy prepaid SIM cards, and queues outside at the discount taxi stand.

It is no coincidence that Malaysia became the hub for Southeast Asia's low-cost aviation networks. Its unusual religious and ethnic diversity—a mix of Malays, Chinese, and Indians, and of Muslims, Buddhists, and Hindus—lends the country a built-in demand for flights that connect it to historical sources of migration, such as China and India. Moreover, Malaysia's extreme dependence on cheap imported labor—which constitute about a quarter of the workforce—demands a high degree of connectivity to cities like Dhaka and Jakarta. These flows are complimented by Malaysia's lax immigration policies and by its reputation as a *shariah*-compliant vacation destination and place of study, which attracts millions of tourists and students from India, Iran, and the Gulf States. It is also an obligatory stop on the so-called Xin-Ma-Tai route, the common holiday circuit through Singapore, Malaysia, and Thailand pursued by Mainland Chinese tourists. Finally, with daily nonstop flights to Jeddah, the LCCT is an important transit hub for Muslim pilgrims en route to Mecca.

All of these groups, in addition to backpackers from Australia, Europe, Japan, and Korea, converge on AirAsia's low-cost terminal at KLIA (Figure 4.10). Two things distinguish them from passengers at the Kurokawa-designed terminal on the other side of the airfield. First, the majority are accompanied by children, who make up about a third of the terminal's population. Second, like budget travelers throughout Asia, passengers at the LCCT are slowed down by an inordinate amount of belongings: bulky duffel bags, overstuffed carry-ons, cardboard boxes filled with instant noodles and Milo. Many try to haul more than their own weight in carry-on luggage onto the plane. It's a practice typical of passengers who fly infrequently and therefore must carry much more luggage, but who want to avoid the fees charged for checked or excess baggage.

Signs in Malay, English, Arabic, and Chinese point passengers toward ticketing windows, just as one might find in a bus station. And indeed, from an aesthetic perspective, the airport terminal is difficult to distinguish from the adjacent long-distance coach terminus, connected to the arrivals area by a covered walkway that follows the airfield's perimeter fence, where passengers transfer to cities throughout peninsular Malaysia. The depot is bounded by the Food Garden @ LCCT, a cafeteria that combines the standard hawker center and airport typologies into a curious hybrid. Nasi padang and mixed rice stalls serve cheap meals to diners who are at once bored and anxious: tucking into Styrofoam plates of rojak and nasi lemak

FIGURE 4.10. Travelers check in for flights at Kuala Lumpur International Airport's Low-Cost Carrier Terminal.

while cautiously eyeing their luggage carts and the status of departing flights, displayed on flatscreens mounted above the food court's plastic tables and chairs.

Trickle-Down Infrastructure: Don Mueang International Airport, Bangkok

Twelve hundred kilometers to the north, a similar scene unfolds at Bangkok's Don Mueang International, an airport whose peculiar sequence of closures and reopenings testifies to how the rapid expansion of low-cost travel has challenged existing modes of infrastructure planning in the Thai capital. In 2006, after many delays caused by regime changes, economic volatility, and cost overruns, the Thai airport authority opened a new, supersized airport hub called Suvarnabhumi, or "Golden Land," on the far eastern periphery of Bangkok.[31] Designed by the Chicago-based practice of Murphy & Jahn, Suvarnabhumi's launch was timed to coincide with the closure of Don Mueang, which had served as Thailand's main gateway since the 1920s and had been largely unrenovated since the 1980s. But in the time between when Suvarnabhumi was planned and when it finally opened, air traffic in the kingdom had grown so quickly that the new airport was operating above capacity within months of its inauguration. Faced with overloaded runways, the airport authority agreed to reopen Don Mueang, on the condition that it only be used for domestic flights.

For the Thai government, the old airport's reinstatement was a source of embarrassment. In the official storyline of Bangkok's urban development, Don Mueang's outdated facilities had been rendered obsolete by Suvarnabhumi, whose massive gabled roof canopy provided megastructural confirmation of Thailand's recovery from the Asian financial crisis, and of Bangkok's transformation from a chaotic Third World city into an orderly twenty-first-century metropolis. Don Mueang's reopening did not sit well within that larger narrative arc: yet it was necessary in order to accommodate the leap in passenger numbers that had overwhelmed Bangkok's transportation networks. In effect, the plans to shift air traffic to Suvarnabhumi had not adequately taken into consideration the deregulation of the Thai airline industry, and with it the surge in low-cost, domestic traffic. Operating on razor-thin profit margins and catering to an extremely price-sensitive clientele, Thai LCCs found Don Mueang's admittedly antiquated but nonetheless functional facilities to be a more appropriate venue than Suvarnabhumi, which charged higher landing fees and was poorly served by public transportation.

In its new iteration, Don Mueang came to serve as a makeshift hub for two budget airlines, Orient Thai and Nok, that offered cheap flights to distant provinces. Surrounded by dilapidated airport office parks, a massive airport hotel, and the pylons of a failed airport railway project, Don Mueang's redevelopment was a bare-bones affair, with flights operating out of just a few gates in a half-shuttered terminal (Figure 4.11).[32] With few services and a notable absence of basic upkeep, Don Mueang's reopening appeared to be a provisory measure: tolerated, but not especially encouraged, by a public infrastructure authority that was disinclined to provide facilities for a segment of the airline industry that was neither lucrative nor prestigious.

Rather than a temporary solution, Don Mueang's revival as a domestic airport proved to be only the first step in a longer process of infrastructural reinvention, fueled largely by a surge in air traffic flowing into Thailand from its immediate neighbors. Specifically, the deregulation of air travel between ASEAN and China in 2012, coupled with political and economic changes in Myanmar, led to an unmanageable increase in flights—many of them operated by LCCs—to previously inconsequential destinations like Mandalay and Changsha.[33] Abandoning the conceptual division between a high-class international airport and a plebeian domestic one, in the fall of 2012 the airport authority agreed to redirect all low-cost flights to Don Mueang and committed to redeploying immigration officers so that the airport could welcome travelers from abroad. In its first year of operation, the "new" Don Mueang hosted 15 million passengers; two years later, that figure had doubled.[34] Whereas the airport had previously only served domestic flights departing from a single concourse, the revived Don Mueang connected Bangkok to destinations throughout China, India, and Southeast Asia, including thirteen flights a day to Kuala Lumpur, six to Singapore, four to Yangon, three to Jakarta, and one each to Phnom Penh, Saigon, and Hanoi. The airport's makeover was decidedly frugal:

FIGURE 4.11. Travelers wait to board a flight to Chiang Mai at Don Mueang International Airport, Bangkok.

apart from a new logo along its access road—rendered in brushed steel and backlit with green LEDs—the airport terminal was largely preserved in a spectral state, with few modifications made to the way it had looked when it was shut down nearly a decade earlier.

As such, Don Mueang is very much a museum of Thai modernism and a repository of late twentieth-century interior design; with small efforts at contextualism embedded in an aesthetic vocabulary of poured concrete walls, acoustic ceiling tiles, and linoleum floors.[35] Mainland Chinese tourists, Buddhist monks in saffron robes, Western backpackers, Thai university students and creative types en route to Chiang Mai all check in for flights in a departure hall adorned with a giant advertisement for Seiko wristwatches (Figure 4.12). Separated from the check-in area by a divider that demarcates the terminal's hastily reinstalled passport control area, the Seiko ad features an abstract rendering of a world map, recalling 1980s computer graphics, and displays the current time in twelve European and North American cities, none of which is accessible from Don Mueang. In their stead are a host of new destinations like Kunming and Wuhan. These air routes were made possible by the ratification of the ASEAN–China Air Transportation Agreement, which opened up inland Chinese cities to nonstop international air travel. Their popularity can be attributed, in part, to the 2012 box-office hit *Lost in Thailand,* a screwball comedy-cum-thriller that stimulated substantial interest in Thailand among Chinese tourists.[36] In the opening sequence of the film, a businessman takes a flight from Beijing to Bangkok, where he plans to transfer to a connecting flight to Chiang Mai in order to secure a promotion from his boss. Upon arrival at Suvarnabhumi, he realizes that an adversary has implanted a tracking device in his mobile phone. He ditches the phone and heads to Don Mueang, where he attempts to buy a last-minute ticket from a Nokair sales agent. Improbably, the businessman's opponent has followed him, and a chase scene ensues in the skybridges above the airport.

While it is not a primary plot point, the film subliminally educates a Mainland Chinese audience—especially those hailing from the country's less urbane inland provinces—about some of the do's and don'ts of international travel. In an early scene, a fellow passenger, donning a red cap typical of Chinese tour groups, admonishes the businessman for not turning off his cell phone before takeoff. The leader

FIGURE 4.12. A wall clock at Bangkok's Don Mueang International Airport displays the current time in twelve American, Australian, and European cities. Similar to the case of Shenzhen (see Figure 3.2), none of these destinations can be accessed from Don Mueang.

of the tour group goes to great pains to explain that Bangkok has, in fact, two separate airports. Stuck in heavy traffic between Suvarnabhumi and Don Mueang, a taxi driver tells the exasperated businessman to *jai yen yen*—calm down—explaining that getting pushy and impatient doesn't produce faster results in Thailand. And at Don Mueang, the Nok Air sales agent explains that Thai law requires him to show his passport if he wishes to buy a plane ticket. The didactic necessity implied by these interchanges was apparently lost, however, on the Thai airport authority, which neglected to install Chinese-language signage at Don Mueang, with the result that disoriented Mainland tourists wandered around the terminal aimlessly until the airport agreed to modify its wayfinding systems.

That was one of the very few modifications made to the original terminal. Arriving passengers whizz past obsolete "health control" desks where travelers were once obliged to produce yellow fever certificates, and retrieve their luggage from aging carrousels in a baggage claim area, emblazoned with teak carvings of pagodas and a kitschy *Sawasdee* sign, that evokes the quaint exoticism of twentieth-century air travel (Figure 4.13). At the entrance to each concourse, an illuminated sign implores visitors to "please send off passenger here"—a relic of the days before airplane

FIGURE 4.13. Defunct health control desks at Don Mueang International Airport, Bangkok.

hijackings and security checks, when friends and relatives were allowed to escort departing travelers to their gates. On the top floor of the terminal, an observation deck overlooking the airfield houses further remnants of Don Mueang's past: an abandoned business-class lounge, a defunct food court. The airfield itself reveals an odd juxtaposition between the high modernist terminal—boxy and ponderous in its prolific use of poured concrete and sharp right angles—and the playful, poppy liveries of the budget airlines that operate out of Don Mueang (Figure 4.14). Here we see the contrast between the modernist airport, designed at a time when both airport architecture and national airlines were conceived as austere emblems of the state; and Don Mueang's revival through low-cost carriers, whose very existence is predicated on the decline of national monopolies and the liberalization of cross-border mobility.

In effect, Don Mueang has embarked on an afterlife as a space populated by less moneyed air passengers. Much in the way that neighborhoods "trickle down" when their comparative advantages fall out of fashion with wealthier clienteles, so too has Don Mueang descended down the socioeconomic food chain. The incipient flying public picks up the infrastructural detritus of the past, which is barely retrofitted for new operators like AirAsia and Nok. Like the LCCT in Kuala Lumpur, Don Mueang is designed to accommodate passengers who have limited access to the

FIGURE 4.14. Jets operated by AirAsia and Nok Air idle on the tarmac of Don Mueang International Airport, Bangkok.

Internet and very little background knowledge about how to fly. (This includes very basic concepts, including the notion of assigned seating on board planes.) Similar to the case of Tung Chung New Town discussed in chapter 1, these airports function as loci of nonpedigreed cosmopolitanism: serving an extraordinarily heterogeneous clientele whose constituents are difficult to classify as either elite or subaltern, who converge on airports like Don Mueang and the LCCT in the pursuit of cheap, flexible, and reliable international transportation.

Conclusion

In *Engineers of Happy Land: Technology and Nationalism in a Colony,* the historian Rudolf Mrázek analyzes the construction of railways in Indonesia during the period of Dutch colonial rule. He charts the "amazing power of attraction" that this new transport technology had on all who came into contact with it. Mrázek writes that "as soon as rails were laid and the first train appeared, people, the whole landscape, turned around and moved to the train." From the 1880s onward, Dutch official publications noted with some astonishment that "particularly the native population makes a great use of the existing railways":

> A special government investigating committee reported that . . . the natives of lower standing, . . . the real masses, traveled more eagerly and often than their higher-ups, native aristocrats, native colonial officials, the Dutch-supported elite, who, in the ideal plan of the empire, should have been transmitting the modern manners in an orderly way to the plebeians of the colony. . . . The native masses . . . were [not] in any perceptible awe over the modern technology. In fact, they did not appear to change their traditional ways very much. . . . Pragmatically, en masse, and with an efficient use of trains, . . . they traveled as they always did, with their goats and their hens sometimes, and with bags of clothes and food.[37]

There are some uncomfortable parallels between the Dutch colonists' displeasure with the railway's unexpected popularity—popularity in two senses of the word—and the visible unease that Asian airport operators display when confronted with the rapid expansion of budget air travel. In 2013, I co-organized a conference at the Singapore Aviation Academy, a training facility where engineers, managers, and ground staff from around the world learn the nuts and bolts of how to run an airport. Hugging the perimeter fence of Changi, one of the world's busiest intercontinental hubs, the academy's conference center mimics the architecture of a tropical resort. Hundreds of koi swim around in a picturesque central laguna, and one might mistake its shaded outdoor walkways and palm tree–fringed swimming pool for a beachfront hotel were it not for the aircraft submerged ten meters below the pool's surface, used to simulate passenger rescue missions at sea (Figure 4.15).

FIGURE 4.15. Trainees use the swimming pool at the Singapore Aviation Academy to simulate maritime rescue missions.

During the two-day event, we invited architects, planners, airport operators, and airline executives to speculate on the innocuous title of the conference: *The Future of Asian Airports.*[38] With very little variation, each speaker presented spiffy PowerPoint slides that highlighted impressive growth figures and terminal expansion plans aimed at extracting new revenue streams from Asia's expanding flying public. Not surprisingly, the effects of budget airlines on airport design emerged as one of the meeting's central themes.

The conference was bookended by two presentations delivered by planning executives from Changi, who were eager to present their designs for a new low-cost terminal, known as T4, which would replace a smaller budget facility that had opened just six years earlier. The executives described the original budget terminal as an eyesore, a "mistake," and an "unwanted child," opened under duress due to the unforeseen boom in low-cost airlines that Changi's original master plan—devised in 1975 and diligently pursued for more than three decades—had failed to anticipate. With its drab finishes, basic layout, and minimal services, the budget terminal represented an embarrassment to Changi and to Singapore's leaders, ever conscious of the city-state's impression on short-term visitors. In the absence of jetways between the departure gates and airplanes, passengers were obliged to walk across the tarmac to enter the building—a common practice at provincial airports in Southeast Asia, but apparently one that would not do in Singapore. According to one of the presenters,

> Typically, Singaporeans are quite pampered so they would like a comfortable experience. At the budget terminal, they park their car over the weekend while they are away on their getaway, and they would like to have a convenient car park near the terminal. Also they would prefer to have aerobridges since in Singapore we have torrential downpours every day and they do not like to use an umbrella to get to their airplane.[39] And they would like better shopping facilities.[40]

The other presenter elaborated, claiming that "the preference of passengers seems to be against the very basic type of terminal with minimum facilities. They are not used to it—maybe in Asia they are just not comfortable with that sort of environment."[41]

The new terminal aimed to remediate these shortcomings, and so much more. In private meetings, airport executives had told me about the urgent need to increase the airport's budget travel capacity.[42] Yet in public presentations and statements to the press, the airport authority assiduously avoided using the term "budget," referring instead to T4 as a "boutique terminal" that would provide a "five-star feel with a three-star cost."[43] In a groundbreaking ceremony in late 2013, Singapore's transport minister announced that T4 would be used as a "test-bed for . . . the use of technology [that] will raise productivity levels and economise the use of space."[44]

Pursuing a "new paradigm of self-service and automation," departing passengers would be "educated" to use "productivity enhancement measures" including "fast-track self check-in terminals, self baggage drop, automated immigration clearance systems, and automated boarding at the departure gates" (Plate 17). While in transit, they would enjoy a "vibrant retail environment" as well as high-tech lavatories, equipped with an "instant feedback system" (Figure 4.16):

> If a passenger finds that a toilet is not as clean as it should be, he or she can easily press a button on a touch screen and the cleaners will receive an SMS immediately to respond to the toilet that needs to be cleaned. This streamlines the deployment of cleaners while improving the ease of toilet cleaning and maintenance.[45]

Changi's planners likewise envisioned that arriving passengers would walk to an adjacent parking lot or to a conveniently located taxi rank, capable of holding three hundred cabs at a time, so that "the moment the passengers get out of the terminal, they can get in a taxi and go home." Through the "multiple integration of systems-, ops-, and design-driven productivity," T4 would thus represent a showcase of technology-driven efficiency, necessary for maintaining Singapore's flagship stature in relation to other Asian metropoles.

An article published in the pro-government *Straits Times* worried that "without T4, airlines would turn to other airports that can better facilitate their growth, and

FIGURE 4.16. A rendering of Terminal 4 at Changi International Airport imagines a budget terminal concourse lined with upscale shops. Courtesy of Changi Airport Group.

Changi would risk losing connectivity, and consequently, its mantle of being Asia's premier hub." Yet the design of T4, and the way in which the airport presented it to both the public and to an audience of experts at the Singapore Aviation Academy, underscores the dilemma that Southeast Asian cities face in their quest to become highly interconnected "first-class hubs" in a part of the world that is growing very quickly but nevertheless remains mired in the challenges typical of developing countries. Terminal 4 is indeed crucial to Changi's future. But the vocabulary used to describe its purpose—a "boutique" terminal serving "narrow-body aircraft" with a "quick turnaround"—obscures its actual function as a vehicle for accommodating, belatedly and begrudgingly, the explosive growth in budget air travel. That purpose becomes clearer when one considers the terminal's design and its relation to the rest of the airport: it will be the only terminal not connected by Changi's elevated skytrain; and the push toward automation is clearly an attempt to reduce operating costs for a clientele that won't be spending much money.

I was curious about how that automation would be implemented, and how quickly T4's "boutique" travelers would adapt to it. I mentioned this in a private conversation with one of the terminal's planners. "Personally, I can't imagine a lot of these travelers being able to check themselves in," I ventured. He laughed and nodded vigorously. "It's definitely a problem. A lot of our budget customers, especially the ones coming from China, from Indonesia, from Vietnam, they're not too familiar with these kinds of things. A lot of them have to go to travel agents to buy their tickets for them. So it will definitely be a problem. But [Changi] wants to reduce our labor expenditures. So it gets to be a bit political."[46]

At the conference, many of those in the audience responded skeptically to the plans for T4. An airport operator from Australia suggested that the automation of check-in and immigration procedures would make it easier for passengers to engage in visa violations and illegal migration practices. A Singaporean planner asked how Changi intended to move budget travelers efficiently between the airport and the city. In a similar vein, a PhD student criticized the absence of public transportation facilities at the terminal, and an architect from Hong Kong noted that relying on cars alone to get people to and from the airport would produce significant congestion problems. Visibly baffled by these questions, one of the planners responded that public transportation was not a priority since "foreseeably taxis will be the predominant mode of transport." He also noted that there would be more short-term parking since "Singaporeans particularly like to send their spouses off on holiday at the curbside."

The response was jarring, given the strong connotations of wealth surrounding car ownership in the city-state. Government taxes make Singapore one of the most expensive places in the world to own a private vehicle—a midrange car, such as a Toyota Corolla, costs about 120,000 U.S. dollars—and Singapore consequently has an extremely low car-ownership rate. Pressed on the matter—this was, after all, a budget terminal, and presumably not everyone could afford to drive a car or take a taxi—the executive defended the choice not to include public transit by arguing that native Singaporeans would not want to carry their luggage onto a bus or a train; and that in the case of migrant laborers, such as construction workers and maids—who collectively constitute one-third of Singapore's workforce—it was the obligation of the employer to pick them up and drop them off at the airport.[47]

That disavowal of responsibility, and the willfully myopic approach of Singapore's airport planners, are symptomatic of a peculiar form of urban planning science fiction that is common throughout Southeast Asia: one that eschews active engagement with the region's socioeconomic divisions and indulges instead in escapist fantasies about an idealized future where every user is wealthy, technologically savvy, and unfailingly efficient (see Plate 18). Wracked with status anxiety and a relentless pursuit of an asymptotic "First World" standard, the business elites, boosters, and technocrats in Southeast Asia's growth poles decouple their ambitions from the social reality of a world region with extremely uneven levels of income and education. At the same time as they strive for ever increasing levels of "connectivity"—a buzzword indelibly ingrained in the ideology of urban "competitiveness"—they appear unwilling to countenance the flip side of what it means to connect regional hubs like Bangkok, Kuala Lumpur, and Singapore to the much poorer and less developed hinterlands surrounding them. If the connectivity afforded by air travel is meant to invest rapidly expanding cities with an air of refinement, and if airport hubs themselves have become an obligatory metonym for global city status, then the exponential growth in low-cost airlines, and in their neophyte clientele, represents an unwelcome intrusion into a romanticized vision of a future city "hardwired" with "cutting-edge" digital technologies and physical infrastructures. It's a vision akin to the "ideal plan of the empire" identified in Mrázek's study of colonial Indonesia, updated with the seductive vocabulary of tech startups and management consultants. The insertion into that picture of millions of people who are flying around Southeast Asia on the cheap, without recourse to digital devices, therefore presents an unwelcome impediment.

Moreover, the dismissive attitude of Changi's planners toward the needs of low-cost travelers—sentiments echoed in the tentative incrementalism of the Thai airport authority—is indicative of a broader gap in knowledge, experience, and perception that divides the technocratic elites who are responsible for managing growth in the region's rapidly developing cities from the wider population that dwells in them. While acknowledging that the rise in air traffic is being driven by LCCs, airport planners are reluctant to engage with the socioeconomic dynamics that are propelling those budget airlines to the fore. By focusing on scenarios where a Singaporean housewife waits patiently inside her car while her husband provides real-time feedback about toilet cleanliness, they effectively ignore more abiding questions such as how to provide affordable ground transportation to the maids, construction workers, students, retirees, and lower-middle-class tourists who make up the majority of the passengers inside the budget terminal.

As the anthropologist Brian Larkin notes, the obvious aim of infrastructural installations such as airports is "to transport vehicles from one place to another, promoting movement and realizing the Enlightenment goal of society and economy as a space of unimpeded circulation." Yet at the same time, Larkin argues that these infrastructures "emerge out of and store within them forms of desire and fantasy; and can take on fetish-like aspects that sometimes can be wholly autonomous from their technical function."[48] Excessive fixation on those fantasies can lead to what Dimitris Dalakoglou calls "infrastructural fetishism": a process by which the aesthetic predilections and utopian ambitions of infrastructure's producers are privileged above the practical needs of its users.[49] A practice that is especially prevalent among governing elites in the developing world, infrastructural fetishism ultimately yields projects whose modernity, to paraphrase the anthropologist Naveeda Khan, far outstrips that of its social and spatial contexts.[50]

Infrastructural fetishism seems to be the preferred mode of development not only in Singapore but throughout many parts of Southeast Asia. In 2012, the Malaysian airport authority went on a public-relations tour to promote the upcoming launch of KLIA2, a new low-cost terminal that would replace Kuala Lumpur's existing LCCT. (It opened in 2014.) In an interview with Bloomberg Television, the authority's chief financial officer explained, "What we've been seeing in the last five or six years is growth coming mainly from the low-cost segment. The current [budget] facility was only doing [*sic*] 2 million passengers back in 2006—and now they've grown to 20 million passengers. So we have no choice but to cater for this new"—he paused—"this new growth that we are seeing in this segment."[51] To generate excitement for the project, the Malaysian airport authority released a video on its official YouTube channel entitled *KLIA 2: The Next Generation Hub. World Class Image.*[52] The video deploys 3D-rendering software to simulate the trajectory of a departing passenger through the future terminal. The clip opens on the "eco-inspired" check-in hall, hovering briefly over a bank of ticketing desks. The visualization then swoops into the retail area, revealing a "variety of shopfronts" affixed with the distinctive logos of Louis Vuitton, Montblanc, and Fabrice Gillotte, the French chocolatier. Finally, the rendering glides upstairs to a departure concourse, designed as a "tropical leisure space" and dotted with "interactive info panels," that is populated predominantly by adult Caucasian passengers (there are no children) and features a huge wall poster, emblazoned with the logos of several budget airlines, that advertises nine-ringgit flights to Indonesia.

The incongruity between an ad promoting tickets for 3 U.S. dollars and a shopping arcade filled with luxury handbags, fountain pens, and French *macarons* was not lost on some of those who watched the video. "What is Louis Vuitton doing in KLIA2, isn't it suppose [sic] to be Low Cost?" asked one member of an online discussion forum.[53] Overwhelmed by the need to impart the practicalities and implicit proprieties of international travel upon millions of novice passengers, airport operators have focused on the didactic potential of the next generation of low-cost terminals: seeing them as a training ground for initiating Southeast Asia's mass-market consumers into the elite cults of technological determinism and class differentiation as encapsulated by the interactive touchscreen and the luxury handbag. As at Changi, KLIA's planners' preference to indulge in future fantasies of orderliness and technological progress—a future where efficient machines have replaced inefficient workers, and where budget travelers have been replaced by "boutique" ones—recalls, somewhat problematically, the dismay that Dutch colonial administrators expressed in response to the vernacularization of modern modes of transport at the beginning of the twentieth century. Mrázek notes that the Dutch aim to roll out a rationally planned network of railways and automobiles clashed with the haphazard reality that emerged in interwar Indonesia—a period of "general disorder in the colony's economy and communications" that was marked by the emergence of "native lorries"—a low-tech, and highly popular version of motorized transport."[54] These "wild trucks," one administrator noted, offered "faster transport, wider selection, with a greater flexibility, and along the routes the native travelers really desired to take."[55] The Dutch, Mrázek notes, found the popularization of the automobile utterly confounding—cars were meant, after all, to be a "*de luxe* means of communication," not a vehicle of the hoi-poloi.[56]

Here again we can draw parallels between the "native lorries" of the early twentieth century and the low-cost carriers of our own time: airlines whose airport ticket windows and downtown travel centers cater enthusiastically to needs of budget passengers. In the interwar period, concerns about these "native lorries," and the growing mobility of the masses, articulated anxieties about an impending paradigm shift in social relations and in the relationship between the subject and the state. Innovations in transport technology were meant to solidify the Netherlands' claim over the broadly dispersed islands of Indonesia and aimed to serve a civilizing mission that reaffirmed the moral position of the Dutch as the curators of modernization. The uncontrolled popularization of these technologically advanced modes of transport posed a significant challenge to that legitimacy. In a similar vein, the current valorization of international mobility as a tool for integrating the fragmented landmasses of Southeast Asia—a goal embraced by ASEAN and its constituent national governments, and manifested in liberalized regimes of cross-border transport and migration—seeks to reaffirm the state's central role in guiding social and economic development. Yet the same proponents of regional integration are made uncomfortable when those liberalized regimes, devised to stimulate high-level trade among multinational corporations and the free movement of skilled professionals, are adapted to support less glamorous forms of mobility, such as the movement of budget tourists, low-income retirees, and migrant workers. While these populations' manual labor and mass consumption crucially underpin economic growth, their unsophisticated deportment does not fit into the sanitized conception of a "global city" that urban boosters are keen to portray. In effect, the banalization and vernacularization of Southeast Asia's airport infrastructure— through hawker stalls, through passengers who squat in the waiting lounges, through the garish advertising of budget airlines—represents a tropical variant of Freud's return of the repressed, wherein sociospatial practices that are perceived as backward and shameful resurface in spite of airport designers' best efforts to paper them over with the science fiction of architectural renderings (Figure 4.17).[57]

The incapacity to reconcile the messy reality of a developing metropolis with the utopian ambitions for a futuristic global city points to a fatal flaw embedded in the logic of infrastructure development in Southeast Asia. Air traffic is growing rapidly as more people join the flying public; hence, airport facilities need to be continuously expanded. Yet the focus on the quantitative aspect of passenger growth, absent acknowledgement of its socioeconomic dimensions, has proven detrimental to the overall processes of planning and design. With few exceptions, Southeast Asian airports are being built for a semimythical clientele of well-to-do passengers who, with each passing year, represent a smaller and smaller proportion of those who are in the air. In Kuala Lumpur, the volume of budget passengers has

FIGURE 4.17. Passengers in transit at Hang Nadim International Airport, Batam, Indonesia.

already reached parity with those flying on full-service carriers. Elsewhere in the region—in national capitals like Manila, but also in secondary cities like Batam—low-cost travelers are the outright majority.[58] Here we see both the promise and the limitations of infrastructural fetishism. While it is adept at enacting aspirational fantasies, it is less skillful in devising inclusive urban programs that address the practical demands of lower- and middle-income constituents. They find their needs reflected more in the services offered by populist entrepreneurs than they do in airport facilities provided by what are, at least ostensibly, public spaces administered by government institutions. These LCCs have developed an ad-hoc network of low-cost mobility that piggybacks on underutilized infrastructures and urban typologies that have little to do with air travel. In so doing, they compensate for the inadequacies of Southeast Asia's physical and digital infrastructures—producing auxiliary urban networks and alternative regional geographies that bypass starchitect airport terminals and displace the flow of travelers into decommissioned airports, retrofitted cargo hangars, and 7–Elevens.

In effect, the typologies of low-cost mobility spatialize the disconnect between the emergence of a socially and economically diverse flying public and the unwillingness of airport operators to adapt their plans to that new demographic reality. Viewed more broadly, the various infrastructural engagements discussed in this chapter serve as a useful lens for understanding how technocratic planning elites in Southeast Asia—a region historically marked by overwhelming poverty interspersed with pockets of wealth—are adjusting to the notion of a mass-market middle class that is on the move. Their upward mobility—both aerial and economic—poses a significant challenge to dominant modes of urban development, premised on a set of binaries that locate poverty, backwardness, and vernacular forms of urbanity in opposition to wealth, modernization, and imported models of urban design. That dichotomy between rich and poor has precluded the development of urban plans tailored to the programmatic needs and aesthetic choices of users who fall in between those two categories. The challenge, then, is to develop urban scenarios that interpolate between the *kampung* and the condo: to emulate, in other words, the relative success that budget airlines have had in developing an infrastructure of low-cost mobility that speaks not only to the future aspirations but also to the current realities of an emerging bourgeoisie.

Similar to the case of China, most discussions on urban development in Southeast Asia have focused on showpiece infrastructure projects like airport hubs and high-speed railways—showering them, by turns, with praise and opprobrium. Instead, in this chapter I have sought to demonstrate how these infrastructures rely on local entrepreneurs and low-profile transport systems in order to integrate the global flow of people into the urban fabric of the contemporary Southeast Asian city. In other words, it's not a simple case of "high-tech" solutions replacing "low-tech" ones—and it's crucial to understand the interdependence between long-term master planning and improvisational pragmatism in order to respond more quickly and efficaciously to changes in the volume and diversity of cross-border mobility flows. For as I argue in the conclusion, the accelerated flow of short-term populations is throwing existing models of urban development into disarray and demands a fundamental reevaluation of prevailing planning mechanisms and design techniques.

CONCLUSION

———————— ◈ ————————

Mobility, Migration, and the Future Asian City

Throughout this book, I have endeavored to study people and places that are not typically associated with international air travel. In so doing, I hoped to demonstrate the expansion of global air traffic and the diversification of the flying public, and to investigate their implications for architecture and urban design in five East and Southeast Asian cities. More broadly, my goal was to use airport design as an unusual yet incisive lens for interpreting broader changes in the social, spatial, and economic landscape of the contemporary Asian city. In effect, the various case studies used airport infrastructure as a lens for interrogating a much larger question: How are Asian cities being redesigned to accommodate much larger flows of migrants and visitors, who are on the move for the short, medium, and long term, and who exist at bewilderingly diverse levels of the socioeconomic order? And how can cities harmonize the needs of migrants and visitors with those of local constituents?

Chapter 1 studied the new airport designed by Hong Kong's architects and planners in the 1990s and compared their prospective top-down planning scenarios with the lived experience of new members of the flying public, such as budget tourists and labor migrants. That contrast is echoed in chapter 4, which focused on the introduction of low-cost airlines frequented by Southeast Asia's emerging middle class and on the belated, and unhelpfully utopian, design responses formulated by the region's airport authorities. Other chapters, meanwhile, demonstrated how the expansion of cross-border air travel has exposed fundamental contradictions between the migration and security policies of Asian nation-states, the logistical demands of transnational economic flows, and the cosmopolitan aspirations of urban policymakers. The resulting incongruities are particularly apparent in the relationship between China and its neighbors to the south and east—and are most palpable along the border between Guangdong province, the locus of the PRC's post-Mao economic transformations, and Hong Kong, its traditional "southern gate" to the outside world. Together with my study of budget airport terminals in Southeast Asia, the two chapters on Mainland China illustrate the dialectical relationship between the aestheticization of global connectivity in pricey show projects—which foreground feats of technical and architectural novelty but are often unable to address basic transport demands—and its actualization in relatively mundane and pragmatically designed urban spaces that elaborate on vernacular mobility practices and adaptively reuse preexisting structures.

A side-by-side comparison of the preceding chapters reveals the emergence of three interconnected themes and problematics. First, the increase in international air traffic has highlighted, and at times exacerbated, the absence of coordination between the local, national, and transnational actors who collectively design and manage Asia's cross-border mobility flows. Among these various professionals—who include architects, planners, and urban policymakers, but also entrepreneurs, airport managers, and immigration authorities—there is very little consensus on the social, physical, and economic contours of the contemporary Asian city; or on its proper place within wider national and global systems of governance. More broadly, the haphazard management of international passenger flows illustrates how temporary populations—such as tourists, migrants, and commuters—are placing new and unpredictable demands on municipal housing, transport, and social welfare systems and are throwing existing models of city planning and administration into disarray.

Second, the everyday experience of cross-border mobility, and the needs of Asia's extremely heterogeneous flying public, stands in stark contrast to the fantastical design concepts advanced by airport planners and architects whose plans rest on the semimythological exigencies of an ideal user moving around a utopian future city. The inability of the resulting airport infrastructures to adequately address the transport demands of Asia's dynamically expanding flying public has led to widespread user-driven adaptations of both airport and non-airport spaces in order to meet their mobility needs. In that sense, the shortcomings of Asia's hugely expensive twenty-first-century airport hubs—evident in the formal and programmatic fantasies enacted at Shenzhen's "international" airport, and in the *couture*-laden renderings of budget terminals in Southeast Asia—echo the excesses of postwar modernist planning practices in the West. These were criticized for ignoring the needs and desires of actual users—*actual* in both the sense of "real" and "present-day"—in favor of an ideal person of the future.[1] Moreover, the deficiencies in airport design reveal a broader, and more problematic, set of contradictions in the urban design concepts put forth by government planners, private developers, and the architectural firms that they employ, who regard the city projectively as a tabula rasa for future economic growth and largely ignore the value of its existing social and spatial organization. The result is a pronounced disconnect between utopian designs, which don't address the basic needs of real existing people, and an over-taxed quotidian urban landscape, dominated by improvisational "quick fixes" that are often lacking in aesthetic quality.

This approach actively avoids engagement with the third and final theme, namely the bifurcation of Asia's middle class into two distinct groups: one that is global, mobile, and expanding; and one that is local, immobile, and shrinking. I argue that urban development in Asia needs to be understood within the context of a nascent, and potentially explosive, intraclass conflict between these two groups. As the case studies in this book reveal, developing and middle-income countries throughout Asia have experienced a surge in middle-class consumers, many of whom have leapt at the previously unthinkable opportunity to gain experience and higher incomes by working abroad, or who depend on remittances from relatives who are doing so. In effect, the geographic mobility of these migrants spatializes their social mobility. At the same time, stagnant economies and limited job prospects have induced millions of Europeans and North Americans to seek their fortunes beyond the West. The career paths of these two groups intersect most often in the growth poles of Asia—that is, in cities like Hong Kong and Singapore—where upwardly mobile migrants encounter a politically and economically disenfranchised middle-class population who were raised in a culturally bourgeois (or at least petit bourgeois) milieu but find it difficult to replicate the professional trajectories of their parents due to fundamental changes in local labor markets. In both cities, increased competition with newcomers—for jobs, for housing, for public space—has fueled populist, antigovernment protest movements whose adherents accuse urban leaders of catering to the needs of foreign tourists and investors while ignoring those of the local middle class.

The crucial role that both the mobile and immobile middle classes will play in shaping the future Asian metropolis has been overlooked for two distinct reasons. First, the civil servants charged with planning major infrastructure projects—whether in postsocialist China or in postcolonial Southeast Asia—have been raised in a professional and cultural context that prizes expert knowledge, hierarchical political structures, and technical and managerial efficiency. The emergence of a moderately educated mass middle class—one that has a modest amount of disposable income and is neither mired in poverty nor entrenched in elite power networks—complicates their worldview and modus operandi. Unaccustomed to incorporating the opinions of "middling" individuals into urban development scenarios, planners struggle to understand the actions and motivations of the incipient Asian bourgeoisie.[2]

The second reason why the middle class as an agent of urban change remains poorly understood reflects the cultural biases of Western observers. In recent decades, academic discourse in the United States and Europe has displayed a legitimate concern for what is usually termed a "disappearing" or "shrinking" middle class and a concomitant polarization of society into "haves" and "have-nots." If one limits one's geographic scope to the trans-Atlantic sphere, where deindustrialization and digitalization have rendered many reliable middle-income jobs obsolete, this is undoubtedly a valid preoccupation. These conversations make quite a lot of sense from the perspective of someone living in, say, the American Northeast, or in the myriad postindustrial regions of Germany, France, and the United Kingdom. Viewed from the sprawling periphery of Shenzhen or Kuala Lumpur, however—where freshly asphalted highways connect factory compounds, office towers, shopping malls, amusement parks, and Levittownesque housing estates, all built within the last two decades—discussions about a shrinking middle class are more likely to be met with incomprehension. Here, the primary societal quandary is how to engage with the political, spatial, and economic demands of a burgeoning bourgeoisie whose rapid expansion has fundamentally undermined established modes of governance, with urban planning being one of the most visible domains of contestation. In that sense, the problematics confronting planners in Asia contrast diametrically with those faced by their colleagues in the West who have struggled to maintain welfare-state planning mechanisms during a period of economic restructuring that has eroded the welfare state's monolithic middle-class client base.

In sum, cities throughout East and Southeast Asia are contending with three major challenges: inadequate coordination between the local, national, and transnational actors who collectively shape urban development; an unhelpfully utopian approach to urban design; and an urgent need to incorporate the spatial demands of both the global-mobile and local-immobile middle classes into future design scenarios. Bearing these themes in mind, I would like to end the book with three questions—directed, respectively, at policymakers, designers, and scholars of the contemporary Asian city:

- First, how can policymakers adjust the traditional metrics of urban planning in order to account for the substantial increase in short-term migrants and part-time residents, particularly in the domains of transport, housing, and recreation?

- Second, how can architects and planners move beyond iconic and monumental approaches to the architecture of "global" cities, and instead devise urban design strategies that more accurately reflect the aesthetic experience of cross-border connectivity and hypermobility in the twenty-first-century Asian city?

- Third, how can scholars revise their conceptual model of Asian cities—which divides the built environment into exceptional urban enclaves designed for itinerant elites and everyday urban spaces populated by immobilized "subaltern" constituents—in order to take into account the shifting geography of the global middle class? More broadly, how can their research findings be better communicated beyond the limited confines of academia?

I struggled with all three of these questions when I moved to Singapore to take up a two-year postdoctoral position at the Future Cities Laboratory—a research center operated jointly by the Swiss Federal Institute of Technology, better known as the ETH Zurich, and by Singapore's National Research Foundation. In the months leading up to my departure, as I began to look for a place to live, a Singaporean friend advised me to apply for a unit in Chip Bee Gardens. I soon understood why. Built as British military housing in the 1960s, the neighborhood of interconnected terrace houses is quite exceptional in Singapore's urban landscape, which is typified on the one hand by high-rise blocks of public housing that accommodate more than 80 percent of Singaporean citizens, and on the other hand by pricey condominiums and low-rise "landed estates," home to the wealthy and well connected. With its narrow, lightly trafficked streets, mango and coconut trees, and Bauhaus-inspired tropical modernism, Chip Bee was indeed unique (Figures C.1a and C.1b).

The application process was quite straightforward. JTC, the state-run developer that managed Chip Bee, had been instructed to prioritize the applications of so-called "foreign talent"—that is, knowledge workers like me, recruited from abroad—who were employed in the research centers and university campuses that were shooting out of the ground like mushrooms in the first ring of suburbs beyond Singapore's central business district.[3] (In Singapore, all migrants are categorized as either "foreign talent"—skilled professionals—or "foreign workers," which include both unskilled and semiskilled employees. In 2013, foreign workers outnumbered foreign talent by a ratio of about six to one.)[4] The policy was in line with broader government initiatives that sought to make suitable, fixed-term accommodation available to recently arrived expatriate professionals.[5] Crucial to my application was a letter from my university confirming both my status as a "foreign talent" and the geographic proximity of the Future Cities Laboratory to Chip Bee Gardens. Not long after moving in, I discovered that six of my colleagues had been housed within a two-block radius. I also discovered that my housemate and I were one of the very few mixed Singaporean–foreigner households living in the enclave: the majority of houses were occupied by Australians and Europeans, along with a handful of Americans and Mainland Chinese. We were also one of the few houses that did not employ a full-time, live-in Filipino maid. One unit on our street was inhabited by six lesbians from London and Perth who were famous for their backyard pool parties. The adjacent house served as an atelier for a Tanzanian-born Indian pop artist whose studio doubled as an off-the-books guesthouse for a primarily *desi* clientele. Walking home from the subway station at dusk, I was greeted by young Europeans speaking Polish, German, Dutch, and Italian, and by smaller groups of Filipinas chatting in Tagalog, Bisaya, and Ilocano while walking their employers' dogs.

Over time, I began to notice just how many of Chip Bee's residents were, like me, engaged in a long-distance relationship. While I Skyped every evening with my

FIGURES C.1A AND C.1B. Chip Bee Gardens, a housing estate favored by expatriate knowledge workers in Singapore. In the photo below, high-rise public housing estates are visible in the background.

husband in Berlin, my housemate did the same with her boyfriend in the Middle East. Next door, both our German neighbor, who worked as a physical therapist and yoga instructor, and her American housemate, who taught in a local primary school, pined for their partners in the United States. Their Filipina maid, meanwhile, spent her time vacuuming, mopping, and folding laundry with an outsized bluetooth headphone affixed to her ear, chatting the day away with her husband, who worked as a construction worker in South Korea, and with her children, who lived with their grandparents in the central Philippines.

The turnover in Chip Bee was nothing short of astounding: after two years, I was one of my street's oldest residents. People came and went, and each time someone moved out—which happened on a semiweekly basis—the entire house was gutted by a team of Bangladeshi workers who dismantled the iron window frames, removed bathroom and kitchen tiles, yanked off the awnings from the front porch, and stripped the walls of paint. These materials were all thrown in the trash: an odd practice, I thought, for a country that posited environmental sustainability as one of its main selling points. Supervised by a Singaporean foreman—local labor laws enforce a so-called "dependency ratio" that obligates construction firms to hire at least one Singaporean citizen for every seven foreign workers—the Bangladeshi crews napped in the shaded outdoor carports during the seering heat of the afternoon, using plastic water bottles as makeshift pillows.[6] Resuming shortly before sunset, they renovated late into the night, washing their clothes by hand in the empty kitchens and listening to music on their cell phones after a long day of work.

Chip Bee was ringed by construction sites: in the short time that I lived there, four massive condominiums sprang up, along with several malls and serviced apartment complexes. The largest of these was the Star Vista, an evangelical megachurch, shopping center, and rock concert arena built by the corporate architecture firm Aedas (Figure C.2). After dinner, I often strolled past the megachurch-cum-megamall's enormous construction site. On any given night, it was teeming with Thai, Bangladeshi, and Mainland Chinese workers, toiling under blinding Klieg lights, repairing to their temporary housing units located on-site, and hanging out by the hundreds on the median strips of the surrounding streets that they themselves had built just a few months before. Relaxing on the patchy cow grass, each held a mobile phone while speaking to relatives back home.

Walking the streets at night along with scores of other recent migrants, I came to feel like the people I passed were physically present but mentally somewhere far, far away—Coimbra, Chittagong, Cebu, Changsha. Present in body but not in mind, their dual existence manifested itself in mobile phones and bluetooth headsets permanently glued to the earlobe, enabling a double consciousness fueled by cheap VOIP calls. That partitioning of the self was also reflected in the abundance of convenience stores and roadside stalls that sold prepaid phone cards, each targeting

FIGURE C.2. The Star Vista, a fundamentalist megachurch-cum-shopping center in Buona Vista, Singapore. Temporary construction workers' barracks and a serviced apartment complex are visible in the background.

a specific clientele—*Jamuna, Smart Pinoy!, Sri Lanka Talk* (see Plate 19 and Figure C.3). These shops, which also offered top-up cards for foreign cell phone networks— China Mobile, Indosat, Tata Indicom—clustered around the downtrodden malls, parks, and interstitial spaces that served as informal gathering points for foreign workers: Lucky Plaza for the Filipinos, Golden Mile for Thais, Peninsula Plaza for Burmese, Lembu Square for Bangladeshis, Geylang Road for Mainland Chinese, City Plaza for Indonesians, and so on (Figure C.4). All of these spaces were marked by the pursuit of cross-border transactions and communications. On Sunday afternoons, long lines snaked around dozens of remittance counters and makeshift telecom tents, which advertised their services in Bangla, Thai, Tamil, Tagalog, Bahasa, and Putonghua. Many of the locals that I met avoided these areas, explaining that they were "too crowded, and make me feel like I'm in a foreign country." In many of these areas, the double consciousness of the migrant was formalized through the density of kiosks, electronics stores, and roadside pushcarts that not only sold phone cards, but also offered "twin-SIM" mobile phones that enabled their owners to toggle between a local and foreign telephone number within the same device (Figure C.5). In effect, these mobile phones emblematized the dual, or dueling, identities of Singapore's migrant population, who keep a sufficient balance on both

FIGURE C.3. Dozens of shops in Singapore's Little India cater to the telecommunication needs of migrant workers.

FIGURE C.4. Foreign workers from Indonesia and the Philippines congregate on their weekly day off in the churchyard of St. Andrew's Cathedral in downtown Singapore.

FIGURE C.5. A shop on Singapore's Serangoon Road sells "twin-SIM" mobile phones.

their Singaporean and home phone accounts in order to maintain a foothold in both countries.

My workplace was designed as a little island in an archipelago of foreign-talent research institutes. Located inside a skyscraper called CREATE—short for the Campus for Research Excellence and Technological Enterprise—the Future Cities Laboratory overlooked a master-planned education district made up of teaching and research institutions operated by Yale, MIT, UC Berkeley, Hebrew University, the Technion, and the Technical University of Munich (Figure C.6). University Town, as the district was known, was also home to three twenty-story dormitories that housed hundreds of foreign students and researchers.

Occupying two floors of CREATE, FCL employed a hundred PhD students, postdocs, and visiting professors hailing from more than thirty countries. Five languages coexisted in the workplace: English, German, Swiss German, Chinese, and Singlish, the local dialect that combines the grammar and vocabulary of English, Hokkien, Cantonese, Teochew, Malay, and Tamil, and that is Singapore's de-facto national language. My immediate colleagues came from China, the United States, Italy, Germany, Holland, New Zealand, and Switzerland. Often, their passports masked more complex personal histories: the student from Michigan was born in Shanghai; the Italian grew up in Kinshasa and Brussels; one of the Germans had been educated in Scotland and Denmark; while the other, half Thai, grew up

FIGURE C.6. The Town Green of University Town, a master-planned higher-education district in Singapore. The towers at the center of the photograph are the campus of Yale University, while those on the right are residential colleges that house a substantial number of foreign students and researchers.

between Hamburg and Bangkok. Several of my European colleagues could trace their ancestry to the Southeast Asian outposts of colonial empires, while many others had Singaporean or Indonesian spouses. Their biographical heterogeneity was a source of endless confusion to many of our partners in the Singaporean government, who had difficulty understanding that only a minority of those working at a "Swiss" university were actually born in Switzerland.

Many of my colleagues belonged to an interstitial class of global migrants: people who were trying to achieve, or in many cases maintain, a middle-class lifestyle by working abroad. They included ambitious young people from developing countries like China, India, Malaysia, and the Philippines, as well as twenty-somethings escaping the high rates of youth unemployment in continental Europe. The overwhelming majority had never lived abroad before and relished the opportunity to try exotic foods, meet people from other cultures, and observe unfamiliar cultural and religious celebrations. They were, in other words, in the process of becoming global citizens. For them, as for most migrants, Singapore represented a step up: in income, in opportunities, and in stature back home. When I had told my friends in the United States and Europe that I was moving to Singapore, quite a few were unclear on whether it was a country and where exactly it was located, believing vaguely that it was either part of China or India. In Bangladesh or the Philippines, on the other hand, having a family member who is working in Singapore is a point of pride and affords definite bragging rights in the countryside, thanks to both the added income flowing in via remittances and to the prestige of being associated with one of the world's richest nations. Many of the young Europeans I met had been attracted by the abundance of interesting and well-paying jobs, or more pragmatically by the low level of taxation, which rarely exceeds a tenth of one's income. Several of my female friends from India, Malaysia, and the Philippines appreciated being able to walk home at night without having to worry about being assaulted or robbed. Others had more complex reasons for migrating to Singapore. Reza, a researcher from Tehran, came to pursue his passion—public health—finding greater opportunity in the dystopian landscape known as Biopolis, one of Singapore's many master-planned research and development hubs (Figure C.7). For him, Singapore represented a perfect place to advance his career: full of research positions and, more importantly, laboratory materials that he could not access at home due to sanctions imposed by the United Nations. The city also welcomed Iranian scientists like him, who found it difficult to obtain a work visa at universities in the United States and Canada. Reza's ultimate plan—and his main reason for staying so long in Singapore, despite admitting that it was "a little boring"—was to apply for citizenship so that he could obtain a passport that would afford him greater global mobility.[7]

While it was easy to meet other migrants like Reza—there were literally hundreds of thousands of "foreign talents" such as myself, many of whom had left their

FIGURE C.7. Biopolis, a research and development center devoted to the biomedical sciences.

friends and family behind—it quickly became apparent that unless I made a concerted effort, I would never get to know any native Singaporeans; and I consider it a personal triumph that I can, in the end, count a number of them as close friends. Having lived in five different countries, I was used to the effects of culture shock and to the challenges of making friends in a new environment, but nowhere had I found these to be as extreme as in Singapore. On a daily basis, I interacted with astonishingly few Singaporeans. Most of my colleagues and neighbors were either Caucasian or from elsewhere in Asia; in addition, the receptionists at the gym, the teller at my bank, the waiters in restaurants, and the handymen who came to fix things around the house were usually Malaysian, Filipino, Bangladeshi, Indian, or Mainland Chinese. When I ventured into the surrounding high-rise housing estates or posh villa neighborhoods, populated almost entirely by Singaporeans, I never felt unwelcome, but I certainly felt out of place. Watching the *uncles* sitting cross-legged in the hawker centers over tall bottles of Tiger beer, or observing wealthy teenagers Instagramming photos of their after-dinner ice creams, had a cinematic quality to it; one that reminded me of the surreal and distant way in which white people are portrayed in films made by the African American director Tyler Perry: occupying the same space in a coffee shop, or on the sidewalk, yet studiously avoiding interaction. Although the widespread use of English made the city easier to navigate than, say, Hong Kong or Shenzhen, the cultural barrier separating locals from foreigners appeared, at least to me, to be much higher than in these other places.

A few months after I arrived, I mentioned my conundrum to a prominent local academic, an Indonesian who had lived in Singapore for more than a decade. He laughed. "Well, Singapore likes to think of itself as a melting pot," he replied. "But actually it's a bento box—not just socially speaking, but also spatially." Indeed, as I spent more time traveling around the city, I came to understand that the lack of interaction between foreigners and Singaporeans was not a coincidence, and was actively discouraged by the city's urban planning guidelines. On the one hand, they enforce strict racial quotas in the allocation of public housing units to avoid the formation of ethnic enclaves; yet at the same time, they effectively segregate the citizen population from the increasingly large foreign workforce. In 2014, only 60 percent of Singapore's 5.5 million inhabitants were citizens. During the same year, 1.6 million people were classified as "nonresidents": that is, foreigners like me who were living in Singapore on fixed-term employment contracts.[8] This "nonresident" population is concentrated in a loose web of upper- and lower-class migrant ghettos that extends across the city. At the top end, the Singaporean government has invested an enormous amount of money and effort into planning downtown lifestyle destinations for the multinational corporate class, who shell out astronomical sums of money for poorly designed condominiums and watered-down martinis. On the opposite end of the spectrum lie Singapore's arrival cities for migrant laborers, such as Little India and Geylang, as well as far-flung dormitory complexes, scattered throughout the island's industrial periphery (Figure C.8). In between are a smaller number of middle- and upper-middle-class enclaves, such as the one where I lived.

In a closed-door discussion on the city-state's future urban development, the prominent businessman Ho Kwon Ping warned against the creeping "Dubaization" of Singapore: arguing that the government devoted huge efforts to maintain racial harmony among the citizen population—a mix of Chinese, Malays, Indians, and Eurasians—but essentially ignored the spatial polarization, and attendant social tensions, between Singaporeans and so-called nonresidents.[9] Moreover, traditional methods of urban planning did not adequately address the infrastructural needs of this "nonresident" population: a fact that became obvious every Sunday, when nearly a million foreign workers overwhelmed the city's subway system as they moved between their homes in distant suburbs and ethnic commercial zones in the inner city. When my Singaporean friends got together—most of whom were ethnically Chinese—a portion of the evening's discussion was often filled with anecdotes about the uncouth behavior of Mainland Chinese immigrants: who, with their nylon track suits, tendency to squat in public, and loud retroflex 'r's were easily distinguishable from their Singaporean counterparts. Some of these stories revolved

FIGURE C.8. Temporary construction workers' housing on the periphery of one-north, a master-planned technology zone that comprises various subdistricts devoted to media, information technology, and biomedical sciences.

around incidents that took place in hawker centers: "Those Mainlanders brought in outside food, spat on the floor, and didn't clear their trash from the table when they left!" "The *char kway teow* has become so salty since *they* started cooking it." Others were set in the subway: "He tripped me in order to get on the train first." "She refused to give up her seat to an elderly woman." "I had to wait for three trains because there were so many Chinese crowded around the doors, not queuing at all." In an uncanny way, these stories of Mainlanders' ill manners reminded me of the reaction that the arrival of Soviet Jews elicited in Jewish communities in the West in the early 1990s: how could we share a similar history and cultural background, yet also be so completely different? Tinged with a subtle form of internalized sinophobia, my Singaporean interlocutors' condemnation manifested a very real panic about the way in which the city's public spaces and communal resources were being pushed to the limits by the unrestrained influx of newcomers, many of whom were rural labor migrants on short-term contracts. In effect, the city-state's migration policies were poorly coordinated with its urban design schemes; and that resulted in overcrowded trains, delayed buses, and a palpable appropriation of in-between spaces by migrant groups: as any median strip, station entrance, covered arcade, or green space doubled as an off-duty gathering space for foreign workers (Figure C.9 and C.10).

FIGURE C.9. Foreign workers from Bangladesh, China, and India gather on a strip of undeveloped land near Paya Lebar station in Geylang, Singapore.

Transportation lay at the heart of these complaints, summarized in one sentence: I can't get home on time because of all these damn foreigners. Staging a photo shoot aboard the East-West Line, an opposition party candidate vocalized the widespread sense of overcrowding by foreigners that many Singaporeans felt in their daily lives, effectively turning a subway platform into a political one. In this fashion, complaints about Singapore's transport crisis operated as an indirect (and sometimes not so indirect) way of criticizing the government's liberal immigration policy, and as a means of expressing anxieties about the erosion of local identity. At the same time, however, these complaints overlooked the fact that many of the city's public transport employees were, in fact, foreigners: people who worked long shifts in stressful jobs considered undesirable by locals. That fact became clear in 2013, when hundreds of Mainland Chinese bus drivers walked off the job, initiating a strike— the city's first in nearly three decades—that grounded Singapore's bus network.[10] Demonstrating for higher wages and better living conditions—workers complained about unsanitary and overcrowded conditions inside makeshift dormitories—the drivers drew attention not only to the crucial role that semiskilled workers played

FIGURE C.10. Throughout Singapore, overcrowded subway trains operate above capacity due to poor coordination between the city-state's migration and urban planning policies.

in keeping Singapore running, but also to the inability of the city-state's existing housing system to provide them with adequate accommodation. Singapore's public transportation system thus became a weathervane not just for voicing the public's discontent with the rising foreign population, but also an emblem of the profound disconnect between the government's ambitious immigration policies and the ability of local planning agencies to deliver the requisite infrastructure in a timely fashion. Emerging from a modernist technocratic tradition, Singapore's housing and public transport agencies made no short-term plans: houses, and subway lines, were built for a permanent, stable number of residents according to complex guidelines with ten-, twenty-, and thirty-year horizons. But could this planning approach adequately address the needs of a city-state whose population was growing by leaps and bounds, with many migrants staying for just two to three years at a time?

Discussing these challenges with local planning professionals made them visibly uncomfortable. During my first month in the city, I had lunch with a researcher from a government think tank charged with promoting Singapore's "urban livability." When she asked what I was working on, I replied that my research focused on how transnational migration effected changes in the planning and design of Asian cities.

She laughed, nervously. "How very interesting. Actually, this is not really a topic in Singapore."

"Really?" I replied. "It seems like there a lot of foreigners moving here right now. Doesn't that require any adjustments to the way you plan the city?"

She smiled tightly. "As I said, this is not an issue in Singapore."

She paused awkwardly, then pointed to the plate of chicken rice in front of me. "Are you familiar with Chinese food? Here, let me show you how to use chopsticks."

After a few similar interactions, I realized that my field of research was not just extremely sensitive—some speculated that dissatisfaction with the growing number of temporary migrants could cost the government the next general election—but also that the accelerated mobility of migrants and visitors was fundamentally reshaping Singapore's social and spatial fabric, with unpredictable results.

Moving back to Hong Kong after two years in the tropics, I found the city in a similar state of flux, likewise induced by a surge in cross-border mobility flows. Unlike in Singapore, however, the main point of contention was not a dramatic increase in labor migrants, but rather in tourists. In the few short years since I had conducted my dissertation fieldwork, Hong Kong's immigration authority had significantly reduced its entry requirements for Mainland Chinese visitors: leading to an enormous rise in the number of tourists, and in illicit and semi-licit cross-border trade.[11] As Hong Kong relaxed restrictions on PRC passport holders—making it easier for them to come for short visits—entire districts of Hong Kong were transformed into shopping arcades, by turns opulent and garish, that cater to Mainlanders' niche consumer desires. These include nouveau-riche status symbols such as foreign shoes, handbags, watches, jewelry, and beauty products, which are much cheaper in Hong Kong than on the Mainland; as well as basic necessities like baby formula and pharmaceuticals, which are often the subject of safety scandals on the Mainland due to lax enforcement of food and drug regulations.[12] From the furthest suburban new towns to the grittiest inner-city neighborhoods, entire blocks that were once composed of mom-and-pop teahouses, bakeries, hardware stores, and fruit stalls have been replaced by uniform strips of jewelry shops and neon-lit dispensaries, stacked from floor to ceiling with Australian milk powder and Japanese facial creams (see Plate 20). In Causeway Bay, one of Hong Kong's main retail and entertainment districts, these shopping boulevards intersect with side streets lined with Indonesian fast-food outlets and mobile phone shops—a reflection of the rising number of Indonesian maids who, like their counterparts in Singapore, congregate in downtown parks and shopping malls on their weekly day off (Figure C.11). At the same time, areas such as Sham Shui Po and Yau Ma Tei, once solidly working-class neighborhoods, host a growing population of young Europeans—French, Spanish, Italian—who are redefining the class boundaries of

FIGURE C.11. As the cheapest form of public transport, Hong Kong's trams are a common mode of travel for the city's Filipino and Indonesian maids. Here, a streetcar advertisement, written in Bahasa Indonesia, promotes cheap rates for phone calls to Indonesia.

what it means to be a Western expatriate. Working under the table as bartenders, waiters, and fitness instructors, or surviving off freelance work conducted online, they live in unrenovated walk-ups, pay their expenses in cash, and rarely bother to apply for a work permit, instead taking a round-trip ferry ride to Macau every three months in order to maintain their status as "tourists."

Given the pronounced shift in the balance of wealth from West to East that has taken place since the end of the twentieth century, it is perhaps no surprise to find many more affluent Mainland Chinese, as well as many not-so-affluent Western-ers, coursing through the streets of Hong Kong. The resulting programmatic and demographic changes—both at the heart of the city, in places like Causeway Bay and Tsim Sha Tsui, as well as in suburban new towns such as Sheung Shui and Tung Chung, discussed in chapter 1—inevitably inspire resentment among long-time residents. The sense of alienation that they experience overpowers any rational awareness of tourists' and migrants' positive socioeconomic contributions, both in terms of creating an endless supply of service jobs for young and inexperienced workers and in providing an equally infinite pool of well-trained caretakers for children and the elderly. Yet the discontent is understandable: if I want to pick up one or two items at my local drug store, I often find myself standing behind an end-less queue of Mandarin-speaking tourists who seem to be buying up every single product within reach. As noted in chapter 3, enormous traffic jams form in front of my apartment several times a day as an armada of buses pulls in and out of two nearby hotels. Traveling by subway to my Cantonese teacher in Tsim Sha Tsui, I often have trouble exiting the subway station due to the high volume of luggage-toting tourists visiting from inland Chinese provinces, many of whom have never been on a subway before and are unfamiliar with how to use a smart card in order to "tap" in and out of the system. (In an attempt to alleviate congestion, the subway authority began stationing employees at the turnstiles and near escalators to assist novice passengers.)

The surge in visitors and migrants has inevitably provoked a counterreaction, particularly in places where daily life has been disrupted on a grand scale—and where, to paraphrase Margaret Crawford, the rapidity of movements has fundamen-tally changed the organization of space.[13] As in Singapore, complaints about the deleterious consequences of lax migration rules and accelerated cross-border mobil-ity fixate upon subway stations and shopping centers. This is not surprising, since it is at these sites that the quickening and thickening mobility flows are most evident, and where the frictions between locals, visitors, and migrants are laid bare. Hand-held videos that document altercations between Hongkongers and Mainland Chi-nese tourists circulate widely on social media platforms. These quarrels—prompted by the violation of metropolitan social norms, such as eating in the subway or allowing a child to urinate on the street—frequently take place aboard crowded trains, or in the commercial zones of neighborhoods whose infrastructure has been stretched to the limit by an influx of tourists.[14] Antipathy toward foreign visitors also manifested itself in a growing resistance to new infrastructure projects—until very recently hailed as signs of progress and modernization—that is paired with a compensatory interest in local traditions, historic architectural forms, and environmental protection.[15] Numerous political parties and NGOs voiced opposition to the construction of a high-speed rail link between Hong Kong and Mainland China and denounced plans to build a third airport runway, arguing that both projects would endanger local wildlife and destroy ancient villages while increasing the number of visitors to unmanageable levels.[16] In Singapore, the turn against infrastructure manifested itself in widespread disapproval of an urban redevelopment plan that aimed to demolish a historic cemetery in order to make room for a four-lane expressway.[17] In one of the city's increasingly common public protests, demonstrators bore signs proclaiming "Road or Roots—Save Singapore's Nature and Heritage." But protestors also carried other, more ominous ones—such as "Singapore for Singaporeans"—that indicated how debates about transport planning could simultaneously function as an outlet for xenophobic sentiments.

In *The Railway Journey: The Industrialization of Time and Space in the Nineteenth Century,* the historian Wolfgang Schivelbusch argued that "a society's space-time perceptions are a function of its social rhythm and its territory. . . . If an essential element of a given sociocultural space–time continuum undergoes change, this will affect the entire structure; our perception of space-time will also lose its accustomed orientation."[18] While Schivelbusch was referring to the social and cultural shifts ushered in by the introduction of rail transport in nineteenth-century Europe, his comments likewise resonate with the profound changes in space–time perception engendered by the advent of frequent, affordable air travel in twenty-first-century Asia. Compared to their European counterparts, the metropoles of East and Southeast Asia are rather far from one another: the distance between Hong Kong and Singapore, for example, is roughly the same as that between Finland and Tunisia. And unlike in Europe, the development of high-speed international road and rail connections have been limited by adversarial foreign relations and impractical topographic conditions.[19] Even within the boundaries of a single country, overland trips are often an all-day endeavor. With a paucity of viable alternatives, air travel has thus become the dominant mode of cross-border transportation, and it is not uncommon when boarding a 7 p.m. flight from, say, Bangkok to Singapore, or from Manila to Hong Kong, to find that there is another plane flying the exact same route at 7:15 and yet another one at 7:25.[20] Aboard low-cost carriers like AirAsia and Jetstar, journeys of three, four, and five hours feel less like a momentous international voyage and more like a ride aboard a Greyhound bus.

Over the past thirty years, two "essential elements" in East and Southeast Asia's "sociocultural space-time" have undergone significant changes: the dominant mode of transportation, as well as the migration regimes that govern the cross-movement of people. The result is a paradigm shift in the spatial consciousness of a world region where, for much of the twentieth century, most people were unable to travel abroad due to intersecting financial, juridical, and infrastructural limitations. Decoupled from its elite connotations, air travel has, in the short span of several decades, become almost banal; and has fundamentally reshaped the mental map of Asia's urban middle classes.[21] Keeping in mind the kinship ties and historical trade routes that have long bound Asian cities to one another across great distances, it is important to note that contemporary cross-border mobility flows are by no means unprecedented. Indeed, many East and Southeast Asian cities are the product of repeated waves of cultural cross-polination, evident in a toponymic panorama—Stone Nullah Lane, Jalan Gereja, Muscat Street—that testifies to previous encounters with Europe, the Indian subcontinent, and the Middle East. Yet the volume of contemporary flows—along with their socioeconomic diversity, acceleration by air, and expansion beyond a few select sites explicitly designed for long-distance transportation—are indeed novel phenomena in the region's urban development. By and large, architects, planners, and urban policymakers have been ill-equipped to deal with this shift in the region's space–time continuum and with the attendant changes in the social and spatial structure of cities. This is evident at the level of public policy, which struggles to grasp the demands of an increasingly large population of tourists, migrants, and transnational commuters, and at the level of urban design, which has not yet developed an aesthetic vocabulary that appropriately reflects the new regime of hypermobility. Citing their transience, urban planners rarely include itinerant urban dwellers in future development scenarios. Yet while the individuals themselves may depart, the phenomenon of short-term and part-time residence is quickly becoming much more common. Its absence from the practice and pedagogy of urban planning points to a perilous disconnect: between the valorization of international mobility by employers, national governments, and institutions of higher learning, and the traditional metrics by which cities are planned. Whereas the former requires the intensified circulation of talent, capital, and labor, the latter is predicated on a stable, full-time population—a conception that is no longer consonant with demographic realities.

As the anthropologist Pál Nyíri argues, "Travel and displacement heighten people's susceptibility to new ideas and interpretations of the world, and relax the boundaries of what is socially acceptable. Therefore, movement often serves as a laboratory for creating new social practices."[22] As this book has revealed, fundamental changes in transportation and migration regimes have contributed to the democratization of cross-border mobility in many parts of East and Southeast Asia, vastly expanding the volume and variety of people traveling across international borders. In effect, these flights are enablers of first contact between neighboring countries, many of which remained isolated from one another due to the ideological cleavages of the post–World War II political order in Asia. Yet the implications of that democratization for the social relations and spatial demands in Asia's urban centers remain thus far unprobed. What happens, for example, when a relatively small city such as Penang or Luang Prabang suddenly becomes accessible to millions of Mainland Chinese tourists hailing from inland provinces, many of whom are unfamiliar with the practicalities of international travel and the implicit proprieties expected of foreign visitors? And what happens when young southern Europeans or Indonesian villagers decide to try their luck in Hong Kong or Singapore, and in so doing unwittingly disrupt the sociospatial order of suburban housing estates that were previously beyond the established pale of migrant settlement? While the advent of cheap international airfares provides the opportunity for personal enrichment and intercultural rapprochement, it likewise harbors the potential to reinforce stereotypes and awaken the impression that urban leaders are prioritizing the desires of visitors and migrants over the everyday needs of local constituents—a particularly divisive issue, it seems, when those visitors and migrants are of a lower or comparable socioeconomic status.

What, then, can be done to address the growing conflict between rooted and mobile segments of the population? Returning to the questions that I posed at the outset of the conclusion, I would like to propose some potential future strategies for urban policy, urban design, and urban research.

At the level of public policy, three changes are imperative. First, policymakers need to move beyond an outdated conception of migrants that categorizes them either as permanent "immigrants," who move once and stay forever in their adopted home, or as temporary "guest workers" whose presence is both brief and inconsequential, and who do not need to be accounted for in long-term urban plans. For many migrants, the truth lies somewhere in the middle—and it is that middle, both socioeconomic and temporal, that needs to be better understood in order to fully grasp the impact of circular migration on the spatial development of Asia's cities. Moreover, it is crucial to incorporate recent arrivals into local decision-making processes and to create a public forum, ideally at the neighborhood level, where grievances between newcomers and long-term residents can be openly discussed and arbitrated. Finally, policymakers should foster global-mindedness among the local, rooted population by expanding opportunities to work, study, and volunteer abroad: encouraging not just top managers and university students to take on foreign assignments, but also emboldening "normal" pupils and workers to do so. In postwar Europe, the establishment of international city partnerships, organized at the municipal level via schools and trade organizations, led to frequent cross-border exchanges of average citizens. These citizens' exposure to other cultures led to improvements in foreign language skills, reduced aversion to people from neighboring countries, and a distinct democratization of cross-border social capital. Might not similar efforts pay off within an institutional context such as ASEAN?

These changes in public policy need to be closely coordinated with innovations in urban design. Most pressingly, it is incumbent upon architects and urban planners to acknowledge the shortcomings of iconic transport megaprojects and to advance design strategies that are more appropriate for rapidly growing and unpredictably changing urban environments. In so doing, they would address a basic challenge that confronts infrastructure planners not just in East and Southeast Asia but in developing regions around the world. Simply stated, the conditions that apply at the start of a given airport's planning process rarely correspond to those that prevail when it is finally opened. As a result, many Asian cities have developed an unfortunate knack for commissioning extremely expensive infrastructure projects that teeter on the edge of obsolescence within months of their inauguration. The bathological displeasure that planners experience when these high-profile installations fail to yield their expected outcomes illuminates the profound limitations of long-term master planning in a rapidly developing urban context. It also reveals the limitations of monumental approaches to transport design, which fixate obsessively on the construction of visually striking distribution hubs while ignoring the opportunity to implement more modest interventions and systemic modifications that would greatly improve the overall organization of cross-border mobility flows.[23]

These shortcomings point to the importance of improvisational design strategies that compensate for deficiencies in the master plan: filling in programmatic gaps overlooked by state-sponsored planning practices and catering more efficiently to end users through flexible and pragmatic urban interventions. These two modes of development can be productively synthesized through the promotion of *incremental design:* an approach that is particularly suited to urban environments that are undergoing long-term changes in their social and spatial organization. Writing on incremental design, the urban planner Kevin Lynch argued:

> In creating a large environment over many years, the perceptual disorder of building—its noise, dust, and inconvenience—can be a serious affair. . . . Processes that may have a desirable conclusion and a well-considered technical order may nevertheless impose frustrating temporary difficulties on the participants and appear to be an incomprehensible chaos. . . . Each brief period in the long process of development must be designed to enhance its quality as a time to be lived in. . . . [T]here must be some sense of completeness at every stage of development so that each generation has some visually stable surroundings, *some feeling*

of living in today rather than tomorrow. In any plan, the temporary traffic systems, amenities, and patterns of activity must be as carefully planned as the "ultimate" ones (italics mine).[24]

Lynch's notion of design by accretion aims to guarantee a degree of built-in flexibility within long-term plans: permitting cities to take advantage of unforeseen opportunities and to circumvent unanticipated obstacles. (It also enables architects, as well as their municipal clients, to celebrate milestones at more frequent intervals, while solidifying support among the general public for multiyear disruptions to the urban landscape.) Moreover, incremental designs allow the urban landscape to respond more gracefully to unpredictable demographic changes as well as to swings in the economic cycle, producing neither an untenable surfeit of grade-A office spaces and luxury condominiums nor a painfully abrupt halt to all construction.

The incorporation of incremental design approaches into existing master-planning techniques thus presents a fruitful avenue for addressing the social, political, and economic uncertainties that confront the contemporary Asian city. At the same time, architects and urban planners will be much better equipped to engage with these societal transformations if *scholars* begin to participate more actively in public conversations about urban development: drawing attention to broader changes in global mobility patterns, and to their implications for urban form, that are often overlooked by policymakers and designers. Moreover, scholars should also seek out more opportunities to converse with their colleagues in other disciplines. Many counterintuitive insights and valuable ideas are generated, and then quietly perish, inside hyperspecialized, hermetically isolated academic institutions and discipline-specific publications. In schools of architecture, an ironic tension exists between an unwavering canonization of the Bauhaus movement and a wholesale disregard for the unity of research, pedagogy, and practice that the Bauhaus founders championed so vociferously. In area studies centers, historians and anthropologists spend years conducting fieldwork and archival research, establishing a depth of knowledge about people and places that cannot be matched by nonspecialists. Rarely, however, do urban scholars disseminate their knowledge to a wider audience: too great is the fear that their research will be "dumbed down" or otherwise compromised or, even worse, deemed erroneous or irrelevant. Yet a review of previous periods of urban expansion reveals how the input of interdisciplinary teams of scholars crucially informed innovations in urban design and planning, and helped to attenuate larger social and economic upheavals.[25] At present, however, few institutions exist that both support rigorous urban research and provide a venue for meaningful interdisciplinary exchange.

In his influential book *What Time Is This Place?* Kevin Lynch defined urban planning as the management of change. "Changes," he wrote, "are meant to lead to more desirable states, or at least to avoid worse ones. Nevertheless, all changes exact costs: economic, technical, social, psychological."[26] Some of the most radical of these urban changes, Lynch suggested, were those that were ushered in by shifts in human mobility patterns. Presciently, he speculated:

> In the future even people of modest means may have access to a string of localities among which they move regularly, following employment, preferred climate, or ritual events in what has been the aristocratic and nomadic tradition. These localities may be no more than empty sites on which mobile housing can temporarily be placed, or they may be permanent dwellings owned by shares or leased for special times of the year. . . . There are obvious advantages in the diversity of settings and relationships, the shifting roles such movements permit, the enjoyment of new climates, the fluidity of mobile manpower.

At the same time, Lynch issued a word of caution:

> People must learn how to cope with multiple houses or frequent moves and how to enjoy them. . . . The shock may be softened in many ways: by increased counseling and other social services; by using roads and telephones to connect the new locale to the old; by moving among the same round of places . . . ; by moving facilities, services, and institutions along with the population; by education to the new. Relocated people may live in "halfway houses," or join temporary organizations for people undergoing similar transitions. . . . Local residents and visitors must learn to live with each other and how to act in large crowds. Beyond any individual adjustments, the moves require mobile environments and services to meet the surges of demand: hotel ships, tent communities, temporary utilities, deployable police and medical care. A public agency of wide or shifting jurisdiction may be required to cope with these tides.[27]

Lynch's comments, and especially his focus on how to properly *accommodate* mobile populations, foreshadowed some of the greatest challenges confronting urban designers and policymakers today. While this book has concentrated primarily on the transport dimensions of global mobility, it is equally important to consider the changes that quickening and thickening cross-border flows of people are producing, and will undoubtedly continue to produce, in the realm of housing. Their imprint is most apparent in the multiplication of short-term dwelling types that are specifically designed to accommodate transient populations. One example is serviced apartment complexes, which much like international passenger flows have expanded throughout Asia by an order of magnitude since the turn of the century. The modular dwelling units and modified shipping containers that house Asia's army of migrant construction workers are another notable instance. Moreover, the growing population of short-term and part-time expatriates in Asian cities can also be observed in the rise of residential education districts, such as Singapore's University Town and Doha's Education City, designed to house foreign students, researchers, and other knowledge workers. It can likewise be seen in the rapid expansion of expatriate retirement communities that support the flow of senior citizens commuting between aging societies such as Japan, Singapore, and South Korea and developing ones like Malaysia, Thailand, and the Philippines. Less visibly, urban housing stocks are being reconfigured by the proliferation of cross-border subletting and property management arrangements, negotiated online via peer-to-peer real estate platforms, which have effectively converted thousands of mid-range apartments into short-term dwelling spaces. Much like the transport infrastructure studied in this book, the rapid expansion of these short-term and part-time housing typologies testifies to the substantial increase in the number of people who are working, training, studying, and retiring outside of their home countries, and it provides physical evidence of these short-term populations' impact on the urban fabric of Asian cities.

The increase in temporary accommodation physicalizes the emergence of an itinerant and socioeconomically diverse class of transnational urbanites, one whose myriad spatial demands and institutional needs often come into conflict with those of local residents. This becomes particularly apparent when the conversion of apartments into temporary dormitories, along with the explosive growth in vacation, retirement, and investment properties, significantly compromise the ability of long-term residents to secure affordable housing. Urban scholars, designers, and policymakers need to address that friction head-on by formulating policies that interpolate between the residential demands of mobile and immobile urban dwellers; by experimenting with various flat-sharing designs and part-time homeownership models; and by engaging in in-depth research into historical prototypes of short-term accommodation. The consequences for not doing so are rapidly becoming evident, as the inability to guarantee an adequate supply of both temporary as well as full-time housing has led to increasing civil unrest in Asia's megacities.

The international mobility of talent, capital, and labor, and its impact on the city, will undoubtedly remain a fraught political topic for the foreseeable future. Both in academic debates and in popular media, most discussions have focused on its socioeconomic extremes: the exploitation of migrant workers, for example; or the gluttonous real estate practices of transnational elites. But these are just the most obvious manifestations of a much larger phenomenon—one that encompasses an astonishing variety of people at all levels of society, who are on the move for an equally diverse number of reasons. In major hubs such as Hong Kong and Singapore, their expanding presence has led to an escalating conflict between mobile and rooted segments of society. Similar sentiments are evident in secondary cities, such as Chiang Mai and Melaka, whose old towns can scarcely accommodate an explosion of tourists and vehicular traffic and whose suburbs are being remade by the arrival of foreign workers and retirees.[28] In many of these places, a permanent condition of temporariness has come to characterize a sizeable proportion of the population. Ignoring their presence and enacting symbolic countermeasures may be effective strategies in the short run, but they are unlikely to reverse the accelerated movement of people across borders and between cities. Ultimately, scholars, designers, and policymakers need to work together in order to explore how cities can productively accommodate a growing number of itinerant inhabitants—and harmonize their needs with those of full-time residents.

Acknowledgments

Many, many people and institutions have supported me throughout the long process of turning an idea into a dissertation, and then turning a dissertation into a book. I am particularly grateful to Margaret Crawford, who first introduced me to southern China and who continually challenged me to take a creative approach to the study of urbanism. I am also thankful to Antoine Picon, whose tutelage was both supportive and no-nonsense; and whose background as an engineer attuned me to the mindset of those who build and manage major infrastructure projects such as airports. I would also like to thank Eve Blau for encouraging me to apply my lifelong passion for maps and mapping toward analytical ends.

Numerous institutions provided crucial intellectual stimulation throughout the life of the project. The Social Science Research Council offered consistent help, supporting both preliminary research through a Dissertation Proposal Development Grant and enabling me to interact with an interdisciplinary group of urban scholars through a series of workshops organized under the auspices of the Inter-Asian Connections program. At Harvard, research grants from the Fairbank Center for Chinese Studies, Weatherhead Center for International Affairs, and Harvard Real Estate Academic Initiative permitted me to conduct long-term fieldwork in Hong Kong and Guangdong province. I am particularly grateful for the support of the former director of the Fairbank Center, William Kirby. A postdoctoral research position at the ETH Zurich's Future Cities Laboratory in Singapore allowed me to expand my fieldwork into Southeast Asia. As a member of the ETH's Airports and Cities research platform, directed by Kees Christiaanse, I was fortunate to be able to engage with many of the world's most influential airport designers and managers. Finally, a research professorship at the Hong Kong Institute for the Humanities and Social Sciences, under the direction of Angela Leung and Helen Siu, provided a supportive home during the final stage of the project.

Above all, I am grateful for the stimulating conversations that have helped me to gain better insight into the broader cultural, political, economic, and artistic forces that are shaping contemporary processes of urbanization in East and Southeast Asia. In Hong Kong and Shenzhen, I greatly benefited from discussions with Jayson Chan, Maria M. Chan, Waisze Choi, Jericho Gozar, Laurent Gutierrez, Tanya Hsu, Sandra Kister, Doreen Liu, Mark McDonald, Euan McKirdy, Matthew Mosca, Julia Ng, Maryann O'Donnell, Valérie Portefaix, Cole Roskam, Shen Jianfa, Jennifer Shum, Dorothy Tang, Lorna Tee, Sunshine Wong, Winnie Wong, and Megan Wycoff. I would also like to thank the four foreign domestic helpers, as well as two businessmen and two retirees, who agreed to speak with me about their cross-border travel patterns on the condition of anonymity. I am also grateful to my interlocutors in Singapore, including Boo Junfeng, Stephen Cairns, Chan Heng Chee, Chang Jiat-Hwee, Anjeline de Dios, Jau Goh, Jon Kher Kaw, Lee Kah Wee, Johan Lindquist, Phua Mei Pin, Andres Sevtsuk, Lily Song, Hallam Stevens, Sharon Tan, and Ying Zhou. Thanks also go to Janepicha Cheva-Isarakul, Ahmad Coo, Gao Jianhang, KJ Kim, Minyoung Kim, Nisha Mathew, Ora-orn Pooencharoen, and Coco Zhao.

I am especially thankful for the feedback and support of friends, colleagues, and mentors, including Anna Barańczak, Annie Bourneuf, Ben Lytal, Maureen Chun, Abby Collins, Kenny Cupers, Igor Demchenko, Laura Frahm, Caille Millner, Łukasz Stanek, and Alla Vronskaya. Thanks also go to Jana Cephas, Gökçe Günel, Erik Harms, Sanneke Kloppenburg, Vladimir Kulić, Li Ji, Jennifer Mack, Pál Nyiri, Bill Rankin, Nathalie Roseau, Christian Salewski, Gonçalo Santos, Robin Schuldenfrei, Rachel Silvey, Jonathan Solomon, Nick R. Smith, Sara Stevens, and Larry Vale.

I'm also grateful for the insights offered by practicing architects, urban planners, and airport managers, including Jan van Benthem, Chan Choy Kee, Howard Eng, Victor Fung, Wilson Fung, Goh Chin Chin, Sujata Govada, Dendi Gustinandar, Fiona He, Ho Beng Huat, Eric Höweler, Huang Weiwen, Khoo Sun Lim, Kjell Kloosterziel, Koh Ming Sue, Rik Krabbendam, Wilfred Kwok, Elisabeth Le Masson, Rafi Lerman, Thomas Müller, Kevin Poole, Lee Sang Jun, Park Sung Soon, Greg Pearce, Maurits Schaafsma, Winston Shu, Desmond Shum, Margaret Tan, Oren Tatcher, Tian Fang, Tim van Vrijaldenhoven, Bert Wee, and Julia Yan.

Christine Boyer, Ed Dimendberg, Charles Maier, and Ken Tadashi Oshima provided helpful suggestions at a very early stage of the project. Engseng Ho, Philip Kuhn, and Lakshmi Subramanian commented on a draft of chapter 2. Swati Chattopadhyay, Martin Collins, Nancy Levinson, Dominique Rouillard, Vanessa Schwartz, and Josh Wallaert offered thoughtful editorial feedback on several articles that resulted from initial fieldwork.

Finally, I would like to thank my father for stimulating my intellectual curiosity, my mother for endowing me with a sharp and creative editorial eye, and my sister for nurturing a multilingual sense of humor. This book is dedicated to Michael Schiefel.

Notes

Preface

1. Westermann quoted in Mark Parry, "Mellon Puts Humanities in Close Touch with Urban Studies," *Chronicle of Higher Education*, November 11, 2013, http://chronicle.com/article/Mellon-Foundation-Puts/142889.

2. Swati Chattopadhyay, *Unlearning the City: Infrastructure in a New Optical Field* (Minneapolis: University of Minnesota Press, 2012), ix.

Introduction

1. For more on the construction of HKIA, see Robert Bruegmann, "Airport City," in *Building for Air Travel: Architecture and Design for Commercial Aviation*, ed. John Zukowsky, 195–211 (Chicago: Art Institute of Chicago, 1996); Alastair J. Budge-Reid, "The Hong Kong Airport Railway," *Japan Railway and Transport Review* 19 (March 1999): 40–41; Hugh Pearman, *Airports: A Century of Architecture* (New York: Abrams, 2004); Peter G. Rowe, *Emergent Architectural Territories in East Asian Cities* (Basel: Birkhäuser, 2011); Zofia Rybkowski and John Seel, "Hong Kong," *Architectural Record*, July 1997, 86; Corinne Tiry, *Les mégastructures du transport: Typologie architecturale et urbaine des grands équipements de la mobilité* (Lyon: Certu, 2008).

2. Howard Eng, executive director, Airport Operations, Airport Authority Hong Kong, interview with the author at HKIA, April 15, 2010.

3. See John Bowen, *The Economic Geography of Air Transportation: Space, Time, and the Freedom of the Sky* (New York: Routledge, 2010).

4. "Will They Still Come?" *The Economist*, August 5, 2010, www.economist.com/node/16743639.

5. See Clive Dimmock and Jason Ong Soon Leong, "Studying Overseas: Mainland Chinese Students in Singapore," *Compare* 40, no. 1 (2010): 25–42.

6. See, for example, the "Malaysia My Second Home" program from Ministry of Tourism Malaysia, www.mm2h.gov.my.

7. In many of these countries, the financial threshold for obtaining legal status as a foreign retiree is relatively low. Thailand, for example, requires proof of either $25,000 in savings or a monthly income of $2,000 (ThaiEmbassy.com, *Retire in Thailand: A Step-by-Step Guide*, www.thaiembassy.com/retire/retire.php).

8. A corollary of this is the rise in medical tourism, as citizens of wealthy countries seek more affordable health care abroad in order to compensate for the dysfunctions and inequalities embedded in their home country's social welfare systems. This development is perhaps most evident in Thailand, a nation that relies on international tourism for nearly one-fifth of its GDP. Bangkok's Suvarnabhumi Airport features several in-house hospitals, acupuncture treatment centers, and dental clinics on the airside of the terminal. On the landside, the main reception hall includes a fleet of medical service counters that offer free transfers to hospitals and treatment facilities around Greater Bangkok (site visit to Suvarnabhumi Airport, Bangkok, January 16, 2011).

9. On circular migration, see Gregory Feldman, *The Migration Apparatus: Security, Labor, and Policymaking in the European Union* (Stanford: Stanford University Press, 2012); Susan Ginsburg, *Securing Human Mobility in the Age of Risk: New Challenges for Travel, Migration, and Borders* (Washington, D.C.: Migration Policy Institute, 2010); Tai-Chee Wong and Jonathan Rigg, eds., *Asian Cities, Migrant Labor, and Contested Spaces* (London: Routledge, 2011).

10. The term "Four Asian Tigers" refers to four Asian countries—Hong Kong, Singapore, South Korea, and Taiwan—that industrialized very quickly during the second half of the twentieth century and currently constitute the continent's most advanced, high-income economies.

11. On the dual socioeconomic status of labor migrants in their country of origin and country of employment, see Jonas Larsen, John Urry, and Kay Axhausen, *Mobilities, Networks, Geographies* (Burlington, Vt.: Ashgate, 2006).

12. This discrepancy in class status is borne out by Brenda Chalfin's ethnography of Ghana's Kotoka International Airport, where the author documented persistent conflicts between unskilled yet relatively wealthy Ghanaian laborers returning from abroad and the highly educated and underpaid customs officers who police them. Similarly, Sanneke von Kloppenburg's study of Indonesian maids returning from the Middle East documents the relative wealth associated with low-skilled labor migrants. Brenda Chalfin, "Affective Sovereignty: Airport Anthropology and the Shifting Contours of Citizenship," in *Neoliberal Frontiers: An Ethnography of Sovereignty in West Africa* (Chicago: University of Chicago Press, 2010); Sanneke von Kloppenburg, "Protecting 'Foreign Revenue Heroes': Terminal 4 and the Arrival of Returning Migrant Workers at Soekarno-Hatta Airport," workshop paper presented at Asia Research Institute, Singapore, August 22, 2013.

13. In addition to Bowen, *Economic Geography of Air Transportation*, and Chalfin, "Affective Sovereignty," noted above, see Kathy Burrell, "Going Steerage on Ryanair: Cultures of Migrant Air Travel between Poland and the UK," *Journal of Transport Geography* 19 (2011): 1023–30; Francesc Muñoz, "Mobility Landscapes: From Multiplex Centres to Low-Cost Airports," *The Challenge of Landscape in Metropolitan Areas: Review Papers of Institut d'Estudis Regionals i Metropolitans de Barcelona* 47 (2008): 94–98; Michael Peter Smith, *Transnational Urbanism: Locating Globalization* (Malden, Mass.: Blackwell, 2001); Michael Peter Smith and Adrian Favell, eds., *The Human Face of Global Mobility: International Highly Skilled Migration in Europe, North America and the Asia-Pacific* (New Brunswick, N.J.: Transaction, 2006). On the shifting demographics of the Chinese diaspora, see Lin Weiqiang, "Beyond Flexible Citizenship: Towards a Study of Many Chinese Transnationalisms," *Geoforum* 43 (2012): 137–46.

14. Most budget airlines are not members of the International Air Transport Association, the trade group of the aviation industry; they also tend to operate exclusive online ticketing systems that are independent of industry-wide booking networks. As a result, aviation data sources exclude or undercount the operations of low-cost carriers and understate the importance of the secondary airports through which they fly. Yet the contribution of these airlines and airports is significant. Throughout the first decade of the twenty-first century, the Irish budget airline Ryanair was the largest carrier of international air passengers, flying many more travelers across international frontiers than so-called "legacy carriers" like Lufthansa and Cathay Pacific. See International Air Transport Association (IATA), *World Air Transport Statistics (WATS)* 53 (2009): Table 4.2.

15. On European hubs, see Tim Cresswell, *On the Move: Mobility in the Modern Western World* (New York: Routledge, 2006); Abderrahman El-Makhloufi, *Spatial-Economic Metamorphosis of a Nebula City: Schiphol and the Schiphol Region during the 20th Century* (New York: Routledge, 2013); David Pascoe, *Airspaces* (London: Reaktion Books, 2001).

16. On starchitect airport hubs and airport cities in the Asian context, see Rowe, *Emergent Architectural Territories in East Asian Cities.* On airport cities in Europe, see Mathis Güller, *From Airport to Airport City* (Barcelona: Gustavo Gili, 2003); Maurits Schaafsma, Mathis Güller, and Joop Amkreutz, *Airport and City* (Schiphol: Schiphol Real Estate, 2009).

17. Stephen Graham and Simon Marvin, *Splintering Urbanism: Networked Infrastructures, Technological Mobilities, and the Urban Condition* (London: Routledge, 2000), 364–69.

18. The result is that much of the scholarship, regardless of whether it is critical or supportive, ends up being a study of illusions rather than reality. As the geographer Michael Crang argues, by "falling for the manipulated image of airports" as projected by airport operators and designers, this literature focuses on the perspective and experience of the seasoned business traveler to the exclusion of all other passenger archetypes. Crang notes that that approach "may speak to a globe-trotting semiotician, but says little to the family with overtired children delayed by lack of connecting buses in Majorca." See Michael Crang, "Between Places: Producing Hubs, Flows, and Networks," *Environment and Planning A* 34 (2002): 573. Danielle Labbé and Julie-Anne Boudreau note a comparable shortcoming in Western analyses of Vietnam's new towns: "Much of this work has relied on the analysis of construction plans and the study of projects under construction, rather than the actual experience of the inhabitants of these areas once they are occupied. As a result, and to use Lefebvre's well-known triad, we can say that the existing scholarship deals with Vietnam's new urban enclaves as 'conceived spaces,' but tells us very little about how they become 'lived' and 'perceived' spaces." Danielle Labbé and Julie-Anne Boudreau, "Exploring Local Integration Experiments in the New Urban Areas of Hanoi: A New Form of Asian Urbanism?," workshop paper presented at Koç University, Istanbul, October 3, 2013.

19. Manuel Castells, *The Rise of the Network Society* (Oxford: Blackwell, 1996); Graham and Marvin, *Splintering Urbanism,* 366–68. See also Marc Augé, *Non-lieux: Introduction à une anthropologie de la surmodernité* (Paris: Le Seuil, 1995); Hans Ibelings, *Supermodernism: Architecture in the Age of Globalization* (Rotterdam: NAi, 2002); John Kasarda and Greg Lindsay, *Aerotropolis: How We'll Live Next* (New York: Farrar, Straus and Giroux, 2011); John Kasarda, *The Rise of the Aerotropolis* (Washington, D.C.: Urban

Land Institute, 2000); John Thackara, *In the Bubble: Designing for a Complex World* (Cambridge, Mass.: MIT Press, 2005).

20. For a critical analysis of this intellectual genealogy, see Charles S. Maier, "Transformations of Territoriality, 1600–2000," in *Transnationale Geschichte: Themen, Tendenzen und Theorien*, ed. Gunilla Budde, Sebastian Conrad, and Oliver Janz, 32–55 (Göttingen: Vandenhoeck and Ruprecht, 2006).

21. See, for example, Saolo Cwerner, Sven Kesselring, and John Urry, eds., *Aeromobilities* (London: Routledge, 2009), 32; Keller Easterling, *Enduring Innocence: Global Architecture and Its Political Masquerades* (Cambridge, Mass.: MIT Press, 2005); Gillian Fuller and Ross Harley, *Aviopolis: A Book about Airports* (London: Black Dog, 2004); Martha Rosler, *In the Place of the Public: Observations of a Frequent Flyer* (Ostfildern-Ruit: Cantz, 1998); Anthony Vidler, *Warped Space: Art, Architecture, and Anxiety in Modern Culture* (Cambridge, Mass.: MIT Press, 2000). Referring to the rise of hub airports at the end of the twentieth century, Hannam, Sheller, and Urry argue that "airport space is a 'space of transition' that facilitates the shrinkage of the globe and the transcendence of time and space, especially by 'seamlessly' connecting major 'global' cities—though mainly for the hypermobile elite." Kevin Hannam, Mimi Sheller, and John Urry, "Mobilities, Immobilities, and Moorings," *Mobilities* 1 (March 2006): 6. For another discussion of the "kinetic elite" in relation to airports, see David Wood and Stephen Graham, "Permeable Boundaries in the Software-Sorted Society: Surveillance and the Differentiation of Mobility," in *Mobile Technologies of the City*, ed. Mimi Sheller and John Urry, 177–91 (London: Routledge, 2006).

22. Johan Lindquist, *The Anxieties of Mobility: Migration and Tourism in the Indonesian Borderland* (Honolulu: University of Hawai'i Press, 2009), 7, 19.

23. For example, by mapping the commuting patterns of automobile workers and department store employees and contrasting them with those of a wealthy university student, Chombart de Lauwe highlighted the role of transport systems in abetting the larger processes of suburbanization and sociospatial segregation in postwar Paris. Whyte's study of pedestrian flows in New York and Montréal revealed how small design interventions—the removal of a door here, the addition of a bench there—can have profound effects on urban sociability. Friedman's *It Is Your Town: Know How to Protect It*, conceived as a how-to guide for the general public, used comic strips to explain the trade-offs between infrastructure development and historic preservation. Finally, Appleyard, Lynch, and Myer's *The View from the Road* illustrated the perceptual shifts engendered by highway driving, and identified ways for architects to retrofit the urban landscape to accommodate those changes. Paul-Henry Chombart de Lauwe, *Paris et l'agglomération parisienne: L'espace social dans une grande cité* (Paris: Presses universitaires de France, 1952); William H. Whyte, *The Social Life of Small Urban Spaces* (Washington, D.C.: Conservation Foundation, 1980); Yona Friedman, *It Is Your Town: Know How to Protect It* (Strasbourg: Council of Europe, 1975); Donald Appleyard, Kevin Lynch, and John R. Myer, *The View from the Road* (Cambridge, Mass.: MIT Press, 1964).

24. By studying these new types of air travelers, the book engages with renewed interest, among architectural historians, in the role of the user in processes of urban transformation. See, for example, Kenny Cupers, *Use Matters: An Alternative History of Architecture* (London: Routledge, 2013); Lukasz Stanek, *Henri Lefebvre on Space: Architecture, Urban Research, and the Production of Theory* (Minneapolis: University of Minnesota Press, 2011).

25. On the role of so-called "VFR" travel in global mobility flows, see Larsen, Urry, and Axhausen, *Mobilities, Networks, Geographies.*

26. Hannam, Sheller, and Urry, "Mobilities, Immobilities, and Moorings," 1. An interest in that interconnection—between processes taking place at the very local level and those that operate on a planetary scale—also lies at the heart of Willem van Schendel's study of the transnational flow of goods and people in the cities and towns that lie along Asia's international frontiers. Specifically, van Schendel argues that the short-distance systems of cross-border mobility "worked out in the world's myriad borderlands have a direct impact on the shape, legitimacy, and organization" of transnational flows of goods and people. Itty Abraham and Willem van Schendel, eds., *Illicit Flows and Criminal Things: States, Borders, and the Other Side of Globalization* (Bloomington: Indiana University Press, 2005), 61.

27. Hannam, Sheller, and Urry, "Mobilities, Immobilities, and Moorings," 8.

28. See Richard J. Neutra, "Terminals? Transfer!" *Architectural Record* 68, no. 2 (1930): 99–104. On the role of mobility in the work of Le Corbusier, see Pier Giorgio Gerosa, *Le Corbusier: Urbanisme et mobilité* (Basel: Birkhäuser, 1978); Le Corbusier, *Aircraft* (London: The Studio, 1935). On Sant'Elia, see Vivien Greene, ed., *Italian Futurism 1909–1944: Reconstructing the Universe* (New York: Guggenheim Museum, 2014); Antonio Sant'Elia, "Il messaggio di Antonio Sant'Elia, 20 maggio 1914," *Architettura* 2, no. 13 (1956): 516.

29. Colin Buchanan, *Traffic in Towns* (Harmandworth: Penguin, 1964). On Hénard, see Peter Wolf, *Eugène Hénard and the Beginnings of Urbanism in Paris, 1900–1914* (Paris: Centre de recherche d'urbanisme, 1968). On Wagner, see Eve Blau and Monika Platzer, eds., *Mythos Großstadt: Architektur und Stadtbaukunst in Zentraleuropa 1890–1937* (Munich: Prestel, 1999).

30. Reyner Banham, *Los Angeles: The Architecture of Four Ecologies* (New York: Harper and Row, 1971); Melvin Webber, *Explorations into Urban Structure* (Philadelphia: University of Pennsylvania Press, 1964). For Banham's views on air travel, see Banham, "The Obsolescent Airport," *Architectural Review*, October 1962, 252–53.

31. Alison and Peter Smithson, *Ordinariness and Light: Urban Theories 1952–1960 and Their Application in a Building Project 1963–1970* (London: Faber, 1970). On Victor Gruen, see Alex Wall, *Victor Gruen: From Urban Shop to New City* (Barcelona: Actar, 2005). Donald Appleyard, Kevin Lynch, and John R. Myer, *The View from the Road* (Cambridge, Mass.: MIT Press, 1964).

32. Smithson and Smithson, *Ordinariness and Light*, 158.

33. James E. Thorold Rogers, *A History of Agriculture and Prices in England* (Oxford: Clarendon Press, 1866), 108.

34. "Mobility, n.2," *OED Online* (Oxford: Oxford University Press, September 2014).

35. That process is not dissimilar from the appropriation of the word "queer" by gay rights activists more than a century later. For more on the use of the term "mobility" in the rhetoric deployed by nineteenth-century workers' movements, see E. P. Thompson, *The Making of the English Working Class* (New York: Vintage Books, 1966), 94. See also John Charlton, *The Chartists: The First National Workers' Movement* (London: Pluto Press, 1997).

36. Pál Nyiri, *Mobility and Cultural Authority in Contemporary China* (Seattle: University of Washington Press, 2010), 61.

37. Ibid., 8.

38. Ibid., 79.

39. Ibid., 4.

40. Qtd. in ibid., 101.

41. Ibid., 61–62. See also Wolfgang Georg Arlt, *China's Outbound Tourism* (New York: Routledge, 2006).

42. For example, until the period of democratic reform in the 1980s, both South Korea and Taiwan heavily restricted their citizens' ability to travel overseas.

43. Sanneke Kloppenburg, "Confined Mobilities: Following Indonesian Migrant Workers on Their Way Home," *Journal of Economic and Social Geography* 103, no. 5 (2012): 530–41.

44. On Vietnamese brides in Taiwan, see Hong-zen Wang, "Hidden Spaces of Resistance of the Subordinated: Case Studies from Vietnamese Female Migrant Partners in Taiwan," *International Migration Review* 41, no. 3 (2007): 706–27. On South Korea, see "South Korea's Foreign Brides: Farmed Out," *The Economist*, May 24, 2014.

45. Brian Larkin, "The Politics and Poetics of Infrastructure," *Annual Review of Anthropology* 42 (2013): 327–43. Xiang Biao and Johan Lindquist, "Migration Infrastructure," *International Migration Review* 48, no. 1 (2014): 122–48. Lin Weiqiang, Johan Lindquist, Xiang Biao, and Brenda S. A. Yeoh, eds., "Migration Infrastructures and the Constitution of (Im)mobilities," special issue, *Mobilities* 11, no. 4 (2016).

46. Swati Chattopadhyay, *Unlearning the City: Infrastructure in a New Optical Field* (Minneapolis: University of Minnesota Press, 2012), x.

47. For example, the construction of Hong Kong International Airport at the end of the 1990s was widely interpreted as a means of reassuring the general public that Hong Kong's global connectivity—a condition of hyperaccessibility upon which influential swathes of the population depend both personally and professionally—would not be compromised by the British colony's handover to China. Two decades later, a resurfacing of existential anxieties over the gradual disappearance of Hong Kong's unique social and cultural norms under Mainland Chinese rule express themselves regularly through track disruptions and construction delays along the Guangzhou–Shenzhen–Hong Kong Express Rail Link, which will connect Hong Kong to the Mainland's high-speed rail network and make it possible to travel from Kowloon to Beijing in less than eight hours.

48. Chattopadhyay, *Unlearning the City*, 247–48.

49. John Leighton Chase, Margaret Crawford, and John Kaliski, eds., *Everyday Urbanism* (New York: Monacelli, 1999).

50. As Crawford notes, "Rather than urban design, urban planning, urban studies, urban theory, or other specialized terms, urbanism identifies a broad discursive arena that combines all of these disciplines, as well as others, into a multidimensional consideration of the city"; Chase, Crawford, and Kaliski, *Everyday Urbanism*, 6.

51. Ibid., 7.

52. Ibid., 4.

53. Michel de Certeau, *The Practice of Everyday Life* (Berkeley: University of California Press, 1984). Henri Lefebvre, *Critique of Everyday Life* (New York: Verso, 1991).

54. As Crawford notes, this approach to urban research "goes against the grain of professional design discourse, which is based on abstract principles, whether quantitative, formal, spatial, or perceptual. Whatever the intention, professional abstractions inevitably produce spaces that have little to do with real human impulses." Chase, Crawford, and Kaliski, *Everyday Urbanism*, 7–8.

55. Ibid., 9. De Certeau's distinction between strategies and tactics draws upon theories of war advanced by the Prussian military strategist von Clausewitz. See Carl von Clausewitz, *Vom Kriege* (Frankfurt am Main: Ullstein, 1994).

56. Chase, Crawford, and Kaliski, *Everyday Urbanism*, 8.

57. Ibid., 7–8.

58. On Schiphol, see Cresswell, *On the Move*; M. L. J. Dierikx, *Building Castles of the Air: Schiphol Amsterdam and the Development of Airport Infrastructure in Europe, 1916–1996* (The Hague: SDU, 1997); El-Makhloufi, *Spatial-Economic Metamorphosis of a Nebula City*; Hugo Gordijn, *De toekomst van Schiphol* (Rotterdam: NAi, 2007); Gijs Mom and Marc Dierikx, *Schiphol: Haven, station, knooppunt sinds 1916* (Zutphen: Walburg, 1999); Martin Kloos, *Schiphol Architecture: Innovative Airport Design* (Amsterdam: ARCAM, 1996).

59. In 1992, air travel within North America accounted for 36 percent of the world's RPKs; by 2012, that proportion declined to 16 percent. During the same period, air travel in Asia increased from 7 to 18 percent of total RPKs. International Air Transport Association (IATA), *World Air Transport Statistics (WATS)* 37 (1992), and 57 (2012). In 2010, the world's top thirty airports by passenger numbers included Beijing, Dubai, Hong Kong, Singapore, Jakarta, Bangkok, Guangzhou, and Shanghai. The shift within such a short period of time is striking: in 1991, 21 of the world's top 30 airports were located in North America; only 5 were located in Asia. By 2010, there were only 13 North American airports in the top 30; while the number of Asian hubs had risen to 10. Centre for Asia Pacific Aviation, "The World's Top 30 Airports: A Disparate Grouping," August 9, 2011, www.centreforaviation.com/news/2011/08/09/the-worlds-top-30-airports-a-disparate -group/.

60. Jane M. Ferguson, "Terminally Haunted: Aviation Ghosts, Hybrid Buddhist Practices, and Disaster Aversion Strategies amongst Airport Workers in Myanmar and Thailand," *Asia Pacific Journal of Anthropology* 15, no. 1 (2014): 47–64; Kloppenburg, "Confined Mobilities," 530–41.

61. Shaw Shih-Lung, Lu Feng, Chen Jie, Zhou Chenghu, "China's Airline Consolidation and Its Effects on Domestic Airline Networks and Competition," *Journal of Transport Geography* 17 (2009): 293–305. See also Jianfa Shen, "Assessing Inter-City Relations between Hong Kong and Shenzhen: The Case of Airport Competition or Cooperation," *Progress in Planning* 73 (2010): 55–73.

62. The Pearl River Delta is divided into five separate territorial entities: Guangdong province, the Hong Kong and Macau Special Administrative Regions (SARs), and the Shenzhen and Zhuhai Special Economic Zones (SEZs).

1. Parallel Lines

1. For more on the structure of the Airport Core Program, see *The New Airport at Chek Lap Kok: Construction Review* (Hong Kong: Building Journal; Construction and Contract News, 1997).

2. The above quote is by Jack So, chairman, MTRC, June 21, 1998; qtd. in Terry Farrell, *Kowloon Transport Super City* (Hong Kong: Pace, 1998), 6.

3. See, for example, John M. Carroll, *A Concise History of Hong Kong* (Lanham, Md.: Rowman and Littlefield, 2007).

4. This conspiratorial account of HKIA's genesis came up in several off-the-record discussions with local architects and urban planners. For a contemporaneous newspaper article that outlines the main arguments, see Stephen Vines, "Chinese Seek Credit for Chek Lap Kok," *The Independent*, June 21, 1998, 12.

5. Moreover, the development of island airports can be read as a typological reaction to the violent political struggles surrounding the expropriation of land entailed by the construction of Tokyo's Narita airport in the 1970s. Ralph M. Parsons Company et al., *Hong Kong Air Transport System: Long Term Planning Investigation*, summary document, Hong Kong, March 1975, 41. For more on the protests at Narita, see Marc Dierikx, *Clipping the Clouds: How Air Travel Changed the World* (Westport, Conn.: Praeger, 2008).

6. Other cities that built bigger, more remote airports included Kuala Lumpur (KLIA, 1998), Shanghai (Pudong, 1999), Guangzhou (New Baiyun, 2004), and Bangkok (Suvarnabhumi, 2006). See Y.-C. Chang, "The Development of Regional Airports in Asia," in *Development of Regional Airports: Theoretical Analyses and Case Studies*, ed. M. N. Postorino (Boston: WIT Press, 2010), 56.

7. Ralph M. Parsons Company et al., *Hong Kong Air Transport System*, summary.

8. Ralph M. Parsons Company et al., *Hong Kong Air Transport System: Long Term Planning Investigation*, site investigation report, Hong Kong, March 1975, 3–8.

9. Lee Sang Jun, interview with the author at Engineering Building, Yonsei University, Seoul, March 9, 2010.

10. Winston Shu, principal, Integrated Design Associates, interview with the author at Innocentre, Kowloon Tong, Hong Kong, February 17, 2010. On London's Stansted airport, see Hubertus Adam, "Alles auf einer Ebene. Foster und Partner: Stansted Airport 1987–1991," *Archithese* 5, no. 2 (2002): 38–41.

11. Farrell, *Kowloon Transport Super City*, 6.

12. Rybkowski and Seel, "Hong Kong," 86.

13. Farrell, *Kowloon Transport Super City*, 13.

14. Freeman Fox Maunsell et al., 1.5.2, 1.5.3, 11.2.24, Greiner International and Maunsell Consultants Asia, *New Airport Master Plan: Final Report: Planning* (Hong Kong: Provisional Airport Authority, December 1991), 3–8.

15. Ibid., 1–2, 5.2.11.

16. Ibid., 11.2.15., 11.2.16, 12.4.5.

17. Ibid., 4.3.2.

18. See Budge-Reid, "The Hong Kong Airport Railway," 40–41.

19. Freeman Fox Maunsell et al., 11.2.6, 11.2.13.

20. Freeman Fox Maunsell et al., *Airport Railway Feasibility Study*, vol. 1: *Text*, Hong Kong Government: Highways Department, Airport Railway Division, 1991, 12.2.5. The authors also note that "an automatic barrier is a deterrent to the passenger with luggage . . . , [so] the objective should be to provide a barrier-free but secure ticket checking system which does not involve the purchase of tickets or the payment of money on board the train" (4.8.4).

21. Ibid., 12.2.8.

22. Greg Pearce, the lead architect working for Arup, noted that "at the behest of the Provisional Airport Authority, MTR insisted that the station must feel like an equal companion to the airport itself. . . . As an infrastructure counterpart, this facility must be on par with the new airport at Chek Lap Kok, and . . . the airport railway as a whole should

be seen as a seamless extension of the airport terminal. Greg Pearce, *Arup: Hong Kong Station* (Stuttgart: Axel Menges, 2001), 9, 12–13.

23. Pearce, *Arup*, 7. Planning for a not yet existent site represented a major challenge, as what would later become the station was, in the early 1990s, a part of Victoria Harbour and Blake's Pier, an area for seaside amusement and seafood restaurants. Greg Pearce, interview with the author at International Finance Center, Hong Kong, January 27, 2010.

24. Pearce, *Arup*, 11.

25. Ibid., 33.

26. Or as the French architectural historian Corinne Tiry calls it, the "tête de pont d'un réseau de nouveaux pôles urbains." Tiry, *Les mégastructures du transport*, 37.

27. At my request, the Airport Authority Hong Kong offered the following estimates: private/company car, 8 percent; bus/shuttle, 46 percent; taxi/limo, 14 percent; rail/subway, 22 percent; rental car, 1 percent; walk/SkyPier, 9 percent. Note that "railway/subway" includes passengers on both Airport Express and the Tung Chung Line. Statistics provided by Carmen H M Chan, Airport Authority Hong Kong, personal communication, April 27, 2010. One airport executive estimated that about 15 percent of air passengers use Airport Express, compared to 45–50 percent who come by bus. Eng interview.

28. MVA Asia, *Transport Study for the New Airport (TRANSNA)* (Hong Kong: Transport Department, December 1996).

29. Ibid., 8.2.

30. Anna (name changed), interview with the author at Water Street, Sai Ying Pun, Hong Kong, and at Hong Kong International Airport, March 22, 2010.

31. *Practical Guide for Employment of Domestic Helpers* (Hong Kong: Labour Department of the Hong Kong Special Administrative Region, September 2013), 8.

32. *Hong Kong Annual Digest of Statistics 2013* (Hong Kong: Census and Statistics Department of the Hong Kong Special Administrative Region, November 2013), x, 43.

33. Cathay Pacific. "Exclusive Domestic Helper Fares," www.cathaypacific.com/cpa/en_HK/offerspromotions.

34. MVA Asia, *Transport Study for the New Airport*, 7.

35. Joseph Chow, senior officer, Airport Authority Hong Kong, interview with the author at Hong Kong International Airport, April 23, 2010.

36. *Hong Kong Annual Digest of Statistics 2013*, 75.

37. MVA Asia, *Transport Study for the New Airport*, 4. MVA's recommendation rehearsed the separation of a high-speed and local line to the airport and Tung Chung, respectively, that was established in the *New Airport Master Plan*. Greiner International and Maunsell Consultants Asia, *New Airport Master Plan*, 8-2.

38. Arlt, *China's Outbound Tourism*, 138. Hong Kong Tourism Commission, *Tourism Performance in 2014*, www.tourism.gov.hk/english/statistics/statistics_perform.html. See also Bettina Wassener and Mary Hui, "Hong Kong Rents Push Out Mom and Pop Stores," *New York Times*, July 3, 2013.

39. Melvin M. Webber, "The Urban Place and the Nonplace Urban Realm," *Explorations into Urban Structure* (Philadelphia: University of Pennsylvania Press, 1964), 79–153.

40. Ibid., 97.

41. Ibid., 98.

42. Ibid., 80.

43. For various examples of the segregation of "native" and colonial populations in nineteenth-century Asian cities, see Laura Victoir and Victor Zatsepine, eds., *Harbin to Hanoi: The Colonial Built Environment in Asia, 1840 to 1940* (Hong Kong: Hong Kong University Press, 2013).

44. Graham and Marvin, *Splintering Urbanism*, 167.

45. The implications of these unsanctioned mobility tactics were not lost on Hong Kong's subway authority: in 2010, it slowly began to replace English-language ads addressed to expatriate tourists and businessmen with posters and brochures written in Cantonese and targeted at a local audience that offered deep discounts to passengers traveling on Airport Express in groups of two or more.

2. Transborder Infrastructure

1. Adam, "Alles auf einer Ebene," 38–41; Donald Albrecht, ed., *Now Boarding: Fentress Airports and the Architecture of Flight* (Denver: Denver Art Museum, 2012); Urbain Cassan, "Ports maritimes et aériens," *L'Architecture d'aujourd'hui* 7, no. 9 (1936): 35–45; Elke Dittrich, *Ernst Sagebiel: Leben und Werk (1892–1970)* (Berlin: Lukas, 2005); Terry Farrell, *Kowloon Transport Super City* (Hong Kong: Pace, 1998); Laura Greco, *Renzo Piano: Dalla macchina urbana alla città dell'informazione* (Venice: Marsilio, 2005); Vittorio Magnano Lampugnani, ed., *Hong Kong Architektur: Die Ästhetik der Dichte* (Munich: Prestel, 1993); Pearce et al., *Arup*; Pearman, *Airports*; Ken Powell, *Stansted: Norman Foster and the Architecture of Flight* (London: Fourth Estate, 1992); Serge Salat, *Paul Andreu: Métamorphoses du cercle* (Paris: Electa Moniteur, 1990); Susana Santala, "Airports," in *Eero Saarinen: Shaping the Future*, ed. Eeva-Liisa Pelkonen and Donald Albrecht, 301–7 (New Haven: Yale University Press, 2006); Ezra Stoller, *The TWA Terminal* (Princeton: Princeton Architectural Press, 1999); Tiry, *Les mégastructures du transport*; Zukowsky, *Building for Air Travel*.

2. Augé, *Non-lieux*; Chalfin, *Neoliberal Frontiers*; Cwerner, Kesselring, and Urry, *Aeromobilities*; Easterling, *Enduring Innocence*; Fuller and Harley, *Aviopolis*; Güller, *From Airport to Airport City*; Ibelings, *Supermodernism*; Kasarda and Lindsay, *Aerotropolis*; Thackara, *In the Bubble*; Corinne Tiry, "Mégastructures urbaines: Grands équipements de transport ou térritoires de l'échange," in *Déplacements: Architectures du transport. Térritoires en mutation*, ed. Anne Grillet-Aubert and Sabine Guth, 137–50 (Paris: Editions Recherches, 2005).

3. Castells, *The Rise of the Network Society*, 413.

4. Graham and Marvin, *Splintering Urbanism*, 364–69.

5. Castells, *The Rise of the Network Society*, 437–39.

6. Graham and Marvin, *Splintering Urbanism*, 348–50.

7. For an anthropological analysis of transborder space, see Willem Van Schendel, "Spaces of Engagement: How Borderlands, Illegal Flows, and Territorial States Interlock," in Abraham and van Schendel, *Illicit Flows and Criminal Things*, 38–60. See also Franck Billé, Grégory Delaplace, and Caroline Humphrey, eds., *Frontier Encounters: Knowledge and Practice at the Russian, Chinese, and Mongolian Border* (Cambridge: Open Book Publishers, 2012).

8. On the role of Guangdong in China's economic ascent since 1978, see Ezra Vogel, *Deng Xiaoping and the Transformation of China* (Cambridge, Mass.: Harvard University Press, 2011), 401–22.

9. Arlt, *China's Outbound Tourism.* The most recent statistics are published quarterly on the website of the China Tourism Academy, www.ctaweb.org.

10. Hong Kong Special Administrative Region, Macau Special Administrative Region, Shenzhen Special Economic Zone, Zhuhai Special Economic Zone, and Guangdong Province.

11. See Yang Xiuyun and Yu Hong, "Deregulatory Reform of China's Airports: Attracting Non-State Investors," *East Asian Policy* 2, no. 2 (2010): 62–72. See also Zhang Anming and Chen Hongmin, "Evolution of China's Air Transport Development and Policy towards International Liberalization," *Transportation Journal*, Spring 2003, 31–49.

12. SkyPier's users come from eight upstream ferry ports in the Pearl River Delta: two each in Shenzhen and Macau, as well as terminals in Guangzhou, Dongguan, Zhongshan, and Zhuhai. HKIA founded a joint-venture company with participating airlines and a handling agent (that is, a ferry operator) to manage these routes and to coordinate the upstream check-in service. The routes are managed by two handling agents: Chu Kong Passenger Transport (CKS), which runs ferries from SkyPier to Dongguan, Macau, Shenzhen, Zhongshan, and Zhuhai; and TurboJET—a joint venture between Hong Kong–based Shun Tak Holdings and China Travel Service (CTS), the Mainland's state-owned tourism corporation—which offers ferry services to Macau and Guangzhou Nansha. However, neither CKS nor TurboJET operate the Mainland routes directly: instead, they subcontract them to half a dozen local ferry operators based in Guangdong province. Eng interview.

13. Site visit to Hong Kong–Macau Ferry Terminal, Humen Town, Dongguan, February 23, 2010.

14. See Philip A. Kuhn, *Chinese among Others: Emigration in Modern Times* (Singapore: NUS Press, 2008). See also Wong Siu-lun, "Deciding to Stay, Deciding to Move, Deciding Not to Decide," in *Cosmopolitan Capitalists: Hong Kong and the Chinese Diaspora at the End of the 20th Century*, ed. Gary G. Hamilton, 135–51 (Seattle: University of Washington Press, 1999).

15. "Population of Dongguan," Dongguan Municipal Website, www.english.dg.gov .cn/population.htm.

16. T. G. McGee, George C. S. Lin, Andrew M. Marton, Mark Y. L. Wang, and Wu Jiaping, *China's Urban Space: Development under Market Socialism* (New York: Routledge, 2007), 97.

17. Ibid., 100.

18. Ibid., 115.

19. In particular, this system of connections offered two benefits: first, informal family connections ensured both a swifter march through China's bureaucratic apparatus; second, the system offered what McGee and Lin refer to diplomatically as a "secured return on investment"—that is, a lower likelihood of being scammed by unscrupulous officials. McGee and Lin, *China's Urban Space*, 78–79, 115.

20. In particular, the region's status as *rural* land prior to Dongguan's incorporation as a city in 1988 permitted a massive influx of migrant workers from the countryside who, impeded by the strictures of China's internal passport system, were barred from moving to urban areas like Guangzhou and Shenzhen. McGee and Lin, *China's Urban Space*, 78–79.

21. The Taiping Passenger Transportation Port was founded in June 1982. Eighteen months later, in January 1984, the People's Government of Dongguan county and the

Huiyang Shipping Bureau established the Humen Passenger Ferry Joint Company, a state-owned enterprise charged with operating ferries between Dongguan and Hong Kong. Shiziyang Sea Express, "Development History," www.hmlw.com.

22. Shiziyang Sea Express, "Congratulating the Official Establishment of Dongguan Longwei Taxi Service Co., Ltd.," press release, September 2003, www.shiziyang.com.

23. During the 2009–10 fiscal year, 204,202 air passengers traveled from Dongguan Humen to HKIA. Statistical analysis provided by Carmen H. M. Chan, Hong Kong Airport Authority, April 26, 2010. In the subsequent two years, traffic increased at an average rate of 37 percent per annum. Government of the Hong Kong Special Administrative Region, "Legislative Council Question 16: Utilisation of Boundary Control Points and the [sic] SkyPier," press release, September 11, 2012.

24. "It's mainly business travelers that use the airport check-in, both Chinese and foreigners. The foreigners are from the Middle East and East Asia. They come to Dongguan because of the clothing markets. The Chinese passengers travel to Europe and America for business meetings. They fly through Hong Kong because there are many more international flights there than in Shenzhen or Guangzhou. And international flights from Hong Kong are cheaper." Interview with Chen Fei, a travel agent who sells air tickets in the run-down shopping center across from the ferry terminal, February 23, 2010.

25. See, for example, Dongguan City Humen Hongxin Garment Factory, http://hongfei1998.com.cn.

26. Discussing the *hukou* system, O'Donnell, Wong, and Bach explain: "Through this long-standing institution, Chinese born in rural villages are designated peasants (with peasants rights of collective property), while Chinese born in cities are given privileges within their particular city of birth. In terms of social mobility, this is a hugely significant institution because educational opportunities, health care access, police protection, and property rights are determined by *hukou*. Nationally speaking, in terms of labor mobility, *hukou* also determines one's place of residence and so it also determines one's place of (legitimate) work." Mary Ann O'Donnell, Winnie Wong, and Jonathan Bach, eds., *Learning from Shenzhen: China's Post-Mao Experiment from Special Zone to Model City* (Chicago: University of Chicago Press, 2016), 14. For more on the *hukou* system, see Chan Kam Wing and Li Zhangi, "The Hukou System and Rural-Urban Migration in China: Processes and Changes," *China Quarterly* 160 (1999): 818–55; Kam Wing Chan and Will Buckingham, "Is China Abolishing the Hukou System?" *China Quarterly* 195 (2008): 582–606; Wang Fei-ling, *Organizing through Division and Exclusion: China's Hukou System* (Stanford: Stanford University Press, 2005).

27. Shiziyang Sea Express, *Fly via Humen: Passenger Guide*, Dongguan Humen Longwei Passenger Ferry Co. Ltd., undated brochure.

28. Nyiri, *Mobility and Cultural Authority in Contemporary China*, 6–7, 153–54.

29. Unless otherwise noted, information in the following section was collected during two site visits to SkyPier on December 16, 2009, and January 23, 2011.

30. Hong Kong Airport Authority, "Airport's New SkyPier and North Satellite Concourse Officially Opened"; press release, January 15, 2010; Hong Kong Airport Authority, "SkyPier and North Satellite Soft Opened"; *HKIA News*, January 2010. 4.

31. Hong Kong Airport Authority, "Airport's New SkyPier and North Satellite Concourse Officially Opened"; Hong Kong Airport Authority, *Annual Report 2011/2012*, Hong Kong International Airport, 2012, 43.

32. SOM Aedas JV, Hong Kong International Airport Contract P250, SkyPier Design and Construction Stage Services, Scheme Design Report, February 18 2005, Fig. 2.10.2: "Pontoon Design—Kit of Parts."

33. Ibid., 1-1, 1-2.

34. "Transfer passengers who have checked in upstream go directly to security screening, then proceed downstairs via escalators/lifts to the secure APM taking them directly to the East Hall in the PTB. Transfer passengers who have not checked in upstream go to the baggage reclaim area, then proceed to check-in, after which they drop their bags at the baggage drop-off point and proceed to security, where they join the other transfer passengers." SOM Aedas JV, Hong Kong International Airport Contract P250, SkyPier Design and Construction Stage Services, working paper 1, December 20, 2004, 10-7.

35. Eng interview.

36. "The baggage containers are lifted from the ferryboats by a crane using a special sling with four hooks that are secured to four handles located on the side of the baggage container. . . . The average time required to unload one inbound baggage container would be 2.5 minutes . . . [and] to load one outbound baggage container would be three minutes." SOM Aedas JV, working paper 1, 8-1, 8-2.

37. Orren Tatcher, principal, OTC Planning and Design, interview with the author at SkyPier, Hong Kong International Airport, December 16, 2009.

38. SOM Aedas JV, Scheme Design Report, 1-1, 1-2.

39. "'SkyPier' may sound good, [but] for the uninitiated this name will not be as easily understandable as 'Ferries,' 'Ferry Transfer,' or 'Ferry check-in area'. . . . All international SkyPier passengers will be required to access the building via the APM where it will not be necessary to expose them to the SkyPier name anywhere along the route." Ibid., 3-3.

40. Reulecke's original phrase "Institutionalisierung der Konfliktaustragung," or the institutionalization of conflict resolution, refers to the role that state bureaucracies played in mediating between the political and economic agenda of rival social groups in late nineteenth-century Germany. See Jürgen Reulecke, *Geschichte der Urbanisierung in Deutschland* (Frankfurt am Main: Suhrkamp, 1985), 130.

41. Castells, *The Rise of the Network Society*, 413.

42. McGee and Lin, *China's Urban Space*, 120.

43. The political scientist Wang Fei-ling notes that "the Chinese traditionally have a low opinion of written law and rely heavily on the administrative capacity of the ruler, allowing and tolerating humane circumvention . . . and some flexibility [that], ironically perhaps, further strengthens the whole system." Wang, *Organizing through Division and Exclusion*, 56.

44. Ludwig Feuerbach, *Das Wesen des Christentums* (Leipzig: Wigand, 1841).

45. "Umweg über Schönefeld." *Der Spiegel* 29/1971, 41. "Unter Brüdern." *Der Spiegel* 18/1985, 103–9. "Volkseigener Köder." *Der Spiegel* 39/1981, 74–76. For more on Interflug, see Karl-Dieter Seifert, *Weg und Absturz der Interflug: Der Luftverkehr in der DDR* (Berlin: Brandenburgisches Verlagshaus, 1994).

46. On the phenomenon of *Gastarbeiter* flights, see Robert Gruner, *Interflug und DDR-Außenpolitik: Die Luftfahrt als diplomatisches Instrument* (Hamburg: Diplomica, 2009), 51–54.

47. Eckhart Stratenschulte, *East Berlin* (West Berlin: Information Center Berlin, 1988), 74.

48. Björn Rosen, "Linientreu: 50 Jahre Interflug," *Der Tagesspiegel*, September 21, 2008.

49. Imtiaz Muqbil notes that "for years, many Asia-Pacific governments have allowed visa-free access to Europeans, Americans, Australians, Japanese and other citizens of industrialized countries. Now, they are totally confused on how to handle the future travellers from China, India, Russia and other countries within the region. Each of these countries has problems with illegal immigrants, crime syndicates, and other undesirables that governments want to keep out. How these issues are sorted out is going to be a major challenge in the future." Imtiaz Muqbil, "Ten Trends That Will Shape the Future of Asia-Pacific Travel," ITB Berlin, press release, 2005; qtd. in Arlt, *China's Outbound Tourism*, 130.

3. Special Zones

1. For an analysis of intercity relations between Heihe and Blagoveshchensk, see Franck Billé, "Surface Modernities: Open-Air Markets, Containment, and Verticality in Two Border Towns of Russia and China," *Economic Sociology* 15, no. 2 (2014): 154–72. On Hekou, see Zhang Juan, "A Trafficking 'Not-Spot' in a China-Vietnam Border Town," in *Labour Migration and Human Trafficking in Southeast Asia: Critical Perspectives*, ed. Michele Ford, Leonore Lyons, and Willem van Schendel, 95–111 (London: Routledge, 2012).

2. On SEZs in Southeast Asia, see Peter J. Rimmer and Howard Dick, "Appropriate Economic Space for Transnational Infrastructural Projects: Gateways, Multimodal Corridors, and Special Economic Zones," Asian Development Bank Institute Working Paper Series 237, August 2010.

3. Jonathan Bach, "Shenzhen: From Exception to Rule?" in O'Donnell, Wong, and Bach, *Learning from Shenzhen*, 333–34.

4. Aihwa Ong, *Neoliberalism as Exception: Mutations in Citizenship and Sovereignty* (Durham: Duke University Press, 2007).

5. Keller Easterling, "Zone: The Spatial Softwares of Extrastatecraft," *Places/Design Observer*, June 2012, https://placesjournal.org/article/zone-the-spatial-softwares-of-extra statecraft.

6. Bach, "Shenzhen," 329. On colonial settlements in Northeast China, see Klaus Mühlhahn, "Mapping Colonial Space: The Planning and Building of Qingdao by German Colonial Authorities, 1897–1914," in Victoir and Victor, *Harbin to Hanoi*, 106, 123n. One might also identify the network of "closed cities" in the Soviet Union, each one dedicated to a specific high-tech industry, such as nuclear energy, as a precedent for special zones in the socialist camp.

7. "Shenzhen International Airport Terminal 3," *Dezeen*, April 12, 2008; Andrew Yang, "Fuksas Wins Shenzhen Airport Competition," *Architectural Record*, June 10, 2008.

8. Fang Tian, project manager, Fuksas, interview with the author at Shenzhen Bao'an International Airport, March 7, 2012.

9. Fuksas developed the terminal facade in collaboration with the German engineering firm Knippers Helbig, which specializes in parametric design. See Florian Scheible

and Milos Dimcic, "Parametric Engineering: Everything Is Possible," paper delivered at annual symposium of International Association for Shell and Spatial Structures, September 2011, www.programmingarchitecture.com/publications/ScheibleDimcic_IASS_2011 .pdf.

10. See Yang and Yu, "Deregulatory Reform of China's Airports," 62–72. See also Zhang and Chen, "Evolution of China's Air Transport Development," 31–49.

11. This arrangement was formalized in October 2008, when HKIA and SZIA signed an agreement that "enables passengers at HKIA or SZIA to check in and obtain boarding passes for connecting flights at either airport." *Media Center—Key Dates and Events,* www.hongkongairport.com/eng/media/key-dates-events.html. See also Shen, "Assessing Inter-City Relations between Hong Kong and Shenzhen," 55–73. On average, flights to Mainland Chinese destinations that depart from Shenzhen are 30 to 40 percent cheaper than those that leave from Hong Kong. Moreover, SZIA offers much more frequent departures to major hubs like Beijing, Shanghai and Chengdu; as well as nonstop service to dozens of provincial capitals and secondary cities.

12. Vogel, *Deng Xiaoping and the Transformation of China,* 403, 404, 406.

13. Ibid., 399.

14. Ibid., 398, 411.

15. Huang Weiwen, director, Shenzhen Center for Design, interview with the author at Shenzhen Center for Design, March 7, 2012. Huang also notes that "these sites of integration with Hong Kong transportation and logistic networks stretched between Mainland China and Hong Kong, informing the development of each stage of Shenzhen's development as well as the conditions through which land use changed. To date, however, there has been insufficient research from this perspective on the development of the city." Huang Weiwen, "Tripartite Origins of Shenzhen: Beijing, Hong Kong, and Bao'an," in O'Donnell, Wong, and Bach, *Learning from Shenzhen,* 110–11.

16. Shaw et al., "China's Airline Consolidation," 293–305.

17. Civil Aviation Administration of China, "从国有独资到产权多元化—民航现代企业制度逐步建立完善," press release, December 16, 2008, www.caac.gov.cn/D1/30years/200812/t20081216_20823.html.

18. Shaw et al., "China's Airline Consolidation."

19. Huang interview.

20. Ibid.

21. Writing in 1991, the authors of the master plan for Hong Kong's new airport argued that the construction of Shenzhen's airport would have little effect on demand at HKIA and would serve chiefly as an "overflow facility" for Guangzhou's Baiyun Airport. Moreover, they projected that traffic at Bao'an would amount to no more than 3.4 million annual passengers by the year 2000. Greiner International and Maunsell Consultants Asia, *New Airport Master Plan. Final Report: Planning* (Hong Kong: Provisional Airport Authority, December 1991), 3-2.

22. Center for Asia Pacific Aviation, "Shenzhen Reports 6% Traffic Growth in 2011," January 12, 2012, www.centreforaviation.com/news/shenzhen-airport-reports-6-traffic -growth-in-2011–136349. Author's own calculations.

23. This position was reaffirmed by the twelfth Five-Year Plan, adopted in 2011. See Xin Dingding, "Airspace Management Reform Urged," *China Daily,* October 30, 2012.

24. "The airspace of the PRD region is very complicated. Three different air traffic management authorities oversee flight movements in the area, using different operation procedures and standards. All are subordinate to the Chinese military in terms of rights of access to the region's air space. . . . In addition, an 'invisible wall' exists between Hong Kong and Macau on the one hand, and the Mainland on the other, the result of three separate aviation information zones. When aircraft leave HKIA airspace, they are required to reach a specific altitude before they are allowed to climb 'over the wall' into Chinese Mainland airspace. This results in extra flight time and fuel consumption, as well as logistical complications for air traffic controllers." One Country Two Systems Research Institute, "Study of Hong Kong's Aviation Industry: Current Challenges and Future Strategies," Central Policy Unit of the Government of the Hong Kong Special Administrative Region, September 2010, 62.

25. Author's own calculations based on data provided by Shenzhen Airport Group. See also Keith Wallis, "HK Airport Outpaces Shenzhen," *South China Morning Post*, January 26, 2012. An article in the British *Independent*, written on the occasion of T3's inauguration, noted that "Shenzhen airport's website boasts a wide range of international destinations, including Dubai, Cologne, and Sydney. But a trawl of sources, including airline websites and the aviation data specialist OAG, failed to find any services to or from these airports. Existing links seem to be purely regional, to cities such as Bangkok, Kuala Lumpur, and Singapore." Simon Calder, "Shenzhen Airport Terminal Three: Vast, Shiny, New—and Empty?" *The Independent*, November 28, 2013.

26. Site visit to Shenzhen Bao'an International Airport, February 23, 2010.

27. Trans-Island Chinalink Ltd., "Cross-Border Transportation Service of Trans-Island Chinalink," www.trans-island.com.hk/eng/china.html; Eternal East Cross-Border Coach Management Ltd., "永东直巴管理有限公司—關於我們," www.eebus.com/combg.asp.

28. Airport Authority Hong Kong, *Together We Make the Future: Annual Report 2011/2012*, 43. See also Huang Fang, "宝安国际机场迎送旅客70万," *Bao'an Daily*, October 8, 2013.

29. Site visit to Futian Coach Terminus, Shenzhen, March 8, 2012; site visit to Shenzhen Grand Theatre, Shenzhen, November 29, 2012; site visits to Kingkey Banner Center, Shenzhen, December 1, 2009, February 22, 2010, March 8, 2012.

30. Eternal East Cross-Border Coach Management Ltd., *EEBus Service 2009 Guide Book*, pamphlet, November 2009, 4.

31. For more on Shenzhen's urban villages, see Wang Ya Ping, Wang Yanglin, and Wu Jiansheng, "Urbanization and Informal Development in China: Urban Villages in Shenzhen," *International Journal of Urban and Regional Research* 33, no. 4 (December 2009): 957–73.

32. Huang, "Tripartite Origins of Shenzhen," 111–12.

33. Ibid., 112.

34. Ibid., 114.

35. Ibid., 113.

36. O'Donnell, Wong, and Bach, *Learning from Shenzhen*, 20.

37. As Mary Ann O'Donnell notes, the area known as Baishizhou emerged out of a collective farm and five adjoining villages. See Mary Ann O'Donnell, "Of Shahe and OCT," *Shenzhen Noted*, weblog, January 31, 2010, http://maryannodonnell.wordpress.com/2010/01/31/tangtou-baishizhou.

38. Jason (name changed), interview with the author at Kingkey Banner Center, Shenzhen, February 22, 2010; follow-up interview at Shun Tak Centre, Hong Kong, April 20, 2010.

39. See Tsang Shun-Fai, "Border Control in Colonial Hong Kong, 1958–1962" (undergraduate thesis, University of Hong Kong, 2010).

40. For an in-depth account of the handover, see Carroll, *A Concise History of Hong Kong*.

41. For more on the history of the Hong Kong-Shenzhen border, and on Hong Kong's immigration regulations, see Y. M. Yeung and Shen Jianfa, eds., *The Pan-Pearl River Delta: An Emerging Regional Economy in a Globalizing China* (Hong Kong: Chinese University of Hong Kong Press, 2008).

42. "旅客资料。个人游计划," Commerce and Economic Development Bureau of the Government of the Hong Kong Special Administrative Region, www.tourism.gov.hk/sc_chi/visitors/visitors_ind.html. As noted in the previous chapter, China's *hukou,* or household registration system, defines how often Mainland citizens can travel outside China according to their place of birth.

43. A complete list is available at "Visitor Information," www.tourism.gov.hk/english/visitors/visitors_ind.html.

44. For more on the economic considerations informing IVS, see Arlt, *China's Outbound Tourism,* 140.

45. "Shenzhen Extends Individual Visit Scheme," China Internet Information Center, www.china.org.cn/travel/2011–01/05/content_21674188.htm.

46. Government of the Hong Kong Special Administrative Region, "Annex to Legislative Council Question 16. Number of passengers using various boundary control points from January to September 2011," press release, September 11, 2012.

47. Site visits to Shenzhen Bay Port Border Control Point, Shenzhen, March 5, 2010, April 3, 2010, January 26, 2011.

48. The Shenzhen Bay border control facility was designed and constructed by JRP, a professional engineering consultancy based in Hong Kong. See J. Roger Preston Ltd., "Hong Kong Shenzhen Western Corridor, Co-location of Boundary Crossing Facilities," www.jrp-group.com.

49. Government of the Hong Kong Special Administrative Region, "Shenzhen Bay Port Hong Kong Port Area Ordinance," Ordinance No. 4 of 2007, April 26, 2007. For more on the design of Shenzhen Bay, see Max Hirsh and Jonathan D. Solomon, "Does Your Mall Have an Airport?," *Log* 19 (Summer 2010): 99–106.

50. Government of the Hong Kong Special Administrative Region, "Legislative Council Question 16: Utilisation of Boundary Control Points and the SkyPier," press release, September 11, 2012.

51. Trans-Island Limousine Ltd., *HKIA Guangdong Deluxe Cross Border Limousine,* undated brochure, retrieved November 2009.

52. According to Victor Fung, the former CEO of HKIA, the airport authority built Terminal 2 in response to an increase in the number of passengers traveling to and from Mainland China: "Terminal 2 . . . isn't really meant as an airport terminal, but rather as a transport hub for land and sea passengers who are coming to the airport." Victor Fung, chief executive officer, Li and Fung, interview with the author at Alexandra House, Hong Kong, February 11, 2010.

53. Site visits to Mainland Coach Terminus, Hong Kong International Airport Terminal 2, June 29, 2009, February 22, 2010, December 10, 2011, November 28, 2012.

54. Lindquist, *The Anxieties of Mobility*, 17.

55. Ibid., 8, 12.

56. Dendi Gustinandar, commercial director, Hang Nadim International Airport, Batam, Indonesia, interview with the author at Hang Nadim International Airport, March 11, 2013.

57. Government of the Hong Kong Special Administrative Region, Census and Statistics Department, *Hong Kong: The Facts*, June 2014.

58. Van Schendel, "Spaces of Engagement," 62. Van Schendel argues that that attitude is a common facet of daily life, and a necessary survival strategy, throughout Asia's border cities: "Inhabitants of borderlands share . . . an uneasiness about dominant conceptions of spatial reality. Their lived experience makes it impossible for them to accept as given, and unproblematic, the contemporary organization of the world as defined by state elites. . . . They cannot restrict their imagination to the territory of a single state, and they see those who do so as imprisoned in a delusion. . . . Around the world, inhabitants of border regions have developed practices and worldviews that take account of the state but never as an undisputed, overarching entity. [They] scale their world in ways that do not coincide with state borders [and that] spill over the spatial limits set by the state's territory." Van Schendel, "Spaces of Engagement," 54, 56.

59. Katha Pollitt, "Learning to Drive." *The New Yorker*, July 22, 2002, 36.

60. Vlad Savov, "Shenzhen's New Airport Terminal Puts the Wonder Back into Flight," *The Verge*, November 28, 2013, www.theverge.com/2013/11/28/5154484/baoan-interna tional-airport-terminal-3-studio-fuksis-design.

4. Cheap Tickets

1. Site visit to Plaza Low Yat, Kuala Lumpur, August 27, 2013.

2. Cebu Pacific Air, "CEB Joins the Mob in Singapore!," YouTube video, www.you tube.com/watch?v=ByhG8qkXsDw.

3. "Consider, for instance, the deregulation of the airline industry and the rise of the cell phone, which have come to structure communication and transportation. Two decades ago the great majority of Indonesian migrants travelling from the island of Lombok to Malaysia would go overland via a complicated network of middlemen and different modes of transportation. Today most fly directly." Johan Lindquist, "Migration Infrastructure in Asia and the Middle East," paper presented at Asia Research Institute, Singapore, August 22, 2013. See also Xiang and Lindquist, "Migration Infrastructure," 122–48.

4. In 2013, the low-cost airline Jetstar released a TV ad in Singapore and Malaysia that showed an elderly couple traveling to Australia to attend their grandson's university graduation. Another ad opened with an establishing shot of an older woman boarding a flight at Singapore's Changi airport, and then cut to the same woman sitting by her daughter's side in an Australian maternity ward. Jetstar Group, "Student PlusBundle," YouTube video, www.youtube.com/watch?v=eIUREao1KrY; Jetstar Group, "Grandmother Plus-Bundle," YouTube video, www.youtube.com/watch?v=JQLnB6WokWA.

5. Guillaume Burghouwt, *Airline Network Development in Europe and Its Implications for Airport Planning* (Aldershot: Ashgate, 2007), 1.

6. As Burghouwt notes, "the trinity of the national government, the national airline, and the national airport dominated the international air transport markets. Little room was left for competition in the air transport regime of bilateralism." Ibid., 1.

7. Bowen, *The Economic Geography of Air Transportation*, 147. The most notable example was Southwest Airlines, which began operating inexpensive flights between Dallas, Houston, and San Antonio in 1971. Southwest Airlines, "Fact Sheet," www.southwest .com. Significantly, Southwest based itself at Dallas's Love Field, which airport planners expected would be rendered obsolete due the contemporaneous construction of the new regional hub at DFW. This portended the role that secondary and/or antiquated airports later played in the expansion of air passenger demographics.

8. Bowen, *The Economic Geography of Air Transportation*, 95.

9. In the decades following ADA, many former intrastate air companies such as Southwest transformed themselves into budget airlines or low-cost carriers operating at the national level. By the late 2000s, Southwest flew more domestic passengers within the United States than any other airline, and it had become the largest domestic carrier in the world. International Air Transport Association (IATA), *World Air Transport Statistics (WATS)* 53 (2009): Table 4.2, 90.

10. Bowen, *The Economic Geography of Air Transportation*, 97.

11. Most often, these were small countries that stood to gain from an increase in international air traffic, either because they had no significant domestic market (such as the Netherlands) or because they saw improved connectivity as a means of compensating for their geopolitical isolation (e.g., Israel and Taiwan). In the case of Singapore, both of these conditions applied. In the 1990s, the United States replaced these ASAs with "Open Skies" agreements, beginning with the Netherlands in 1992, which further liberalized operations between member parties, removing limits on capacity, frequency, pricing, and codesharing. Moreover, deregulation in the transatlantic market led to the use of smaller aircraft flying into many new gateways, thus expanding the focus of international travel beyond traditional transatlantic hubs like Heathrow, JFK, and Charles de Gaulle. Bowen, *The Economic Geography of Air Transportation*, 104, 106.

12. The first step in that direction came in 1984, when the Netherlands and the United Kingdom deregulated air traffic across the English Channel. Burghouwt, *Airline Network Development in Europe*, 2.

13. "Summary of the EU Packages of Deregulation Measures," qtd. in Burghouwt, *Airline Network Development in Europe*, Annex 6.

14. Apart from removing restrictions on ticket prices, the most significant "freedoms" included the right to *full cabotage,* which permits a foreign airline to operate domestic flights in another country, along with "seventh freedom rights," which allow an airline to operate an international route between two countries, neither of which is the home country of the carrier. Burghouwt, *Airline Network Development in Europe*, Annex 2.

15. "Ryanair: The 'Southwest' of European Airlines," case study (Hyderabad: IBS Center for Management Research, 2003). As Bowen notes, "The large Irish immigrant and guest worker population in Britain and the substantial number of travelers then crossing the Irish Sea by ferry made the market fertile ground for the upstart low-cost carrier. . . . In the three years [after] Ryanair launched its low-fare service, London–Dublin traffic doubled." Bowen, *The Economic Geography of Air Transportation*, 162.

16. The Schengen Agreement was signed by ten members of the European Community in 1985 and was implemented a decade later. Together with the euro, the creation of the Schengen Area was probably the most palpable effect of European integration, as it facilitated the cross-border movement of millions of travelers. Significantly, the boundaries of the twenty-five Schengen countries are not coterminous with those of the EU: several non-EU countries like Switzerland and Norway are members; while some EU members, notably the UK, have refused to join. Schengen is not the only example of such supranational border regimes, but it is the most far-reaching iteration insofar as it extends the right to passport-free movement to all travelers within the Schengen Area, regardless of citizenship or residency. Thus a Chinese tourist who obtains a Schengen Visa can travel without restrictions across any of the member states' borders.

17. Bowen, *The Economic Geography of Air Transportation*, 169.

18. Burrell, "Going Steerage on Ryanair," 1024.

19. In 2006, ASEAN ratified the Framework Agreement on Visa Exception (FAVE), which permits citizens from any ASEAN nation to travel to other member states for up to two weeks.

20. Two key pieces of legislation were the Multilateral Agreement on Air Services, adopted in 2008, which liberalized air routes between all ASEAN capital cities; as well as the Multilateral Agreement for the Full Liberalization of Passenger Air Services (MAFLPAS), enacted in 2010, which theoretically deregulated air traffic between Southeast Asia's secondary cities.

21. For more on ASEAN Open Skies and the ASEAN Common Visa Initiative, see Jennifer Meszaros, "Giant in the Making," *Business Traveller Asia-Pacific*, June 2014, 30–35. See also CAPA Centre for Aviation, "ASEAN's Single Aviation Market: Many Miles to Go," http://centreforaviation.com; "PH, Three Other ASEAN Nations Agree to Work On Common Smart Visa," *Newsbytes Philippines*, June 5, 2013.

22. Teresa S. C. Poon and Peter Waring, "Lean Production Aviation in Asia: The Case of AirAsia," working paper #21 (Hong Kong: School of Business Administration, Open University of Hong Kong, February 2007), 3–4.

23. As Poon notes, "This is a fact that is sometimes overlooked in the business press and airline literature that although the terrorist attacks resulted in reduced demand (especially in Western countries), it also enabled low cost carriers to capitalize on the fall in aircraft leasing costs. Ibid., 8–9.

24. The LCC penetration rate varies significantly within ASEAN: from 25 percent in Singapore to an astonishing 85 percent in the Philippines. In 2012, the two biggest carriers in the region were Lion Air and AirAsia—launched in 2000 and 2001, respectively— which each controlled about one-third of the industry. The remainder was made up of smaller carriers like Nok, Firefly, Cebu Pacific, and Vietjet. CAPA Centre for Aviation, "Airasia's 2013 Outlook Marred by Intensifying Competition and Continued Losses at New Affiliates," http://centreforaviation.com.

25. In essence, Fernandes rebranded the airline according to the principles that had brought success to LCCs in Europe: tenets that were summarized by one former AirAsia executive as "many point-to-point [flights], high aircraft utilization, . . . small catchy adverts constantly, high bullshit factor; CEO involved in publicity stunts; seek opportunities to appear in the media as often as possible." Qtd. in Poon and Waring, "Lean Production Aviation in Asia," 7.

26. "Tiger Airways Introduces E-pay in Malaysia," *Tiger Tales*, November 2010, 108.

27. Site visits to AirAsia Travel Center, Tesco Lotus Rama I, Bangkok, August 31, 2013, October 17, 2014.

28. Site visit to AirAsia Travel Center, Stesen Sentral, Kuala Lumpur, August 27, 2013.

29. Site visits to Kuala Lumpur Low-Cost Carrier Terminal (LCCT), April 16, 2012, August 28, 2013.

30. The LCCT's construction was also thirty times cheaper than the Kurokawa terminal, which ultimately cost more than 3 billion U.S. dollars to build. Kuala Lumpur International Airport, "Comparison between KLIA, LCCT, and KLIA2," www.klia2.info.

31. For an in-depth ethnographic account of Suvarnabhumi's construction, see Ferguson, "Terminally Haunted," 47–64.

32. Site visit to Don Mueang International Airport, Bangkok, January 19, 2011, January 23, 2011.

33. The inability of Suvarnabhumi to cope with the added demands placed on its facilities became evident during the Chinese New Year holiday of 2012—one of the busiest traveling seasons throughout much of East and Southeast Asia—when the airport's immigration facilities became overloaded with passengers, causing unbearable delays and challenging the viability of operating Suvarnabhumi as Bangkok's only international airport. Site visit to Suvarnabhumi International Airport, Bangkok, January 20 and 25, 2012.

34. "Airports Record 20% Rise in Travellers," *Bangkok Post*, October 8, 2013.

35. Site visits to Don Mueang International Airport, Bangkok, July 16 and 23, 2013.

36. *Lost in Thailand* (人再囧途之泰囧), dir. Xu Zheng (Enlight Pictures, 2012).

37. Rudolf Mrázek, *Engineers of Happy Land: Technology and Nationalism in a Colony* (Princeton: Princeton University Press, 2002), 10–13.

38. "Future of Asian Airports," conference at Singapore Aviation Academy, August 19–20, 2013.

39. In inclement weather, ground staff kindly distributed giant maroon umbrellas among the passengers. Site visit to Budget Terminal, Changi International Airport, Singapore, April 14, 2012.

40. Koh Ming Sue, senior vice president, Engineering and Master Planning, Changi Airport Group, "Development of Terminal 4 at Singapore Changi Airport," presentation at Singapore Aviation Academy, August 19, 2013.

41. Ho Beng Huat, advisor and chief specialist, Changi Airport Group, "Airport Development in Singapore," presentation at Singapore Aviation Academy, August 19, 2013.

42. Meetings at Civil Aviation Authority of Singapore, July 24, 2012, August 27, 2012.

43. Saifulbahri Ismail, "Changi Airport's T4 to Be Used as Test-Bed for New Concepts," *Channel News Asia*, November 5, 2013.

44. Ibid.

45. Koh, "Development of Terminal 4."

46. Conversation with L (name withheld) at Changi Airport, Singapore, August 20, 2013.

47. Koh, "Development of Terminal 4." He then elaborated: "Singaporeans will not want to carry their luggage. On the bus it can be quite squeezed with others. And with the train, during peak hours, during office hours . . ." He paused, looking for the right words.

"The MRT [subway] is experiencing quite, uhh, capacity concerns. And after taking the train to somewhere near their house they would probably have to switch over to a shuttle bus to get to their housing estate before they reach home. And before you reach home you have to walk in the rain or the sunshine between the bus stop and your house. So that will prevent a lot of people from taking the train. More likely taxis and private cars will be the dominant form of transport. For foreign workers, typically the company that employs them *may* send some kind of transport to pick them up in one group. Or if it's a maid working for a household the employer will drop them off and pick them up at the airport."

48. Larkin, "The Politics and Poetics of Infrastructure," 329, 333.

49. Dimitris Dalakoglou, "The Road: An Ethnography of the Albanian–Greek Cross-Border Motorway," *American Ethnology* 37, no. 1 (2010): 132–49.

50. Naveeda Khan, "Flaws in the Flow: Roads and Their Modernity in Pakistan," *Social Text* 24, no. 489 (2006): 87–113.

51. Faizal Mansor, chief financial officer, Malaysia Airports Holdings Berhad, *Asia Edge*, Bloomberg TV, October 18, 2013.

52. Malaysia Airports Holdings Berhad, *KLIA 2: The Next Generation Hub. World Class Image*, YouTube video, www.youtube.com/watch?v=BnE9UPUURWc.

53. Soorox, "KLIA2—New Mega Low Cost Carriers Terminal," *Malaysian Wings Forum*, Internet forum. www.malaysianwings.com.

54. Mrázek, *Engineers of Happy Land*, 17.

55. Ibid., 18.

56. Ibid.

57. Sigmund Freud, "Die Verdrängung," *Internationale Zeitschrift für Psychoanalyse* 3 (1915): 129–38.

58. On a visit to Batam's Hang Nadim International Airport, I asked Dendi Gustinandar, the airport's commercial director, whether the airport devises different planning mechanisms for flights operated by legacy carriers and budget airlines. He chuckled at the question: "Well you know, almost all of our flights are low-cost. Before the budget airlines came, there wasn't really much traffic here." Dendi Gustinander, commercial director, Hang Nadim International Airport, interview with the author and Anna Gasco at Hang Nadim International Airport, Batam, March 11, 2013.

Conclusion

1. For critiques of modernist planning approaches, in particular as they relate to urban mobility and long-distance transportation networks, see Reyner Banham, *Theory and Design in the First Machine Age* (New York: Praeger, 1960). See also James Holston, *The Modernist City: An Anthropological Critique of Brasília* (Chicago: University of Chicago Press, 1989); Vikramaditya Prakash, *Chandigarh's Le Corbusier: The Struggle for Modernity in Postcolonial India* (Seattle: University of Washington Press, 2002).

2. It is telling in this regard to reflect on my interactions with airport authorities in Hong Kong and Singapore over the past five years. While my questions to them covered a wide range of topics—planning, design, finance, institutional framework—most of the questions that I fielded from airport managers and planners circled around two issues. In Hong Kong, one executive quizzed me on what exactly motivates budget air travelers—where they live, why they are flying, what they expect from the airport. It was clear from his questions that he had very little background knowledge, even bungling the names of

low-cost airlines that would be familiar to anyone who watches the ads that air during prime-time TV shows or in between YouTube clips. In Singapore, meanwhile, several urban planners asked me informally for documents that would help them to understand the process by which European airports consult local stakeholders—that is, how to organize public meetings and statistical surveys that would solicit the opinions of average citizens who live near the airport as well as those who commute there on a regular basis. There was simply no existing blueprint for doing so, and they were grateful for even the most basic information that I could provide.

3. An article in the developer's newsletter boasted that "JTC's wide range of housing facilities for foreign professionals and work permit holders include terrace and apartments in . . . Chip Bee Gardens; artistic niche of Wessex Estate for the creative and scientific community" and "serviced apartments at Fusionopolis for short-term accommodation and easy access to business support services." JTC Corporation, "Creating Vital New Connections: New Business, Housing and Amenity Development Cluster Report," *Periscope: A Magazine for Customers of JTC Corporation* 04/2010 (September 2010), 12.

4. Ministry of Manpower Singapore, "Foreign Workforce Numbers," www.mom.gov .sg/documents-and-publications/foreign-workforce-numbers.

5. "JTC Gradually Phasing Out Scheme for Housing Foreigners: Lee Yi Shyan," *Channel News Asia*, March 12, 2013.

6. Ministry of Manpower Singapore, "Levies and Quotas for Hiring Foreign Workers," www.mom.gov.sg/passes-and-permits/work-permit-for-foreign-worker/foreign-wor ker-levy.

7. Reza (name changed), interview with the author at Coffee Bean and Tea Leaf, Holland Village, Singapore, October 19, 2013.

8. Department of Statistics Singapore, "Latest Data: Population and Land Area," June 2014, www.singstat.gov.sg/statistics/browse-by-theme/population-and-population.

9. Ho made the remarks during a conference called "Lee Kuan Yew and the Physical Transformation of Singapore," held at Singapore's Regent Hotel on September 18, 2013. A heavily edited account of his remarks was subsequently published in the *Straits Times*. See Amelia Tan and Janice Heng, "Foreign Workers 'Need to Be Integrated,'" *Straits Times*, September 21, 2013.

10. John O'Callaghan and Kevin Lim, "Strike by China Bus Drivers Tests Singapore's Patience," *Reuters*, November 28, 2012.

11. In 2009, 29.5 million tourists visited Hong Kong, of which 17.8 million (60 percent) were from Mainland China. In 2013, 54.3 million tourists visited Hong Kong, of which 40.7 million (75 percent) were Mainlanders. Hong Kong Tourism Board. *Work Plan for 2011–12*, 2; Hong Kong Tourism Commission, *Tourism Performance in 2014*, 5.

12. Imported products are heavily taxed in Mainland China. See chapter 1. On China's food and drug safety scandals, see Eric Meyer, "China's Food and Drugs Saga: The Never-Ending Milk Scandal," *Forbes Asia*, August 10, 2014.

13. See introduction.

14. The disappearance of retail outlets that cater to the local population, and their replacement by shops geared toward visitors, represents another flashpoint of contention. In the spring of 2014, activists initiated an antitourism campaign in Tsim Sha Tsui, disrupting sales at jewelry and brand-name shoe stores, and publicly asking Mainland shoppers

to leave Hong Kong. See Ng Kang-chung, "Scuffles Break Out as Protesters Hurl Slurs, Abuse at Mainland Chinese Tourists," *South China Morning Post*, February 17, 2014.

15. See Max Hirsh, "Techno-Pastoral Fantasies at Hong Kong International," *Places Journal*, July 2013, https://placesjournal.org/article/techno-pastoral-fantasies-at-hong-kong-international/.

16. That sea change in public opinion, which divides Hong Kong's younger and older generations, was reflected in the redesign of the city's currency. In the 1990s and early 2000s, bank notes depicted skyscrapers and major infrastructure projects, such as the new airport and a suspension bridge. In 2010, however, the Hong Kong Monetary Authority issued new bills, which primarily featured images of nature reserves and traditional Chinese festivals.

17. For more on the protests surrounding the redevelopment of Bukit Brown cemetery, see Kate Lamb, "Singapore Cemetery Demolition Angers Residents," *Voice of America News*, January 25, 2013.

18. Here, Schivelbusch is elaborating on Émile Durkheim's argument that "a society's space-time perceptions are a function of its social rhythm and its territory." Wolfgang Schivelbusch, *The Railway Journey: The Industrialization of Time and Space in the 19th Century* (Berkeley: University of California Press, 1986), 36.

19. Current plans to extend China's high-speed rail network into Southeast Asia may change this situation in the medium term. See Geoff Wade, "Changing Asia: China's High-Speed Railway Diplomacy," *The Strategist: The Australian Strategic Policy Institute Blog*, December 2, 2013, www.aspistrategist.org.au/changing-asia-chinas-high-speed-railway-diplomacy/.

20. Interestingly, whereas Google Maps provides driving directions between even the most distant pairs of cities in the United States and Europe, in Asia the site's search engine automatically defaults to flight times, with a helpful link to individual airline websites.

21. For example, when I first moved to Singapore, I asked one of the secretaries in my office if she had any recommendations for interesting things to do on the weekends.

"Have you been to Bali?" she inquired. "That's nice for a night or two. Oh, and KL [Kuala Lumpur] has great food."

"Actually, I meant things to do in Singapore."

"Oh," she replied, then rattled off the usual list of tourist attractions: Sentosa Island, the Nighttime Safari, Marina Bay Sands.

"Is that where *you* go on the weekends?" I asked, skeptically.

"No," she paused. "I've visited them before, and also they're too expensive."

"More expensive than flying to Malaysia?"

"Actually, yes!" She replied animatedly, and drifted into Singlish. "Last week I booked a ticket to KL. Only thirty dollars round-trip! And the food and drinks are *so* cheap over there! Can eat eat drink drink all you want and dun need to worry about the bill. Also you can buy lots of groceries, very very cheap."

22. Nyiri, *Mobility and Cultural Authority in Contemporary China*, 139.

23. Reyner Banham outlined the limitations of monumental airport design in a 1962 review of New York's Idlewild Airport. In it, he argued that monumental airport terminals in fact arrested mobility flows, and were "by definition dead, superseded before they were designed" because they could not keep pace with rapid technological changes in the airline industry. A more rational approach to airport design, he contended, would

emphasize "the continuity of the process of transportation rather than the monumental halting places along the way." Banham, "The Obsolescent Airport," 252–53.

24. Kevin Lynch, *What Time Is This Place?* (Cambridge, Mass.: MIT Press, 1972), 196, 198.

25. On the role of academic research in the reconstruction and urban development of postwar European cities, see Stanek, *Henri Lefebvre on Space*. See also Kenny Cupers, *The Social Project: Housing Postwar France* (Minneapolis: University of Minnesota Press, 2014).

26. Lynch, *What Time Is This Place?*, 190.

27. Ibid., 203–4. He also suggested that "prior to moving, [emigrants] may be instructed about the new area, see movies of its people and places, practice living in simulations of its settings. On arrival, they can be systematically educated to the possibilities of the new location, so that they rapidly become actively engaged in it. . . . Communications between old and new places may be so improved that permanent moves are unnecessary and separated individuals can remain in contact with one another and the familiar location. The old place may become a summer retreat or a symbolic rallying point." Ibid., 192.

28. See Morshidi Sirat and Suriati Ghazali, "Migrant Labour, Residential Conflict, and the City: The Case of Foreign Workers' Invasion of Residential Neighbourhoods in Penang, Malaysia," in Wong and Rigg, *Asian Cities, Migrant Labor and Contested Space*, 175–200. See also "Anti-Chinese Feelings in Thailand High As Influx of Tourists Angers Locals," *South China Morning Post*, April 15, 2014.

Index

MAX HIRSH is research assistant professor of the history and theory of architecture and urban planning at the Hong Kong Institute for the Humanities and Social Sciences, University of Hong Kong.